CLEP® AMERICAN LITERATURE

Jacob Stratman, Ph.D.

Dean, College of Bible, Humanities, and Arts

Professor of English

John Brown University

Siloam Springs, Arkansas

Research & Education Association

www.rea.com

Research & Education Association
1325 Franklin Ave., Suite 250
Garden City, NY 11530
Email: info@rea.com

CLEP® American Literature with Online Practice Exams, 2nd Edition

Published 2024

Copyright © 2015 by Research & Education Association.
Prior edition copyright © 2010 by Research & Education Association. All rights reserved. No part of this book may be reproduced in any form without permission of the publisher.

Printed in the United States of America

Library of Congress Control Number 2014944527

ISBN-13: 978-0-7386-1175-4
ISBN-10: 0-7386-1175-1

Cover Image: FogStock/Alin Dragulin/Thinkstock

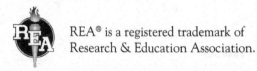

CONTENTS

About Our Author

Dr. Jacob Stratman is Professor of English and Dean of the College of Bible, Humanities, and Arts at John Brown University, Siloam Springs, Arkansas. He has taught English I and II, American Literature to 1900, World Masterpieces, and the Young Adult Literature course. Dr. Stratman earned his B.A. in English and Secondary Education from William Jewell College and his M.A. in English with an emphasis in Creative Writing from Missouri State University. He completed his Ph.D. in English - English & American Literature from Marquette University. His research and teaching interests include Christianity and literature, young adult literature, disability studies, pedagogy and hospitality, and American literature.

A Note from Our Author

It is important for me to tell you a few things about this text before you begin reading. First, to paraphrase one of my colleagues and co-CLEP-prep writers, this book is merely a synthesis of syntheses on American Literature. In other words, I used the great work of many anthologies and works on American Literature to summarize author biographies, literary themes, and cultural contexts for you. My principal sources were *The Norton Anthology of American Literature, The Bedford Anthology of American Literature,* and *The Heath Anthology of American Literature.* These anthologies were invaluable to me as I crafted, outlined, and wrote each section of this book. Please take my advice and use one of these resources yourself — along with this book — to study for your CLEP exam.

This brings me to my next point. This book should be used to complement your reading of primary texts. It is essential that you read the primary works of American Literature and then use this book to help you to understand the lives lived by the authors, the cultural contexts in which the literature plays out, and the literary themes and devices you will discover in those primary texts. I have intentionally created the "Must Read" box for each author with the sincere hope that you will create your own American Literature course. I cannot overstate the importance of actually reading the literature if you want to be successful on the CLEP American Literature exam.

After you take the practice tests, be sure to read all of the test question explanations. The explanations will continue to teach you about American Literature and show you the key differences among the possible answers. Don't just skim this very valuable section!

Finally, and most personally, I hope that you enjoy reading the literature of the United States. I tell my students that the best way to truly understand a culture is to engage with its art: literature, drama, visual art, dance, music, and film. You will better understand what it means (and meant) to be an American by reading our country's poetry, essays, sermons, songs, short stories, and novels.

Enjoy the journey,

Dr. Jacob Stratman

Author Acknowledgments

This work could not have been completed without the support and hard work of several individuals. I would like to acknowledge Diane Baumann for her insight, opinions, and positive engagement with the content editing of each chapter. Diane helped fine-tune this work in numerous ways. Many thanks also go to the diligent work of my teaching assistant, Annaka Ailie, for her hard work on the really tedious research that a project like this requires. Lastly, I would like to thank my colleague, Preston Jones, and my wife, Julia, for encouraging me to take on this project. I am now a better teacher of American Literature for having finished this book.

About REA

Founded in 1959, Research & Education Association (REA) is dedicated to publishing the finest and most effective educational materials—including study guides and test preps—for students of all ages.

Today, REA's wide-ranging catalog is a leading resource for students, teachers, and other professionals. Visit us at *www.rea.com* to see our complete catalog.

Publisher Acknowledgments

In addition to our author, we would like to thank Larry B. Kling, Editorial Director, for his project management of this revised edition; Pam Weston, Publisher, for setting the quality standards for production integrity and managing the publication to completion; John Cording, Technology Director, for coordinating the design and development of the online REA Study Center; Diane Goldschmidt, Managing Editor, for project management of the first edition; and Jennifer Calhoun for file prep.

We also gratefully acknowledge Carolyn Duffy and Julie Clark for copyediting, Ellen Gong for proofreading, Terry Casey for indexing, and Kathy Caratozzolo of Caragraphics for typesetting. This second edition has been revised and updated with the valuable editorial assistance of S4Carlisle Publishing Services and John Kupetz, Associate Professor, English/Journalism, College of Lake County, Grayslake, Ill.

Chapter 1

Passing the CLEP American Literature Exam

Congratulations! You're joining the millions of people who have discovered the value and educational advantage offered by the College Board's College-Level Examination Program, or CLEP. This test prep focuses on what you need to know to succeed on the CLEP American Literature exam, and will help you earn the college credit you deserve while reducing your tuition costs.

GETTING STARTED

There are many different ways to prepare for a CLEP exam. What's best for you depends on how much time you have to study and how comfortable you are with the subject matter. To score your highest, you need a system that can be customized to fit you: your schedule, your learning style, and your current level of knowledge.

This book, and the online tools that come with it, allow you to create a personalized study plan through three simple steps: assessment of your knowledge, targeted review of exam content, and reinforcement in the areas where you need the most help.

Let's get started and see how this system works.

Test Yourself & Get Feedback	Assess your strengths and weaknesses. The score report from your online diagnostic exam gives you a fast way to pinpoint what you already know and where you need to spend more time studying.
Review with the Book	Armed with your diagnostic score report, review the parts of the book where you're weak and study the answer explanations for the test questions you answered incorrectly.

Ensure You're Ready for Test Day	After you've finished reviewing with the book, take our full-length practice tests. Review your score reports and re-study any topics you missed. We give you two full-length practice tests to ensure you're confident and ready for test day.

THE REA STUDY CENTER

The best way to personalize your study plan is to get feedback on what you know and what you don't know. At the online REA Study Center (*www.rea.com/studycenter*), you can access two types of assessment: a diagnostic exam and full-length practice exams. Each of these tools provides true-to-format questions and delivers a detailed score report that follows the topics set by the College Board.

Diagnostic Exam

Before you begin your review with the book, take the online diagnostic exam. Use your score report to help evaluate your overall understanding of the subject, so you can focus your study on the topics where you need the most review.

Full-Length Practice Exams

Our full-length practice tests give you the most complete picture of your strengths and weaknesses. After you've finished reviewing with the book, test what you've learned by taking the first of the two online practice exams. Review your score report, then go back and study any topics you missed. Take the second practice test to ensure you have mastered the material and are ready for test day.

If you're studying and don't have internet access, you can take the printed tests in the book. These are the same practice tests offered at the REA Study Center, but without the added benefits of timed testing conditions and diagnostic score reports. Because the actual exam is internet-based, we recommend you take at least one practice test online to simulate test-day conditions.

AN OVERVIEW OF THE EXAM

The CLEP American Literature exam consists of approximately 100 questions to be answered in 90 minutes.

The exam covers the material one would find in a college-level survey course. It tests your knowledge about literary works written in the United States from precolonial times to the present.

The approximate breakdown of topics covered on the exam is shown in the following chart:

What's on the Exam—by Topic

Topic	Range of Coverage on Exam
Ability to understand and interpret short poems or excerpts from long poems and prose works	35% to 40%
Knowledge of particular literary works—authors, characters, plots, style, settings, themes, etc.	25% to 30%
Knowledge of the historical and social settings of specific works, their relations to other literary works and to literary traditions, and the influences on their authors	15% to 20%
Familiarity with critical terms, verse forms, and literary devices	15% to 20%

Source: College Board, 2023. Percentages are approximate.

The subject matter of the CLEP American Literature exam is drawn from the chronological periods shown in the following chart:

What's on the Exam—by Literary Period

Literary Period	Time frame	Coverage on Exam
The Precolonial, Colonial, and Early National Period	Beginnings to 1800	15%
The Romantic Period	1800 to 1865	20%
The Period of Realism and Naturalism	1865 to 1910	20%
The Modernist Period	1910 to 1945	20%
The Contemporary Period	1945 to Present	25%

Source: College Board, 2023. Percentages are approximate.

CLEP and technology-enhanced questions

While most of what you find on your CLEP exam will be standard multiple-choice questions, the College Board has also incorporated some technology-enhanced items. Such questions may ask you to fill in a numeric answer; shade areas of an object; or put items in a list in the correct order.

The Optional Essay Section

An optional essay section can be taken in addition to the multiple-choice test. The essay section requires that two essays be written during a total time of 90 minutes.

The first essay requires test-takers to write a well-organized essay on a common theme that runs through American literature. A list of major American authors is provided and candidates are asked to discuss how this theme is handled in works by any two of the listed authors.

For the second essay, test-takers are asked to respond to one of two topics — one requiring analysis of a poem, the other requiring analysis of a prose excerpt. In each case, the specific poem or prose excerpt is presented and relevant questions are offered to guide your response.

The essay section is graded by faculty at the institution from which you wish to earn credit and is administered in paper-based format. Be aware that there is an additional fee for taking this section, payable to the institution where you take the exam.

ALL ABOUT THE CLEP PROGRAM

What is CLEP?

More adult learners use CLEP than any other credit-by-examination program in the United States. The CLEP program's 34 exams span five subject areas. The exams assess the material commonly required in an introductory-level college course. Based on recommendations from the American Council on Education, a passing score can earn you at least three credits per exam at more than 2,900 colleges and universities in the U.S. and abroad. Policies vary, so check with your school on the exams it accepts and the scores it requires. For a complete list of the CLEP subject examinations offered, visit the College Board website: *clep.org*.

Who takes CLEP exams?

CLEP exams are typically taken by people who have acquired knowledge outside the classroom and wish to bypass certain college courses and earn college credit. The CLEP program is designed to reward examinees for prior learning—no matter where or how that knowledge was acquired.

CLEP appeals to a wide spectrum of candidates, including home-schooled and high school students, adults returning to college, traditional-age college students, military personnel, veterans, and international students. There are no prerequisites, such as age or educational status, for taking CLEP examinations. However, because policies on granting credits vary among colleges, you should contact the particular institution from which you wish to receive CLEP credit.

How is my CLEP score determined?

Your CLEP score is based on two calculations. First, your CLEP raw score is figured; this is just the total number of test items you answer correctly. After the test is administered, your raw score is converted to a scaled score through a process called *equating*. Equating adjusts for minor variations in difficulty across test forms and among test items, and ensures that your score accurately represents your performance on the exam regardless of when or where you take it, or on how well others perform on the same test form.

Your scaled score is the number your college will use to determine whether you've performed well enough to earn college credit. Scaled scores for the CLEP exams are delivered on a 20–80 scale. Institutions can set their own scores for granting college credit, but a good passing estimate (based on recommendations from the American Council on Education) is generally a scaled score of 50, which usually requires getting roughly 66% of the questions correct.

For more information on scoring, contact the institution where you wish to be awarded the credit.

Who administers the exam?

CLEP exams are developed by the College Board, administered by Educational Testing Service (ETS), and involve the assistance of educators from throughout the United States. The test development process is designed and implemented to ensure that the content and difficulty level of the test are appropriate.

When and where is the exam given?

CLEP exams are administered year-round at more than 2,000 test centers* in the United States and abroad. To find the test center nearest you and to register for the exam, contact the CLEP Program:

> CLEP Services
> P.O. Box 6600
> Princeton, NJ 08541-6600
> Phone: (800) 257-9558
> Fax: (610) 628-3726
> Email: *clep@info.collegeboard.org*
> Website: *www.collegeboard.org/clep*

---

* You may be able to take your exam at home. Learn more at *https://proctortrack.com/clep*.

The CLEP iBT Platform

To improve the testing experience for both institutions and test-takers, the College Board's CLEP Program has transitioned its 34 exams from the eCBT platform to an internet-based testing (iBT) platform. All CLEP test-takers may now register for exams and manage their personal account information through the "My Account" feature on the CLEP website. This simplifies the registration process and automatically downloads all pertinent information about the test session, making for a more streamlined check-in.

OPTIONS FOR MILITARY PERSONNEL AND VETERANS

CLEP exams are available free of charge to eligible military personnel as well as eligible civilian employees. All the CLEP exams are available at test centers on college campuses and military bases. Contact your Educational Services Officer or Navy College Education Specialist for more information. Visit the DANTES or College Board websites for details about CLEP opportunities for military personnel.

Eligible U.S. veterans may apply for reimbursement of CLEP exam fees pursuant to provisions of the Harry W. Colmery Veterans Educational Assistance Act of 2017, commonly called the "Forever GI Bill." For details on eligibility and how to apply for reimbursement, visit the U.S. Department of Veterans Affairs website at *benefits.va.gov/gibill.*

SSD ACCOMMODATIONS FOR CANDIDATES WITH DISABILITIES

Many test candidates qualify for special accommodations when taking CLEP exams. Accommodations include, among other things, extra time, screen magnification, modifiable screen colors, and untimed rest breaks that don't cut into test time. You must make arrangements for these accommodations in advance. For information, contact:

College Board SSD Program
P.O. Box 7504
London, KY 40742-7504
Phone: (844) 255-7728
TTY: (609) 882-4118
Fax: (866) 360-0114
Email: *ssd@info.collegeboard.org*
Website: *accommodations.collegeboard.org*

6-WEEK STUDY PLAN

Be sure to set aside enough time—at least two hours each day—to study. The more time you spend studying, the more prepared and relaxed you will feel on the day of the exam.

Week	Activity
1	Take the Diagnostic Exam at the online REA Study Center. Your score report will identify topics where you need the most review.
2–4	Study the review focusing on the topics you missed (or were unsure of) on the Diagnostic Exam.
5	Take Practice Test 1 at the REA Study Center. Review your score report and re-study any topics you missed.
6	Take Practice Test 2 at the REA Study Center to see how much your score has improved. If you still get a few questions wrong, go back to the review and study the topics you missed.

TEST-TAKING TIPS

Know the format of the test. Familiarize yourself with the CLEP computer screen beforehand by logging on to the College Board website. Waiting until test day to see what it looks like in the pretest tutorial risks injecting needless anxiety into your testing experience. Also, familiarizing yourself with the directions and format of the exam will save you valuable time on the day of the actual test.

Read all the questions—completely. Make sure you understand each question before looking for the right answer. Reread the question if it doesn't make sense.

Read all of the answers to a question. Just because you think you found the correct response right away, do not assume that it's the best answer. The last answer choice might be the correct answer.

Use the process of elimination. Stumped by a question? Don't make a random guess. Eliminate as many of the answer choices as possible. Remember, your score is based only on the number of questions you answer correctly.

Don't waste time! Don't spend too much time on any one question. Your time is limited, so pacing yourself is very important. Work on the easier questions first. Skip the difficult questions and go back to them if you have the time. Taking our timed practice tests online will help you learn how to budget your time.

Look for clues to answers in other questions. If you skip a question you don't know the answer to, you might find a clue to the answer elsewhere on the test.

Be sure that your answer registers before you go to the next item. Look at the screen to see that your mouse-click causes the pointer to darken the proper oval. If your answer doesn't register, you won't get credit for that question.

THE DAY OF THE EXAM

On test day, you should wake up early (after a good night's rest, of course) and have breakfast. Dress comfortably, so you are not distracted by being too hot or too cold while taking the test. (Note that "hoodies" are not allowed.) Arrive at the test center early. This will allow you to collect your thoughts and relax before the test, and it will also spare you the anxiety that comes with being late.

Before you leave for the test center, make sure you have your admission form and another form of identification, which must contain a recent photograph, your name, and signature (i.e., driver's license, student identification card, or current alien registration card). You may not wear a digital watch (wrist or pocket), alarm watch, or wristwatch camera. In addition, no cellphones, dictionaries, textbooks, notebooks, briefcases, or packages will be permitted, and drinking, smoking, and eating are prohibited.

Good luck on the CLEP American Literature exam!

Chapter 2

The Precolonial, Colonial, and Early National Period (Beginnings–1820)

Because this chapter covers over two hundred years in American literary history, I decided to write a brief introduction for each section instead of a larger introduction. I hope you find each section and its introduction useful as you attempt to place these authors and their works in a particular cultural/historical context.

NATIVE AMERICAN LITERATURE: BEFORE THE BEGINNING

Europeans, as a whole, did very little to understand the complex and rich history and literature of the native peoples of the new world. "America" was filled with hundreds and hundreds of societies that maintained their own language, history, literature, and lifestyle. Unlike European countries, these native societies passed down the traditions and histories of the people through song, dance, and storytelling. Much like the ancient Greeks, Native Americans used stories, now called **myths**, to explain cultural, historical, religious, and scientific phenomena. It was not until the nineteenth century that Euro-Americans started to take seriously the history of these people, which led numerous historians, writers, and ethnographers to translate these histories, stories, poems, and songs into English. What is common to most of these societies is the creation story. All cultures pass down stories that explain the creation of the world. Most anthologies include the Iroquois Creation Story as translated by David Cusick, a Tuscarora, who was educated in a Christian mission school in New York. His translation, titled *A Tale of the Foundation of the Great Island (Now North America), the Two Infants Born, and the Creation of the Universe*, is summarized here:

> There existed two worlds: the lower world filled with darkness and the upper world filled with mankind. On the upper world, a woman was to give birth to twins. In labor, the woman begins to slip down into the

lower world. To save her, one of the creatures dives into the great waters to secure a piece of earth, while a great turtle, with a piece of earth on his shell, descends to retrieve the woman. During labor, the twins begin to feud with each other, which leads to the woman's death once they are born. Still in the darker lower world, the turtle grows into a large island, and the twins prosper. One twin is named the "good mind," while the other is named the "bad mind." The good twin decides to bring life to the lower world, so he begins to create the universe.* Eventually, the bad mind challenges the good mind to battle for control of the universe. The good mind wins; however, the bad mind, before cast into the lower world, declares that he will have "equal power over the souls of mankind after death." (Baym et al. 2008, 21)

EUROPEAN EXPLORATION: THE BEGINNINGS

It is important to understand that American literature does not begin with white English settlers in 1620. Although most courses (and tests, for that matter) usually begin with the Puritans, please take the time to read a few excerpts from the works of European explorers and the Native Indians that were so influential to American literature. The makeup of this country's literary background becomes quite complex when we add the different elements of Spain, England, France, Africa, and the many other countries that sent immigrants to its shores from the fifteenth to the seventeenth centuries.

Christopher Columbus (1451–1506)

American students have been raised on facts surrounding Columbus and his explorations of America. This young seaman found great favor and support from Spain's monarchs, Ferdinand and Isabella. This relationship gave him the financial and moral support to sail to the west several times from 1492 to 1504. Although older history books usually gloss over how these voyages affected the native peoples, writings from the time clearly indicate conflict between the Spaniards and the Native Americans. Modern scholars are lucky to have the journal that Columbus wrote of those voyages along with many letters that he penned concerning life at sea and on the new land. Take note that Columbus's *Journal of the First Voyage to America* was more than likely summarized and collected by Bartolome de las Casas, so many anthologies include Columbus's letters in its stead. I suggest reading the excerpts of those letters.

---

* Note that this description is very similar to the Hebrew narrative recorded in the Bible; some scholars argue that Cusick, a Christian, molded and shaped the Iroquois story to mirror a Christian worldview. Keep in mind that American literature also alludes often to the Christian creation story. Students unfamiliar with that narrative are advised to read the book of Genesis in the Bible or at least read a good summary of it.

Alvar Nuñez Cabeza de Vaca (ca. 1490–1558)

If you peruse any current anthology, you will notice that de Vaca is getting a lot more space than Columbus. The reason could be that his history of exploration in America is much more appealing to the adventurous reader. *The Relation* [or *Narrative*] *of Alvar Nuñez Cabeza de Vaca* was first published in Spain in 1542 and then again in 1555 as an address to Charles V about an expedition that occurred around 15 years previously. This highly tumultuous trip involved Hispaniola, Cuba, and, eventually, Florida, where many men were lost in explorations. De Vaca, on the other hand, continued his explorations, eventually landing in Texas where he was imprisoned and enslaved by local Indian tribes. He spent many years after that time in Mexico (and parts that are now the United States), but he eventually returned to Spain where he hoped to write of his adventures and expose European explorers to the rights and lives of Native Americans. Because of "creative differences" with other explorers and politicians, de Vaca was exiled to Algeria in 1551. Each major anthology now includes several selections from his narrative. I suggest reading several sections and comparing the tone and details with those of Columbus's narrative.

THE COLONIAL PERIOD: LITERATURE FROM 1620 TO 1750

In most scholarly circles, it is agreed that the novel as a genre did not exist until the eighteenth century. So what is American literature if it is not fiction? Well, literature that makes up early American literature is filled with Native American creation stories, European exploration diaries, spiritual autobiographies, captivity narratives, drama, poems, and various genres such as epics and romances that are considered precursors to the novel. Not only should you be able to recognize various authors and texts in their cultural context, but you should also be able to define and discuss the myriad of literary genres that were used during the beginning decades of American literature.

John Smith (1580–1631)

Born in Willoughby, England, Smith worked on the family farm until around the age of 15 when he became an apprentice to a shopkeeper. Smith's father died in 1596, which allowed the young boy to live out his dream of travel and seafaring. As a soldier, Smith fought in the Netherlands to help the Dutch secure their independence from Spain's Philip II. After many stints in Europe, Smith joined the Austrian army as they battled with the Turks (1593–1606). It was during one of these battles that Smith was captured and imprisoned by the Turks, only to escape after murdering his master and returned to England in 1605.

During this time, exploration became more of a corporate venture than a heroic one. Under the royal guidance of England's James I and the financial backing of various investors who desired to colonize North America, Smith joined the **Virginia Company** and landed in Virginia in 1607. ("Virginia" was the territory between Canada and Florida.) As a councilman, and later the president or governor of the new colony at **Jamestown**, Smith was labeled as stubborn, high-tempered, arrogant, and generally troublesome.

Smith has been popularized by his own narrative of how he was captured by **Powhatan**, chief of the Chesapeake Bay Indians, and was then rescued by the chief's daughter, **Pocahontas**. Scholars argue whether the event actually happened, or at least whether Smith's portrayal of his capture, imprisonment, and eventual rescue is factual. Regardless, the narrative (see "Must Read" box) addresses the ongoing conflicts between European colonizers and the native peoples of America and the many struggles the settlers faced in the New World: disease, lack of food and supplies, and the weather.

After several more explorations in the New World, Smith began writing of his adventures in America in an attempt to encourage others to settle there: *A True Relation of Such Occurrences and Accidents of Note as Hath Happened in Virginia* (1608); *A Map of Virginia, with a Description of the County* (1612); *A Description of New England* (1616); *New England's Trial's* (1620 and 1622); and later, *The True Travels, Adventures, and Observations of Captain John Smith, In Europe, Asia, Africa, and America* (1630). The most famous, and most anthologized, of his writings is *The General History of Virginia, New England, and the Summer Isles* (1624), which contains six books of collected and original writings; therefore, Smith has been considered more of an editor than an author. Here, he details the construction of the Virginia colony along with explorations of New England and Bermuda. This collection is considered one of the first histories of the English colonies in America.

Must Read

From The General History of Virginia, New England, and the Summer Isles. From the Third Book. From Chapter 2: *What Happened till the First Supply.*

The Pilgrims (1620)

Although the settling of Jamestown, Virginia, is largely discussed as a commercial venture, the settling of New England by the **Pilgrims** and the **Puritans** revolves around the religious unrest in England. The sixteenth to seventeenth century was a time of much political and religious unrest in England. After the Protestant Reformation, King Henry VIII established the Church of England and published the first authorized Bible in English (1534). In 1553, a Catholic Queen, Mary Tudor, assumed the throne. However, Elizabeth I reestablished the Church of England after the death of Queen Mary in 1558. This history is important to establish the state's powerful involvement in church affairs. At this time, there were sects of Christian reformers who struggled to "purify" the Church of England of any resemblance to Roman Catholicism. These Puritans were not liked by English royalty, including James I, who authorized an official English translation of the Bible, now called the King James Bible. Later called Pilgrims by their leader **William Bradford**, these separatists formed independent churches, which King James considered treasonous.

Bradford was influenced by nonconformist preaching as a boy and joined the separatists in 1606. Fleeing the country in 1608, the Pilgrims landed in the Netherlands where they enjoyed the beauties and freedoms of that country. Bradford followed in 1609, immigrating to the Netherlands to live with the separatist community; there he learned weaving as a trade. Poverty, language differences, and difficulty farming, however, forced the Pilgrims to petition for a land grant in the American territories then governed by England's Virginia Company. In 1620, the *Mayflower* landed in **Plymouth, Massachusetts** (a name given by John Smith). Their first winter in the New World was harsh, but the Pilgrims were assisted by the **Wampanoag Indians**, their leader, Massasoit, and **Squanto**, a Patuxet Indian who spoke English.

In 1621, Bradford was named the first governor of the Plymouth colony and established himself as the primary authority of the new colony. Also in that year, forty signatures, including Bradford's, cemented the Mayflower Compact as the governing document of the colony. Obviously influenced by religious separatism, the Mayflower Compact established the protection of individual rights against governmental tyranny.

William Bradford (1590–1657) and *Of Plimoth Plantation*

Written over a period of twenty years, Bradford's history of the Plymouth colony was never meant for publication. The first part of the history was written at the beginning of the Great Migration (1630); this year showed an increase in English migration to the New World. Scholars note that *Of Plimoth Plantation* existed in manuscript form before it was published in its entirety in 1856 by the Massachusetts Historical Society. The publication was returned to the state house of Massachusetts in 1897 after years of legal battles and negotiations.

Because of the document's great importance in narrating life in early America, its contents, prior to publication, were used by several historians and writers in their own works: Nathaniel Morton's *New England's Memoriall* (1669); William Hubbard's *History of New England* (1683); and Cotton Mather's seminal work on early America, *Magnalia Christi Americana* (1702).

It is also important to note that the prose is written in what is called **plain style**. Bradford wrote his history for a general readership, using common language and sentence structure to enable the common reader to easily understand the narrative. Here is an excerpt from *Of Plimoth Plantation*, book 1, chapter 9, "Of Their Vioage, & How They Passed The Sea, and Of Their Safe Arrivall At Cape Codd":

> Our faithers were Englishmen which came over this great ocean, and were ready to perish in this willdernes; but they cried unto the Lord, and he heard their voyce, and looked on their adversitie, &c. Let them therfore praise the Lord, because he is good, & his mercies endure for ever. Yea, let them which have been redeemed of the Lord, shew how he hath delivered them from the hand of the oppressour. When they wandered in the deserte willdernes out of the way, and found no citie to dwell in, both hungrie, & thirstie, their sowle was overwhelmed in them. Let them confess before the Lord his loving kindnes, and his wonderfull works before the sons of men. (Belasco 2008, 135)

Must Read

Of Plimoth Plantation by William Bradford

Book 1, chapter 9, "Of Their Vioage, & How They Passed The Sea, and Of Their Safe Arrivall At Cape Codd"

Book 1, chapter 10, "Showing How They Sought Out a Place of Habitation; and What Befell Them Theraboute"

Book 2, chapter 11, "The Remainder of Anno 1620; Difficult Beginnings; Dealings with the Natives"

Book 2, chapter 23, "Anno 1632 [Prosperity Weakens Community]"

The Puritans (1630)

The biggest difference between the Puritans and the Pilgrims was separatism: unlike the Pilgrims, the Puritans had no intention of separating from the Church of England. However, years of conflict between the Puritans and the Church of England culminated in the **Great Migration**. Led by **John Winthrop** upon the flagship *Arbella*, a group of Puritan settlers left England aboard a fleet of ships and landed in the Massachusetts Bay in 1630. These Puritans, although not official dissenters of the Church of England, adopted religious practices much different from those of their homeland. Although this trip was heavily financed by English investors and many of the immigrants had capitalistic dreams, what marks this migration to America was its religious import. As you will read in John Winthrop's "A Modell of Christian Charity," the Puritans regarded themselves as modern-day

Hebrews responding to God's call to flee England and reestablish God's covenant in the New World—the promised land. Later called the "errand into the wilderness" by preacher Samuel Danforth, this migration was thought by many as divinely authorized.

Puritan theology was widely influenced by the Swiss theologian John Calvin. Both the Pilgrims and Puritans believed in the "total depravity" of mankind. Simply stated, humans were born of a sinful nature and needed Christ's salvation. Calvin's concept of election was also important to the Puritan preachers. The doctrine of election stated that God has called those he has chosen to save and those he has chosen to damn. These theological principles molded much of the literature of this time, including the works of John Winthrop, **Cotton Mather**, **Edward Taylor**, and **Jonathan Edwards**.

John Winthrop (1588–1649)

Unlike Bradford, who came from meager circumstances, Winthrop was raised on a prosperous farm in Groton, England. His father bought the land from Henry VIII, which allowed Winthrop to grow up in relative economic advantage. He was educated at Cambridge University and later studied to become a lawyer instead of managing his family's estate. Scholars note that during his time at Cambridge, Winthrop was heavily influenced by the Puritan beliefs held by many students. After completing school, and with the assistance that his privileged upbringing provided, Winthrop joined the **Massachusetts Bay Company**, and in 1629, the company obtained a charter that would allow them to establish a colony in America based on Puritan ideals and theology. He was elected governor in the same year, and along with seven hundred others, sailed to New England in 1630. (Remember, this voyage marked the beginning of the Great Migration.)

Scholars disagree about when Winthrop delivered his most famous sermon, "A Modell of Christian Charity." Popular belief has long promoted the idea that Winthrop addressed the passengers on the flagship *Arbella* during the voyage west; however, recent scholarship argues that it more likely occurred just before the ship left England's harbors. Regardless, this famous address proposed the religious ideals that would frame this new colony in America. As mentioned earlier, these Puritans believed that their migration was divinely inspired; therefore, their new land must be devoted to living out God's mission and acting in Godly ways towards one another: "This duty of mercy is exercised in the kinds, Giving, lending, and forgiving." The organization of the address also shows Winthrop's lawyer training as well as his religious education. Parts of the sermon resemble sixteenth-century catechisms such as the Scots Confession (1560), the Heidelberg Catechism (1563), and the Second Helvetic Confession (1566). Catechisms were used in religious training in the form of questions and answers. In this way, Winthrop hoped to teach these Puritans the foundations of the faith and practices that would secure their success in America.

▶ TRENDS

Jeremiad: The term was coined and made popular by scholar Perry Miller and later by Sacvan Bercovitch. Simply put, the jeremiad is a loud lament against society's moral ills. It is, as some scholars have described it, a place where the pulpit meets the town house. The term is an eponym, named after prophet Jeremiah and his book of lament against the sins of the Hebrews. This genre is most commonly found in Puritan writing. Preachers such as Cotton Mather, John Winthrop, Jonathan Edwards, and Michael Wigglesworth continually rebuked their congregations for their spiritual backsliding and disobedience to God at a time when spiritual obedience was strictly tied to societal success. Remember Winthrop's exultation that America was to be a "City on a Hill." To these writers and preachers, religious devotion was expressly tied to civic responsibility. This genre, however, is not strictly tied to the seventeenth century. Jeremiads were also popular during the Civil War as writers used religious rhetoric to preach for and against slavery and secession. The civil rights and environmental movements of the twentieth century also provided a space for the jeremiad. What is most important about this genre is its reformative power. Therefore, jeremiad is commonly stereotyped as a complaint; however, the genre depends upon the repentance of its listeners and then, the ultimate reformation of the society.

As the title suggests, the primary theme of Winthrop's text is Christian charity. Although it is said that Winthrop could be overzealous at times, it is clear that he was committed to teaching the importance of community, selfless living, and harmony. At the beginning of the address, he remarks that "there are two rules whereby wee are to walke one towards another: justice and mercy." Again, he states that "wee must be knit together in this work as one man." Note, however, that Winthrop's definition of community did include a particular social structure. He believed that this "caste" system was divinely inspired and operated. At all times, he writes, "some must be rich, some poor, some high and eminent in power and dignity and others low in subjection" (Belasco and Johnson 2008a, 155–156).

He believed ardently that the world would be watching, and ultimately judging, this American "experiment." Readers get the feeling that Winthrop inflected great urgency into his sermon, so his listeners would understand the great burdens of establishing a Christian colony in New England. This idea is made evident in Winthrop's most famous and widely quoted passage:

For wee must Consider that wee shall be as a **Citty upon a hill** [emphasis added]. The eies of all people are upon Us, soe that if wee shall deale falsely with our god in this worke wee have undertaken, and soe cause him to withdrawe his present help from us, wee shall be made a story and a by-word through the world. We shall open the mouthes of enemies to speake evill of the ways of god, and all professours for God's sake. (Belasco and Johnson 2008a, 166)

Must Read

"A Modell of Christian Charity" by John Winthrop: Most anthologies of American literature contain the sermon in its entirety.

Women in Colonial America

Anne Bradstreet (ca. 1612–1672)

One of the passengers on the flagship *Arbella* was a young, educated, and well-to-do woman named Anne Bradstreet. She traveled with her father, Thomas Dudley, who was an estate manager of a wealthy Puritan earl, and her husband, Simon, who was a Cambridge University graduate and associate of her father's.

We know very little of Bradstreet's life in America, except that is was harsh, full of disease and sickness, and strained by birthing and raising eight children. Scholars are also not certain as to why and when she began writing poetry; however, it is certain that her poems of spiritual meditation and reflection, along with depictions of New England life, were not meant for publication. Her first and only published volume of poems, *The Tenth Muse*, was printed in England in 1650 under the authority of her brother-in-law, Pastor John Woodbridge. Although she wrote and revised many poems after this date, including a preface to a second collection called "The Author to Her Book," a second collection (*Several Poems Compiled with Great Variety of Wit and Learning—1678*) was not published until after her death in 1672. Here are the first four lines of that poem:

> Thou ill-formed offspring of my feeble brain,
> Who after birth didst by my side remain,
> Till snatched from thence by friends, less wise than true,
> Who thee abroad exposed to public view,
> (Kennedy and Gioia 2005, 23)

This stanza refers to her first collection of poems that she wrote for personal use, yet were taken to England by her brother-in-law. The first complete edition of Bradstreet's poetry was published in 1867.

The Tenth Muse was the first published book of poetry in the English colonies. This is an important fact because women were not given much flexibility to live literary lives. Not only were readers skeptical of women's ability to write successful poetry, but they also questioned whether poetry should take precedence over more domestic matters. In "The Prologue," Bradstreet writes, "If what I do prove well, it won't advance, / They'll say it's stol'n, or else it was by chance" (Kizer 1995, 27). Bradstreet did not include her name on the title page; instead, readers will see "a Gentlewoman in those parts."

The most popular poems of this collection recall her intimate reflections upon her husband and children. Readers will notice a significant tone shift as she becomes more confident and assertive when she discusses her family and domestic matters. Several poems reveal Bradstreet's keen observations of the natural world, her understanding of science, history, theology, and philosophy, as well as her sophisticated opinions of gender matters and the fears that accompany colonial life.

Here is an excerpt from one of her most anthologized poems, "To My Dear and Loving Husband":

> If ever two were one, then surely we.
> If ever man were loved by wife, then thee;
> If ever wife was happy in a man,
> Compare with me, ye women, if you can.
>
> (Hunter 1996, 19)

In her prose piece, "To My Dear Children," she recounts her faith journey as a child in England to her adult life in the colonies. She remarks, "He [God] hath never suffered me long to sit loose from Him, but by one affliction or other hath made me look home, and search what was amiss" (Baym et al. 2008, 113). Bradstreet reminds her children that the suffering in life is brought on by an act of God in order to bring his children back to his will.

Must Read

Poetry of Anne Bradstreet

"The Prologue"

"The Author to Her Book"

"Before the Birth of One of Her Children"

"To My Dear and Loving Husband"

"To My Dear Children"

"Here Follows Some Verses upon the Burning of Our House"

"The Flesh and the Spirit"

Mary Rowlandson (ca. 1636–1711)

The only reason modern readers are familiar with Mary Rowlandson is that she was captured by a group of Wampanoag Indians during **King Philip's War**, which began in 1675. Although Bradford established relative peace with Massasoit's people, conflicts began to arise between the native people and the colonists. The chief's son, **Metacomet** (he was called King Philip by the colonists), led attacks in New England: burning houses, killing colonists, and capturing women and children. Thousands of people were killed and many were imprisoned.

A minister's wife in Lancaster, Massachusetts, Rowlandson was taken captive on February 20, 1676, and was not released for 11 weeks. Not much is known of her life after her ordeal; however, scholars claim she moved to Connecticut where her husband died in 1678, married Captain Samuel Talcott in 1679, and then later returned to Lancaster where she began writing her account of her captivity. Her manuscript, *The Sovereignty and Goodness of God, Together with the Faithfulness of His Promises Displayed; Being a Narrative of the Captivity and Restoration of Mrs. Mary Rowlandson*, was published in 1682. In Boston, it sold more than a thousand copies, thus becoming the most popular American text in the seventeenth century.

▶ *TRENDS* _____

Captivity narrative: Mary Rowlandson's *Narrative* was the first of many accounts that are now referred to as captivity narratives. Though the genre is most associated with the sixteenth to nineteenth century, many scholars argue that the elements of captivity narrative can be found in modern/contemporary literature as well. Known as the best-sellers of their time, these narratives followed a relatively tight archetype: a devoutly religious person, usually a woman, is forced to stay fast to her religious faith in the face of great temptation and pagan indecency. The Indians and their practices are metaphors for evil, sin, and godless lifestyles. The captive relies on God's power alone to deliver her from her torment and place her back into the "fold."

There are several interesting elements in Rowlandson's *Narrative*. First, it is organized into **removes**, or episodes. Her captors transported her from one camp to another during her captivity; thus, she narrates each remove. The *Narrative* begins with the attack on her home, the killing of one of her children, and the eventual separation between her and her other children, who were also taken captive. Her husband was away in Boston during the attacks. Obviously, she uses angry rhetoric when referring to the Indians. You'll notice phrases such as "murderous wretches," "bloody heathens," "merciless, hell-hounds," "barbarous creatures," and "pagans," just to list a few. Although her anger towards her captives is clear, what is also clear in the text is her devotion to God and her faith that God will deliver her from such evil. In The Second Remove, she exclaims, "But God was with me in a wonderful manner, carrying me along, and bearing up my spirit, that it did not quite fail" (Belasco and Johnson 2008a, 199). Rowlandson was relegated to a slave's role for one of the Indian women. As well, one of her young children died in her arms during her captivity; however, she was reunited with her husband and several other children a couple months later. Second, Rowlandson does depict benevolent natives. In the Twelfth Remove, she recounts how she was kicked out of her wigwam and forced to find shelter elsewhere. After many failing attempts, an old Indian and his wife gave her food, comfort, and rest. Her language, however, is still filled with bitterness and prejudice. Third, the narrative can also be read as a spiritual meditation. Throughout the text, Rowlandson alludes to biblical stories and characters, as well as quotes Scripture, in order to reflect on particular truths she learned during her captivity. In the Twentieth, and final, Remove, she remarks on her spiritual education:

> Yet I see, when God calls a person to anything, and through never so many difficulties, yet He is fully able to carry them through and make them see, and say they have been gainers thereby.
>
> (Belasco and Johnson 2008a, 228)

Must Read

A Narrative of the Captivity and Restoration of Mary Rowlandson (also called *The Sovereignty and Goodness of God*) by Mary Rowlandson

Introduction

First Remove

Second Remove

Third Remove

Twentieth Remove

If you have time, I recommend reading the entire *Narrative*.

The Puritan Preachers

Edward Taylor (ca. 1642–1729)

Now anthologized as a major colonial poet, Taylor did not publish any poetry in his lifetime. The noted Emily Dickinson scholar, Thomas H. Johnson, found

Taylor's library of poetry in the Yale University Library and ultimately published his complete works in 1939, almost 200 years after his death. Much of his poetry was fashioned after the popular British poems published in the seventeenth century: lyrics, elegies, long narratives. However, Taylor is most noted for his poems written in preparation for particular religious services, collected as *Preparatory Meditations*. Each of these poems was written before Taylor served monthly communion. Here is an excerpt from "Meditation 8, John 6:51, I am the Living Bread":

> Did God mould up this Bread in Heaven, and bake,
> Which from his Table came, and to thine goeth?
> Doth he bespeak thee thus, This Soule Break take.
> Come Eate thy fill of this thy Gods White Loafe?
> Its Food too fine for Angells, yet come, take
> And Eate thy fill. Its Heavens Sugar Cake.
>   (Belasco and Johnson 2008a, 232)

Taylor immigrated to America in 1668 from England because he would not sign an oath of loyalty to the Church of England. As a Puritan, he found his home, first, at Harvard, where he studied for several years. Then, he took a pastoral call in Westfield, Massachusetts, which was a frontier village 100 miles from Boston. He stayed there his whole life, raised a family, married twice, and remained minister to that small congregation.

Cotton Mather (1663–1728)

Mather is most noted by contemporary scholars for two primary reasons. First, in 1702 he finished a voluminous history of Christianity in New England. He titled it *Magnalia Christi Americana*, which translates to "a history of the wonderful works of Christ in America." In its seven books, Mather celebrates the people who transformed the "wilderness" of the new world into God's Promised Land, such as Bradford and Winthrop, just to name two. Take note that the tone of the collection is very nostalgic; Mather attempts to recall a time of ecclesiastical order and church authority, so contemporaries will not forget the people and ideologies that first settled America.

Unfortunately, Mather is also well-known for his involvement in the **Salem Witch Trials**. Although he was not actually at the trials, he was (and is) accused of not using his great authority to speak out against the injustices towards innocent people. Moreover, he has made it clear in subsequent writings that he was not always convinced of the evidence brought forth against the accused. He writes in *The Wonders of the Invisible World*, "I was not present at any of them; nor ever had I any personal prejudice at the persons thus brought upon the stage." However, in 1692 Governor William Phips of Massachusetts ordered the trials to take place and Mather found himself, at the request of the judges, an observer and eventual narrator of the court proceedings. The following excerpt from "The Trial of Martha

Carrier" does reveal Mather's contempt for witchcraft and ideology in direct opposition to Christianity:

> This rampant hag, Martha Carrier, was the person of whom the confessions of the witches, and of her own children among the rest, agreed that the devil had promised her she should be Queen of Hebrews.

These writings were published in his defense of the trials in 1692. (Baym et al. 2008, 146 and 149)

As the descendent of prominent Puritans, including his father **Increase Mather** and his grandfather John Cotton, Mather found himself the heir apparent of American Congregationalism during the last decades of the Puritan hold on New England. Students should also note that Mather's retelling of the captivity of Hannah Dustan in *Magnalia* was considered a popular captivity narrative at the time.

Jonathan Edwards (1703–1758)

Born just a year after Mather published *Magnalia*, Edwards is now considered the most widely anthologized preacher of colonial America. Although the symbolic weight of Puritanism died with Cotton Mather, Edwards is a part of the second generation of Puritans; therefore, I include him in this section simply because of his ideological and theological connections with Winthrop, Mather, and Taylor. However, one of the primary contrasts between Edwards and previous Puritan preachers was the prominence of the **Enlightenment** at the beginning of the eighteenth century. Because of discoveries in physics by Isaac Newton and new theories in psychology by philosopher John Locke, the human mind became a more important tool for understanding the universe than the human soul.

After graduating from Yale and holding several leadership posts, Edwards replaced his grandfather, the influential Puritan preacher Solomon Stoddard, in 1727 as an ordained minister of Northampton, Massachusetts. There, he published many sermons to high acclaim, later collected in *A Faithful Narrative of the Surprising Works of God in the Conversion of Many Hundred Souls in Northampton and Neighboring Towns* (1736) and *Discourses on Various Important Subjects* (1738). In an attempt to revive the American Christian spirit, Edwards became inextricably tied to the **Great Awakening**, which swept the colonies in the mid-1730s and 1740s. This spiritual revival is usually defined as a period of increased religious commitment and engagement in America.

It was during this time that Edwards delivered, and later published, his most well-known sermon, "Sinners in the Hands of an Angry God" (1741). Two years later, he published *Some Thoughts Concerning the Present Revival of Religion in New-England, and the Way in Which It Ought to Be Acknowledged and Prompted* (1743). His zealous behavior on the pulpit, including a great conflict over the practice of communion, eventually led to his dismissal as pastor of the Northampton Church in 1750. After a short stint as a missionary to the Indians in western Massachusetts, Edwards was called to preside as president of the College of New Jersey

(Princeton). Unfortunately, he died of smallpox just three months into his presidency. Later publications include *Freedom of Will* (1754) and *The Great Christian Doctrine of Original Sin Defended* (1758).

► **TRENDS** _____

Spiritual autobiography: Students will recognize the overabundance of personal writing in seventeenth-century America. Some scholars assert that the sermon was the first American genre. Religious writing was a popular form of writing in colonial America, as it took the form of sermons, captivity narratives, poems, and especially spiritual autobiographies. The spiritual autobiography is relatively formulaic: the author depicts his/her life as it progresses from a state of sin to a state of grace, detailing cycles of sin and repentance on the journey to salvation. The writer explores his/her relationship with God's natural world, the Bible, other believers and nonbelievers, and theological conflicts such as election or original sin. St. Augustine's *Confessions* is a classic example, and John Bunyan's *Pilgrim's Progress* is a popular fictional example. Puritans were known for keeping scrupulous diaries, so the narrative form of spiritual autobiographies became popular. Edwards' *Personal Narrative* is a brief example of a spiritual autobiography, as well as the most famous in Puritan literature. I also mention this genre now, so you can contrast its themes and conventions with eighteenth-century Enlightenment-influenced autobiographies such as Benjamin Franklin's.

"Sinners in the Hands of an Angry God"

Unfortunately, Edwards has been pigeon-holed as the "fire-and-brimstone preacher" because of this highly anthologized sermon. It is recorded by many historians that Edwards delivered this sermon using an even temperament and soft tone, which contrasted with the cries and audible moans of his congregation. Although his imagery is frightening and his theological assertion is daunting, Edwards published and preached many more sermons on Christ's hope and love. This is a must-read for students because of its poetic nature. Here is a sample of the literary imagery and rhetoric Edwards uses throughout the piece:

> The God that holds you over the pit of hell, much as one holds a spider, or some loathsome insect, over the fire, abhors you, and is dreadfully provoked; his wrath towards you burns like fire; he looks upon you as worthy of nothing else, but to be cast into the fire; he is of purer eyes than to bear to have you in his sight; you are ten thousand times so abominable in his eyes as the most hateful venomous serpent is in ours.

> (Baym et al. 2008, 200)

This excerpt includes the image of the spider dangling over a fire. Note that this sermon is filled with **extended metaphors** (also called a **conceit**) that are developed throughout the sermon.

Must Read

Works by Edward Taylor

Preparatory Meditations, Meditation 8 and Prologue

Huswifery

Works by Cotton Mather

Anthologies vary widely regarding Mather. Consider reading an excerpt of *The Diary of Cotton Mather* as well as an excerpt from *The Wonders of the Invisible World*. I recommend the section titled "The Trial of Martha Carrier."

Works by Jonathan Edwards

"Sinners in the Hands of an Angry God"

Personal Narrative

EARLY NATIONAL PERIOD: LITERATURE FROM 1750–1820

Political Writings

The Age of Enlightenment heavily influenced the minds of American colonists, including Benjamin Franklin, Thomas Paine, Thomas Jefferson, James Madison, and Alexander Hamilton, just to name a few. As Puritanism, and the authority of the Bible and the church, began to lose hold on the colonies, many popular thinkers considered themselves **deists**. These thinkers allowed for a supreme being who created the earth but one who does not interfere with human actions. Population increases, especially those from Europe, also added to the ethnic, theological, and ideological mix of people. No longer did Puritan England have the only show in town. It is also said that religion ruled the first half of the eighteenth century and politics ruled the second half.

This section will highlight several political figures who also wrote extensively.

Benjamin Franklin

Franklin's autobiography was not only one of the most popular autobiographies of all time, but it also constituted a personal and literary undertaking completely different from any memoirs of the past. As I've already stated, the practice of spiritual self-reflection, meditation, and journal writing was very important to Protestant colonists. Self-examination and metaphorical writing were mainstays in seventeenth-century writing; however, due in part to the Enlightenment, the autobiography genre changed dramatically. Because individual reason trumped collective theology, readers became more interested in the travels and travails of the ordinary individual. Also, instead of focusing on the next world, new writers, beginning with Franklin, focused on securing happiness and vocation in this world. He was not interested in the state of the soul but more in the state of the human relationship. Some scholars even note that Franklin's apprenticeship and eventual separation with his older brother is analogous to America's life as a colony and then as an independent nation.

Franklin began writing his life's story in 1771, but the first part of the manuscript was not published in English until 1793. Ironically, it was published in France first in 1791 and not titled *The Autobiography of Benjamin Franklin* with all four parts until 1868. Sadly, the narrative only encompasses Franklin's life before 1758. His prolific years as scientific observer, statesman, and Constitutional writer were years away.

Franklin wrote this first part the *Autobiography* while in England and addressed it to his older son, William Franklin. He begins the narrative recollecting abstractly on his life and his happiness with his choices and incidents, even the errors. Franklin then gives his son a brief history of the Franklin family, as well as his own schooling to become a minister before embarking on a life in printing. Most notably, Franklin tells of how he used the nine-year printing apprenticeship to his brother to indulge his great love of reading and writing. His first published works were essays that he placed on his brother's desk signed by Silence Dogood. Although the elder brother was furious when he was convinced that his apprentice was now a writer, the popularity of the essays gave young Franklin great confidence in writing and publishing. Later, Franklin runs away to Philadelphia where he begins to make connections. With advice and promises of a job and future advancement by the governor of Pennsylvania, William Keith, Franklin travels to England to buy printing equipment. Take note that Franklin usually calls his youthful errors "**errata**." Trusting Keith, leaving his brother, and fathering an illegitimate child are examples of his errata. On his return to America, and his new adopted home, Philadelphia, Franklin begins his career in printing. Thus, the end of the first part focuses on the trials and errors of publishing life in New England.

The second part of the manuscript was written 13 years later in France. After the American Revolution, Franklin begins where he left off in the telling of his life. However, what is most notable about this relatively brief section is his desire to reach "**Moral Perfection**." With this desire, he commits to perfecting one virtue a week until he has succeeded in each and every one: temperance, silence, order, resolution, frugality, industry, sincerity, justice, moderation, cleanliness, tranquility, chastity, and humility. This section is simply an intimation of virtue and the value they have for people of all religions.

Must Read

The Autobiography of Benjamin Franklin, parts 1 and 2: The first two parts of the *Autobiography* are the most widely anthologized; however, it would be wise to be knowledgeable of the content of parts 3 and 4.

Thomas Paine (1737–1809)

Born in England, Paine did not immigrate to America until he was well into his thirties; however, this "rebel" spent much of his energies speaking and writing for American independence. He anonymously published the famous pamphlet *Common Sense* in 1776 directly after the opening battles of Concord and Lexington. Take note of this popular line from the Introduction: "The cause of America is in a great measure the cause of all mankind" (Baym et al. 2008, 326). *Common Sense* sold over a half million copies, so the anonymity of the author did not hold long. Due to his new-found fame, Paine joined the Revolutionary Army and served as a personal assistant to high-ranking officers. His writing continued, however, with a series of pamphlets called *Crisis*. *Rights of Man* was published in 1791–1792, and the best-selling *The Age of Reason*, a treatise for deism that challenged organized Christianity, the inerrancy of the Bible, and the political alignment of the church in America, was published in 1794 (completely in 1807). Although his popularity and effectiveness as a writer waned, Paine still remains one of the most popular statesmen who committed his writings to a plain style in order to reach the common American.

Must Read

Common Sense by Thomas Paine: If you do not have the time to read *Common Sense* in its entirety, read the excerpts published in most anthologies. I recommend the section from the third edition titled "Thoughts on the Present State of American Affairs."

The Federalist

From 1787 to 1788, New York newspapers published about 85 essays advocating support for strong federal government. Although each essay was signed "Publius," most informed readers knew that they were penned by **Alexander Hamilton**, John Jay, and **James Madison**. The essays were later collected into two volumes, and the resulting work is now referred to as *The Federalist*. Its sole function was to convince New Yorkers to vote for a proposed new Constitution, advocating that a strong central government and the freedom of individual rights are not mutually exclusive. Hamilton proposes in his first essay "after an unequivocal experience of the inefficacy of the subsisting federal government, you are called upon to deliberate on a new Constitution for the United States of America" (Baym et al. 2008, 347). The unified states under a new Constitution, argued the Federalists, would ensure national defense, enforce unity between the states, improve commerce and national wealth, and act as a voice for individual states.

Must Read

The Federalist: Although anthologies vary widely on the essays they include, I recommend reading an example each from Alexander Hamilton and James Madison. Try numbers 1, 6, and 10.

Thomas Jefferson (1743–1826) and the Declaration of Independence

Jefferson's life is the making of a great trivia game. After graduating from William and Mary College in Virginia, he was admitted to the state bar and then elected into the legislature of the Virginia House of Burgesses. Due to his bright mind and skills as a writer, Jefferson was asked to draft a **Declaration of Independence** in 1776, and he is still considered the sole author of that document even though Congress edited several sections, much to Jefferson's dismay. It should be noted that Jefferson drafted a section that rejected slavery, though, as scholars point out, he preferred African colonization to American citizenship for Blacks. Here is arguably the most famous excerpt from that document:

> We hold these truths to be self-evident: that all men are created equal; that they are endowed by their Creator with inherent and inalienable rights; that among these are life, liberty, and the pursuit of happiness.
> (Belasco and Johnson 2008a, 448).

Jefferson not only founded the University of Virginia, but he also helped design several of its buildings. His home in Virginia was called **Monticello**, and his personal library lay the foundation for the Library of Congress. After a stint in France as an American ambassador with Benjamin Franklin, Jefferson became vice president to the United States under John Adams in 1796 and then president in 1800; he was the first president to be inaugurated in Washington, D.C.

Must Read

Declaration of Independence: Students should read the version included in *The Autobiography of Thomas Jefferson*. In this version, Jefferson includes the original draft and those sections "struck out by Congress."

Philip Freneau (1752–1832)

Known as the "Poet of the American Revolution," Freneau worked as a journalist, satirist, and as a translator in Philadelphia where he honed his poetic and rhetorical skills. Born into a wealthy New York family, Freneau was well educated and well traveled, with many famous acquaintances to boast. His love for the sea, however, sent him to the West Indies in 1776 where he saw firsthand the atrocities of slave labor. After several years at sea, Freneau returned to America where he continued his love of writing poetry. He published several books of poetry: *The American Village* (1772) and *Poems* (1809). Freneau's poems became more politically and socially aware after the Revolutionary War; however, his love for lyric and the pastoral is still evident in many anthologized poems. Although Freneau is still considered a minor American poet, more and more professors choose to include his poetry as a preface to the movement of a "national literature."

Must Read

Poetry of Philip Freneau

"The Wild Honey Suckle"

"The Indian Burying Ground"

"To Sir Toby"

DIARIES AND JOURNALS
OF THE EIGHTEENTH CENTURY

In this section, I will introduce the multivocal America not always included in typical college classrooms. Here, you will find information and excerpts from journals depicting the lives of women, American Indians, Africans and other foreigners, and various religious groups. One of the great effects of the Enlightenment was the acknowledgment that the individual voice was important, even if that voice was not male, white, Puritan, or wealthy. Although these works are considered minor texts, I recommend being familiar with the names, works, and general themes of these diaries and journals. If you have time, read the several excerpts published in the anthologies.

Samson Occom (1723–1792)

A Short Narrative of My Life (1768) was found in the Dartmouth College archives and not published until 1982. As a Christian convert, Occom, a Mohegan Indian, ministered to several New England Indian tribes, including the Montauks of Long Island. Occom was ordained by the Presbyterian Church in 1759 and taught at an Indian charity school, which later became Dartmouth College when it moved to Hanover, Connecticut. His autobiography was originally written as a ten-page manuscript, and it details his life as an Indian minister.

John Woolman (1720–1772)

The Journal of John Woolman has never been out of print. Born into a Quaker family in New Jersey, Woolman adopted many of the Quaker beliefs that at once put the Quakers at odds with their Puritan brethren. Although both groups of Christians denounced the Church of England, Quakers did not ascribe to Calvin's doctrine of election or predestination; they believed Christ's death and resurrection redeemed all humankind. Each individual was filled with the "inner light," which was Jesus Christ. Because of this philosophy of the equality of all humans, Quakers denounced slavery and later became leaders in women's suffrage. When Woolman was a young worker, he was asked to draw up a bill of sale of a slave woman for his employer. Although he grudgingly complied, Woolman regretted the decision. His religious convictions also persuaded him to stop wearing suits with dyed wool and eating sugar because of the exploitation of slave labor in the United States and the West Indies. Like early Puritan diaries, Woolman's journal is less an account of the mundane than it is a spiritual autobiography. However, what clearly differentiates this journal from Puritan spiritual autobiographies is Woolman's commitment to marry his spiritual convictions with his earthly activities.

J. Hector St. John de Crèvecoeur (1735–1813)

Highly successful in England and France, de Crèvecoeur's *Letters from an American Farmer* was published and revised several times in the late eighteenth century for European readership during a time of American fascination. The most anthologized section of his autobiography is titled "What is an American?" This is an important question from a man who spent most of his life outside of America. Born in France under the name Michel-Guillaume Jean de Crèvecoeur, he immigrated to England and Canada before settling in New York, although this did not stop him from traveling back to France where he eventually remained.

Elizabeth Ashbridge (1713–1755)   42 years approx.

Born to Anglican parents in England, Ashbridge eventually rejected the religion of her parents for a theology more accepting of women in leadership roles. Her first husband died soon after their marriage, and because her parents disproved of her elopement, Ashbridge lived with a Quaker relative in Dublin. Soon she immigrated to New York, and after a stressful marriage, she became a Quaker minister in 1738. Her spiritual autobiography, *Some Account of the Fore Part of the Life of Elizabeth Ashbridge*, was one of the first of its kind published by a woman.

Sarah Kemble Knight (1666–1727)

Although Knight lived most of her life well before the other writers in this section, I include her here because her journal was not published until the nineteenth century. In addition, her journal is filled with mundane and ordinary observations of life in the eighteenth century, thus making her work very different from the spiritual diaries written around her birth. What is most notable about Madame Knight was her acquaintance with prominent Americans. She kept a boarding house and taught many children, which could have included Benjamin Franklin and the Mather children. Most anthologies include the section of her diaries that retell a long journey she took on horseback from Boston to New York in 1704.

Africans in the Eighteenth Century

I don't have to tell you that Africans lived in America in the seventeenth century. Thousands of slaves worked plantations in the Carolinas at the turn of the century. Some scholars assert that African slaves made up around 40 percent of the total population in the mid-eighteenth century. During this time, slavery supplanted foreign indentured servitude and Native American work. The following authors are the most anthologized Black writers of the American eighteenth century.

Olaudah Equiano (ca. 1745–1797)

Where and when Equiano was born is up for scholarly debate. According to his autobiography, *The Interesting Narrative of the Life of Olaudah Equiano, or Gustavus Vassa, the African* (1789), Equiano was born along the Niger River in an Ibo Village of Africa. (The famous twentieth-century African novelist Chinua Achebe sets his fiction in the same place.) Although he was raised to be a chief leader of his people, slave traders captured him and his sister when they were young and took them to America in 1756. Recent scholarship suggests a different story. According to naval records and baptismal records, Equiano most likely was born in the Carolinas in 1747 and sold to a British navy officer and taken to England around 1754. Critics are quick to point out, however, that any "storytelling" on Equiano's part was done in an effort to narrate the African's plight as cargo upon the **Middle Passage**. Ultimately, his narrative voice becomes representative of thousands of silenced voices.

His history beginning in America and England is fully confirmed by historical evidence. Equiano's master, Michael Henry Pascal, renamed him Gustavus Vassa—the name of the first Swedish king who led his people in rebellion against Danish rule. He was educated in London, served in the navy, and sold back into slavery. His next master was a Quaker named Robert King who allowed Equiano to purchase his freedom for forty pounds in 1766. The rest of his life was spent speaking and writing on behalf of the one million slaves who were transported to America during the middle part of the eighteenth century. As a Christian convert, he used Christian sentiment to persuade societies to give up the sinful practice of slave trading. Note the following passage from chapter 2:

> O, ye nominal Christians! Might not an African ask you—Learned you this from your God, who says unto you, Do unto all men as you would me should do unto you? Is it not enough that we are torn from our country and friends, to toil for your luxury and lust of gain.
>
> (Baym et al. 2008, 368)

His now famous, and much studied, autobiography was widely read even through the nineteenth century.

Phillis Wheatley (1753–1784)

In my opinion, Wheatley's story is the most extraordinary and fascinating literary tale of the eighteenth century. She was under the age of twenty when her first book of poems was published. Since American publishing houses would not print a book written by a young, Black, female slave, Wheatley's master's son took Wheatley and her manuscript to England where she met influential people, including Benjamin Franklin, and eventually saw her work in print. What is most remarkable about *Poems on Various Subjects, Religious and Moral* (1773), besides its moving lines, is the preface that was attached to the manuscript. Because white society could not fathom such words coming from a slave, young Wheatley was required to defend that she actually wrote the poems in front of an official court in Boston comprised of powerful and highly respected Americans: John Hancock, Governor Thomas Hutchinson, and Andrew Oliver. She passed the test, so a letter of authentication was placed upon the first book published by a Black woman.

Not much of Wheatley's life is known after this momentous occasion. Her masters died soon after the publication of her book; she was married to a freedman named John Peters in 1778; and she died in 1784. Scholars agree that a second volume of poems and letters was slated to be published, but that project never came to fruition. Most likely she lived out her freedom in poverty and obscurity.

The first poem to make her famous was an elegy for the famous English preacher, George Whitefield. Many of her poems were dedicated to individuals who influenced her in various ways. Wheatley was not shy to discuss politics, religion, and even the ills of slavery. Although some critics believe that her poetry reveals an African who has been totally assimilated into white, Christian, American culture, it is important for students to read her poems carefully, looking for those poignant attacks on hypocrisy and avarice. Here is a sample:

On Being Brought From Africa to America
'Twas mercy brought me from my Pagan land,
Taught my benighted soul to understand
That there's a God, that there's a Saviour too:
Once I redemption neither sought nor knew.
Some view our sable race with scornful eye,
"Their colour is a diabolic die."
Remember, Christians, Negros, black as Cain,
May be refin'd, and join th' angelic train.

(Wheatley 1995, 12)

Must Read

The Interesting Narrative of the Life of Olaudah Equiano, or Gustavus Vassa, the African by Olaudah Equiano, chapter 2: Anthologies vary widely on the sections and lengths of the autobiography to publish; however, most include chapter 2 in its entirety.

Poetry of Phillis Wheatley

"On Being Brought from Africa to America"

"To the University of Cambridge, in New-England"

"On the Death of Rev. Mr. George Whitefield"

"To S.M. A Young African Painter, on Seeing His Works"

"To His Excellency General Washington

"To the Right honorable William, Earl of Dartmouth"

REFERENCES

Belasco, Susan, and Linck Johnson. 2008a. *The Bedford Anthology of American Literature*, Vol. 1, *Beginnings to 1865*. Boston: Bedford/St. Martin's.

———. 2008b. *The Bedford Anthology of American Literature*, Vol. 2, *1865 to the Present*. Boston: Bedford/St. Martin's.

Baym et al. 2008. *The Norton Anthology of American Literature*, shorter 7th ed. New York: W. W. Norton.

Hunter, J. Paul. 1996. *The Norton Introduction to Poetry*, 6th ed. New York: W. W. Norton.

Kennedy, X. J., and Dana Gioia. 2005. *An Introduction to Poetry*, 11th ed. New York: Pearson/Longman.

Kizer, Carolyn. 1995. *100 Great Poems by Women: A Golden ECCO Anthology.* Hopewell, NJ: Ecco Press.

Wheatley, Phillis. 1995. *Poems of Phillis Wheatley: An African and a Slave.* Bedford, MA: Applewood Books.

Chapter 3

The Romantic Period (1820–1865)

THE AMERICAN RENAISSANCE AND A NEW NATIONAL LITERATURE

The 1830s in American literary history was the beginning of what many scholars refer to as the **American Renaissance**—a birth of sorts of literary imagination that was predominantly and uniquely "American." However, it is worth our efforts to spend a little time with those authors who are credited with moving America towards a renaissance. So before we study Emerson, Whitman, Melville, Hawthorne, Poe, Thoreau, Stowe, and Dickinson, I want to introduce you to Washington Irving, William Cullen Bryant, and James Fenimore Cooper. Although many students might not be familiar with these three writers, their contemporaries and readers considered them the great American writers of their day. The first list I gave you is filled with writers who struggled to gain literary recognition and readers in their day; some, like Dickinson, published only a handful of poems during their lifetime.

"It seems stupid to have discovered America only to make it into a copy of another country" (Wharton 1994, 151). Although Edith Wharton's character, Madame Ellen Olenska, spoke these words in *Age of Innocence* (published in 1920 but set in the 1870s), the sentiment rings true to the 1820s. During this time, many newspaper writers and socialites called for a "new national literature." After the **War of 1812** with England, and after witnessing the French Revolution years prior, Americans felt that their identity, their nationality, was vulnerable and imitative. So most historians note that before the 1830s most Americans desired literature at par with their British contemporaries. However, it was not necessary, at this point, for emerging American writers to break completely from the traditional literary conventions of their once parent country. To be compared to William Wordsworth, Alexander Pope, Lord Byron, Edmund Spenser, or John Milton was enough. Bryant's poems, Cooper's novels, and Irving's stories share a love of the landscape and a belief that it would be that American landscape that would construct a distinct American persona. These writers were not afraid to discuss topics such as national expansion, Indian relations, wealth and identity, as well as issues related to American identity.

Washington Irving (1783–1859)

It was during this time in American literary history that a new type of hero was constructed: this man came from humble beginnings, not attached to aristocracy or the English monarchy, or possessed great knowledge or wealth. This new American hero would embody the ideals of the new America, one beholden, but not attached, to England. Irving became the first American international literary superstar. His famous works include a satirical magazine called *Salmagundi* that he wrote in 1807 with his brother; *A History of New-York from the Beginning of the World to the End of the Dutch Dynasty* (1809), a parody and political satire; and his most famous work, *The Sketch Book of Geoffrey Crayon*, which was written during a 17-year stay in Europe and published in a two-volume set in 1820. This work houses Irving's most enduring and mythologized stories, "The Legend of Sleepy Hollow" and "Rip Van Winkle." Note also that Geoffrey Crayon is a loosely autobiographical character. Irving's subsequent and somewhat less successful works include *Bracebridge Hall* (1822) and *Tales of a Traveller* (1824). In 1828, however, Irving published *The Life and Voyages of Christopher Columbus* after living and reading manuscripts in Spain for several years. It is recorded by scholars that this work was used in classrooms for generations to come. During the "Spain years," Irving also wrote *The Conquest of Granada* (1829), *Voyages and Discoveries of the Companions of Columbus* (1831), and *The Alhambra* (1832). Irving returned to America and explored the West, which resulted in several works, including *The Prairies* (1835), *Astoria* (1836), and *The Adventures of Captain Bonneville, U.S.A.* (1837). Even after a long literary life, Irving's *Sketch Book* still remains his most influential, especially for the next generation of American writers.

"Rip Van Winkle"

Before the narrative begins, an unknown narrator tells readers that the following story "was found among the papers of the late **Diedrich Knickerbocker**." This is the same character who "wrote" *A History of New-York* in 1809. Irving created the persona of Knickerbocker for satirical purposes; however, he uses this preface to "Rip Van Winkle" to smooth over any wrinkles caused by the publishing of Knickerbocker's last book. Although this unknown author calls the *History* a "book of unquestionable authority," he is also quick to include "that he never intended to injure or offend." Thus, he introduces a lost and posthumous work by Diedrich Knickerbocker (Belasco and Johnson 2008, 530).

Rip Van Winkle lives in the **Catskill Mountains** in southeastern New York among the descendants of great Dutch immigrants. Irving calls him "a simple good natured fellow . . . a kind neighbor, and an obedient, henpecked husband." Van Winkle is popular with the other wives of the village and especially popular with the children, as he is one to play games, tell stories, and revel in leisure. "The great error," writes Irving of Rip "was an insuperable aversion to all kinds of profitable labour" (Belasco and Johnson 2008, 532). Although Van Winkle is unwilling to work his own sad plot of land, he is quick to run little errands for the other wives in the village. One day, he retreats to the high mountains for squirrel hunting and relaxing. Upon meeting a stranger with a keg of old Dutch gin, Van Winkle follows him up another crevice to a place where a group of gentlemen are playing nine-pins. Drinking too much, he falls into a deep sleep. When he wakes up, Van Winkle notices that the men are gone and the place where they'd played nine-pins seems not to have ever existed, so he returns to his village only to find his house in ruins, strangers in the village, new buildings, and even his dog, Wolf, who doesn't recognize him. He does meet a group of young men, and through his discussion with them, surmises that his sleep on the mountain lasted twenty years. Discovering his daughter, now with child, and his son, a spitting image of his father who spends his days lying underneath a great tree, Van Winkle picks up where he left off those years ago, doing nothing but gossiping and walking the nearby hills. His story is affirmed by another old man in the village who argues that the stranger Van Winkle met on the mountain was none other than a long-dead Henry Hudson (the English navigator) and his gang of explorers who keep an eye on the river and play tricks on unsuspecting travelers. The funny part is that Van Winkle slept through the Revolutionary War and the creation of the United States of America.

One of the major themes of the story is the concept of confusion among and the subsequent response by American colonists who "woke up" one morning only to discover that they were now citizens of their own country and not subjects of another. The irony is that only after his long sleep does Van Winkle find his true calling: to tell the story of the past and to recall a time before the Revolution. Some scholars note that Dame Van Winkle's lectures resemble the Puritan sermons of old. But now that she is dead, Van Winkle can live his life in simple satisfaction. "Rip Van Winkle" is sometimes called the first American story for much of the above reasons.

Must Read

"Rip Van Winkle" from *The Sketch Book of Geoffrey Crayon* by Washington Irving: Most anthologies include only this story from *Sketch Book*; however, you should consider reading "The Legend of Sleepy Hollow" or "The Wife" for a good representation of Irving's work.

James Fenimore Cooper (1789–1851)

Cooper remains one of the most popular authors of the early nineteenth century who is seldom read today. Other than *The Last of the Mohicans* (a book that became a popular, award-winning movie starring Daniel Day Lewis in 1992), his work is losing interest among students and professors (and space in anthologies).

Cooper is best known for his **Leatherstocking series**. In a series of five novels, Cooper reveals the underbelly of American nationalism, especially as it conflicted with the American Indians. The protagonists of the series are the trader and frontiersman Natty Bumpo and his Indian companion, Chingachgook. Each book describes a burgeoning nation as it conflicts with the native people: *The Pioneers* (1823), *The Last of the Mohicans* (1826), *The Prairie* (1827), *The Pathfinder* (1840), and *The Deerslayer* (1841).

Cooper became a voracious writer, publishing over forty books in his lifetime. Aside from the Leatherstocking series, Cooper also wrote one of the first historical romances of the American Revolution, *The Spy* (1821). It was this book that sent him to New York to try his hand at a full-time literary career. In New York, he helped found a literary society called the **Bread and Cheese Club**, which housed **romantic painters of the Hudson River School** and even William Cullen Bryant. He spent several years traveling Europe and writing, although these novels did not receive the same attention as his earlier work. In fact, in 1833 he swore he would never write a novel again. Seven years later, he wrote another series of novels. Cooper's later work includes a controversial take on the military titled *History of the Navy of the United States of America* (1839) and a series of novels ("Littlepage" novels) exploring issues of land ownership.

William Cullen Bryant (1794–1878)

Many scholars appropriately link Bryant to a group of famous poets known as the **Fireside or Schoolroom Poets**: **John Greenleaf Whittier**, **Oliver Wendell Holmes Sr.**, **James Russell Lowell**, and **Henry Wadsworth Longfellow**. The label was given to this group based on their poetry's accessibility to memorization and public recitation. (Ask a person over the age of sixty to recite a poem from their school days and I bet it will be a line or two from one of these poets.) Although their poetry was nationally known and extremely popular, their style, meter, rhyme scheme, and poetic structure were imitative of the great British poets: William Wordsworth, Percy Bysshe Shelley, John Keats, and Lord Byron, among others. Therefore, modern critics denounced their work as simplistic, trite, overly didactic and moralizing, and imitative. Their themes were mostly domestic and lyrical. However, each poet was known to explore politics and social issues, as well as write long narrative poems of those issues. Remember, these poems were published at a time when most Americans called for a literature that was competitive with, rather than entirely different from, that of their British counterparts. The Fireside Poets were the answer.

Bryant's literary career—and his popularity—began with the publication of his volume of poetry titled *Poems* (1821). These poems were lyrical intimations on the natural world and the cycle of life. He was an educated man, but because of his family's meager finances, Bryant left Williams College after his first year; nevertheless, he continued his love of learning and writing poetry. In 1815, Bryant was admitted to the Massachusetts bar. Along with his poetry, Bryant was an accomplished newspaper man. His work with the *New York Evening Post* endured for almost fifty years. Like most of the Fireside Poets, Bryant was socially and politically minded; therefore, his loathing of slavery forced him to leave the Democratic Party and aid in the establishment of the Republican Party. (Fun Fact: Abraham Lincoln was the first Republican president.)

Many scholars consider Bryant's poetry part of (or at least a precursor of) **American romanticism**. As you read his lyrics on nature, pay attention to the metaphors and symbols at play. Bryant finds great truth and spirituality in the natural world and landscape. Also, note that most of Bryant's poetry contains some moral lesson or truth. His most read and anthologized poem is "Thanatopsis." The title can be translated to mean "a meditation on death." In the poem, Bryant reminds the reader that death is a very natural and consistent part of life. Subsequently, he intimates that death should not be feared or hated, but that it should be treated as a "going home" of sorts. Community is a major motif of this poem. Read this famous excerpt:

> When thoughts
> Of the last bitter hour come like a blight
> Over thy spirit, and sad images
> Of the stern agony, and shroud, and pall,
> And breathless darkness, and the narrow house,
> Make thee to shudder, and grow sick at heart;—
> Go forth under the open sky and list[en],
> To Nature's teachings, . . .

(Hollander 1996, 56)

 Must Read

Poetry of William Cullen Bryant

"Thanatopsis"

"To a Waterfowl"

AMERICAN ROMANTICISM

The individual is at the heart of any definition of romanticism. And, although this idea is similar to that espoused by the Enlightenment, the romantics reacted against a life of reason for a life of sentiment and feeling. For the romantics, individuals are the very center of the literary act; therefore, expressing feeling, emotion, and attitude are the key components of the literary act. As a result of this freedom of expression, writers at this time did not feel constrained by traditional conventions of literature, nor did they feel trapped by the politics and social mores of the day. Take note that romanticism (like most other literary movements) was a reaction to a previous cultural era (the Age of Enlightenment). Sparked by the French Revolution in 1789 and also influenced by the Industrial Revolution, romanticism rejected scientific reasoning as the only way to understand the universe or human nature, and claimed the idyllic life of the rural areas of America instead of the growing urban sections.

Ralph Waldo Emerson (1803–1882)

There is simply not enough room in this study guide to appropriately and effectively depict Emerson's importance and influence on American letters and social thought. Born in Boston in a Unitarian family, Emerson was raised by his Calvinist aunt, Mary Moody Emerson, and sent to Harvard College to become a minister. He was ordained in 1829 as one of the pastors at Boston's Second Church (the same church where Cotton Mather preached); however, **New England Unitarianism** was certainly more popular than the Calvinist theology brought over by the Puritans. Although Unitarians at this time still held onto the Bible as God's revealed word, they rejected the Puritan idea that humans were totally depraved, and many Unitarians started to strongly question the divinity of Christ.

Scholars have spilled a lot of ink discussing the causes for Emerson's struggles with and criticisms of Christianity. What is important is that Emerson did break with the Unitarian Church (and orthodox Christianity as a whole) for several reasons:

- He refused to administer the Lord's Supper (communion/Eucharist) because he simply found no reason to do so.

- As stated before, Emerson questioned the divinity of Christ. His position is made clear in his famous Divinity School Address given to the graduates of Harvard College in 1838.

- Emerson also became very skeptical of religious dogma that focused on the past and/or structures that seemed to oppress individuality. These themes permeate most of his writings after 1832.

After a few years of speaking on the lecture tour, Emerson remarried and settled in Concord where he self-published a short essay called *Nature*. This book became the transcendental manifesto for many writers and thinkers of the 1830s and beyond. This book explored humankind's relationship to nature and depicted the "signs" that individuals should recognize in nature in order to transcend nature. Many intellectuals, including Bronson Alcott (father of Louisa May Alcott, who wrote *Little Women*), Henry David Thoreau, and Margaret Fuller, met in Emerson's home to discuss the ideologies present in *Nature*. Eventually, Thoreau, Fuller, and Emerson published their transcendental ideas in the *Dial*, a journal that ran from 1840 to 1844. During this time and beyond, Emerson lectured on various topics all over the country, which culminated into two widely read collections of essays: *Essays* (1841) and a second series of *Essays* (1844).

Emerson's ideas of social reform were interesting. Although he fully supported the antislavery movement and women's suffrage, he refused to participate in group reform efforts. Therefore, he declined an opportunity to live at **Brook Farm**, a utopian community dedicated to social reform and transcendental teaching. (Nathaniel Hawthorne wrote a fictional satire of this utopian community titled *The Blithedale Romance* in 1852.) Anthologies vary widely in what they include from Emerson's vast catalog of essays and poems. My recommendation is to read those works that explore his transcendental ideas of individuality and spirituality. Beyond the selections I mention in the Must Read box, if you have time, I recommend reading "The Poet," the Divinity School Address, "Experience," and "Friendship."

A good way for students to remember how influential Emerson remains is to keep in mind that *The American Scholar*, the magazine of the Phi Beta Kappa Society, took its name from his famous speech. Emerson's own influences included the Scottish philosopher and writer Thomas Carlyle and the British philosopher and poet Samuel Taylor Coleridge. Carlyle's influence included his chapter about "Natural Supernaturalism" in his novel, *Sartor Resartus*. Supernaturalism held that nature, including human beings, commands the power and authority traditionally associated with omnipotent deities. Coleridge was an English poet and philosopher and is considered a major force of the English romanticism that influenced American transcendentalism.

Must Read

Works by Ralph Waldo Emerson

Nature

"Self-Reliance"

"The American Scholar"

Selected poems

   "Each and All"

   "Merlin"

   "Brahma"

   "Concord Hymn"

   "The Rhodora"

TRANSCENDENTALISM

The term "transcendentalism" can be slippery and misunderstood. You should, however, be familiar and aware of particular tenets of transcendentalism as espoused and lectured on by Emerson. Simply, the term refers to the ability to transcend, or to rise above. The implication is that individuals do have the ability to rise above the doctrines, dogmas, and teachings of the present to reach a more ideal spiritual state—one found within themselves. Students should also keep in mind that Emerson's thoughts were heavily influenced by German philosophy (especially **Immanuel Kant** and German idealism), European mystic **Emanuel Swedenborg**, and English romanticism (especially **Samuel Taylor Coleridge**); however, students should also note that Emerson's beliefs were also a reaction to Calvinist theology, the philosophy of **Thomas Locke**, and the structure of American Protestantism.

Here is a short list of transcendental ideas to keep in mind:

- The individual mind can obtain spiritual truths without help from the senses, or without guidance from past institutions or religious dogmas. (Thus, the fact that many students claim to believe what Emerson believed might make the old man cringe.)

- Truth and knowledge are best sought by observing nature.

- Autonomy and individuality are the center of this ideology.

- Independence of mind should bring forth the "inner divinity." Emerson believed in the individual divine soul.

- Intuition and creativity overpower reason. When individuals connect with their own creativity/intuition/divinity, then they are connected with all things in the universe. This moment was called the **oversoul** in transcendental circles. Although a bit reductionist, think of Buddhism's "state of nirvana."

- Everything on earth contained this "divine spark," so nothing was evil; the chief end of an individual is to be fully aware of his "spark" and then fully aware of his connectedness to everything else on earth.

Made famous in Emerson's essay "Self-Reliance," transcendentalism preached that conformity was to be avoided. Emerson wrote that "consistency is the hobgoblin of little minds."

One of the major forces in transcendentalism was Frederic Hedge, a Unitarian minister. He helped found the Transcendental Club for these American thinkers to gather and discuss their ideas as well as to write about them in the club's journal, *The Dial*.

Margaret Fuller (1810–1850)

Fuller is usually associated with Emerson because of her tireless work on the *Dial* from 1840 to 1842 and her membership in the **Transcendental Club**. Note that Fuller shared many of the same transcendental ideas as Emerson and Thoreau; however, her most lasting contribution to American letters revolves around women's rights and, later, coverage of the Italian Revolution (1846–1850). She was given a rigorous education from her father when she was young; she attended a school for only one year before returning home and continuing her self-education. During these years, according to most scholars, Fuller nurtured a fascination with European romanticism, especially the writings of **Johann Wolfgang von Goethe** (although some scholars argue that Goethe was only a precursor to romanticism). Throughout her life, Fuller wrote articles on Goethe as well as translated many of his works into English. When she was in her mid-twenties, her father died, which forced her out of learning and into the workforce. Fuller taught at two prestigious schools: **Bronson Alcott's Temple School** in Boston and the Greene Street School in Providence, Rhode Island. It was Alcott's progressive ideas on education and gender that probably continued to influence Fuller's idea that gender is socially constructed.

Her first book, *Summer on the Lakes*, was published in 1844, recounting her travels in the American north during 1843; it is part travel diary, part philosophical treatise, and part poetry. Fuller's most celebrated work was published just a year later (1845) while she was working as literary editor of the *New York Tribune*. Originally published in essay form—"The Great Lawsuit: Man versus Men. Woman versus Women"—in the *Dial*, the expanded book version was titled *Woman in the Nineteenth Century*. It is now considered one of the most important early works of the feminist movement. The major premise of the book is the notion that gender is socially constructed, and that those constructions are inevitably damaging to both men and women. She proposes that both genders be aware of the structures and strictures society places on gender, and that both genders intentionally work to liberate men and women from those traditional conventions.

From 1846 to her death, Fuller lived, traveled, and wrote in Europe. Many of her essays from this time period have been collected and anthologized. (Many anthologies will include one or two essays from her European travels; consider reading them.) Her work depicting the Italian Revolution was published in the *Tribune* in 1848; however, this time also brought much personal drama. She became pregnant and fell in love with an Italian Catholic, Giovanni Ossoli. Fuller being Protestant, Ossoli's family rejected the match; moreover, they could not find a church that would marry them. When little Angelo was born, Fuller persuaded Giovanni to immigrate to America where they would have more freedoms. Tragically, their ship wrecked off the coast of New York and all three were killed.

Students should note that scholars have said Fuller may have provided Nathaniel Hawthorne with the inspiration for Hester Prynne in *The Scarlet Letter*, Zenobia in *The Blithedale Romance*, and Beatrice in "Rappaccini's Daughter."

Must Read

Woman in the Nineteenth Century by Margaret Fuller: All anthologies that include Fuller will include an excerpt from this work. Some, however, still refer to the work as "The Great Divorce." Read these excerpts and pay attention to her claims about gender.

Nathaniel Hawthorne (1804–1864)

Hawthorne was quite skeptical of transcendentalism, especially after living on (and investing in) Brook Farm in 1841 and not feeling suited for the demands of utopian communities. His work in general contains a healthy sense of skepticism and social critique, especially as it relates to Puritans and Calvinist theology. Many of Hawthorne's stories and novels are morally ambiguous. What I mean is that, unlike his literary ancestors and contemporaries, Hawthorne was unwilling to prescribe a solitary moral or religious lesson upon his narratives; however, it is important to recognize **allegory** and **symbol** in Hawthorne's tales.

It is important to be aware that many American writers at this time were familiar, and even friendly, with each other. In 1842, Hawthorne and his family moved to Concord, Massachusetts, and became acquainted with Emerson, Thoreau, and Fuller. He also developed a rather complex relationship with Herman Melville while he and his family lived in Lenox, Massachusetts, in the early 1850s. Historians note that Emerson, Oliver Wendell Holmes, James Russell Lowell, and Henry

Wadsworth Longfellow were among the few pallbearers at Hawthorne's funeral in 1864.

Many of Hawthorne's early tales were published in magazines and literary journals, most notably *The Token*. With the help of an old college friend, a collection of tales, *Twice-Told Tales*, was published and well received in 1837. This collection includes a couple of well-anthologized stories: "The Minister's Black Veil," "The Maypole and Merrymount," and "The Gentle Boy." For the next several years, Hawthorne focused on publishing children's books and histories of the nation. This is also the time that the family moved from Boston to Brook Farm and eventually settled in Concord, living in a home owned by Emerson's family ("The Old Manse"). In 1846, *Mosses from an Old Manse* was published to great success as well. Herman Melville wrote a star review of the collection called "Hawthorne and His Mosses." This book included "Young Goodman Brown" and "The Birth-Mark." After this publication, however, the Hawthornes fell on hard financial times, so a friend secured a position for Hawthorne at the Salem Custom House. He faced much agitation at this time, and it is important to note that this period in Hawthorne's life spawned the introduction to *The Scarlet Letter*, which he titled "The Custom House." This important novel was published in 1850. Later novels include *The House of Seven Gables* (1851), *The Blithedale Romance* (1852), and *The Marble Faun* (1860). Although these works are certainly worth your time to read, it is *The Scarlet Letter* that has endured. My hope is that you read this wonderful novel that explores the nature of sin and evil in a religious community. Most anthologies do not include the novel because of its length, but it will be important for you to understand the major characters, conflicts, and themes of the work. The stories noted in the "Must Read" box are usually taught in an American Survey course.

Must Read

Works by Nathaniel Hawthorne

"My Kinsman, Major Molineaux"

"Young Goodman Brown"

"The Minister's Black Veil"

"The Birth-Mark"

The Scarlet Letter

As I stated earlier, the novel begins with an introduction by an anonymous narrator who happened upon a bundled manuscript while working in a Massachusetts Custom House. The antiquated manuscript was labeled with the letter "A." Intrigued, the worker, after leaving his job at the Custom House, decides to write a fictional account of what he discovered in that two-hundred-year-old bundle.

▶ **TRENDS** _____

Romance: Many scholars refer to Nathaniel Hawthorne's novels as romances. Be clear that this label does not necessarily refer to the romantic movement of the nineteenth century or to the paperback novels you may see in grocery-store aisles. The romance is usually more interested in plot (or action) than character, it creates a large space for fictional incidents, it is episodic in nature, and it chooses love and religious conflict as its key themes. Hawthorne's prefaces to his novels usually say a few words about romance. In the preface to *The Blithedale Romance*, for example, he succinctly states that the actions of the story offer "an available foothold between fiction and reality."

The setting of the novel is Puritan America in the 1600s. The protagonist is a young woman named **Hester Prynne**. The major conflict of the novel, and its opening, reveals that Hester has had an affair and birthed a child—Pearl—out of wedlock. Her husband, supposedly lost at sea, sent her to America while he stayed in England. At the beginning of the novel, readers see a young Hester, with baby in hand, publicly humiliated as she is forced to wear a scarlet "A" on her chest for her punishment. To further complicate the matter, she refuses to reveal the identity of Pearl's father.

The course of the novel follows Hester and her daughter as they live on the margins of town and are aided by the local minister, **Arthur Dimmesdale**. Readers should gather quickly that it is the minister who fathered Pearl. Reverend Dimmesdale seems to be failing in health, which readers discover is a result of psychological and spiritual torment, but also due to physical torment as he whips himself nightly for his sins. Conflict arises when Hester's husband reveals himself to Hester, having already been established in the Boston medical community under the name **Roger Chillingworth**. As he discovers the connection between Dimmesdale and Hester, he resolves to revenge himself against the minister by moving in with him and "aiding" in his recovery.

Towards the end of the novel, Dimmesdale, Hester, and Pearl promise to flee to Europe where they can live in peace together. Unfortunately, this does not happen. Dimmesdale dies, and Hester and Pearl discover a scarlet letter branded into his chest. A year later, Chillingworth dies, so Hester and Pearl leave Boston for many years. On her return, Hester lives in the same cottage and continues her charitable work in the community, while Pearl has married a European aristocrat. She dies in her dotage and is buried next to Dimmesdale under a shared tombstone on which is inscribed the letter "A."

Henry Wadsworth Longfellow (1807–1882)

It may be hard for twenty-first-century students to understand that a poet could receive rock-star status, but Longfellow, one of the Fireside Poets, was *the* most popular writer and poet of his generation. His birthdays were actually celebrated by whole towns and schools. And, it is known that he was the first American poet to be enshrined in the poet's corner of England's Westminster Abbey. It is sad, however, that modernism regarded these Fireside Poets as overly simple, trite, and didactic. Because of this unfair assessment, many anthologies and courses minimize (and sometimes ignore) their work.

Longfellow was born in Maine and attended Bowdoin College; he was a class-mate of Nathaniel Hawthorne. His love of languages provided him many good years in Europe as well as a teaching post at Bowdoin and later at Harvard. His first book of poetry, *Voices of the Night*, was published in 1839. His most important work include *Poems on Slavery* (1842), which garnered much press because of its strong abolitionist leanings; *Evangeline* (1847), a narrative love poem that is set during the French and Indian War; *The Song of Hiawatha* (1855), a narrative poem about the life, culture, and history of the American Indians; *The Courtship of Miles Standish* (1858), another love narrative, this time taking place in Puritan America; and *The Poets and Poetry of Europe* (1871), a nonfiction work that promoted the literary history of Europe to new American readers. These books made him wildly popular and rich. After his wife's tragic death in 1861, Longfellow did continue to write and publish poetry, as well as travel abroad. However, his most enduring work was behind him.

Anthologies usually publish a few poems. It is important to know a few important elements about *The Song of Hiawatha*. It is an epic poem about the **Ojibway Indians** of the American north, but particularly, it follows an Indian youth named **Hiawatha** and his love, **Minnehaha**. Scholars assert that Longfellow used the style of Finnish folk epics—specifically the epic *Kalevala*—to create his "American" epic. Scholars also note that Longfellow used another source for the content of his poem: the journalistic work of **Henry Schoolcraft**, the superintendent for Indian Affairs in Michigan from 1836 to 1841. Undoubtedly, the poem is also about the Indian's assimilation into the white, colonized America. Hiawatha leaves his people in a mythical departure, but leaves them with the charge to take off the war paint and light the peace pipe in honor of the strangers from abroad.

Must Read

Poetry of Henry Wadsworth Longfellow

"A Psalm of Life"

"The Jewish Cemetery at Newport"

"My Lost Youth"

"The Slave's Dream"

John Greenleaf Whittier (1807–1892)

Whittier rounds off our discussion of the Fireside Poets. Like Longfellow and Bryant, Whittier was immensely popular, provocative, and well read during his day; however, anthologies and courses cover very little of his work. Whittier's popularity quickly waned after the poet's death in 1892. Since then, critics have dismissed Whittier's poetry for its didacticism and moralizing, while also labeling his "sentimental" abolitionist poetry as mere propaganda. However, in an apologia to the 1888 Riverside edition of his collected works, Whittier defended his anti-slavery poems:

> Of their defects from an artistic point of view it is not necessary to speak . . . they were protests, alarm signals, trumpet-calls to action, words wrung from the writer's heart, forged at white heat."
>
> (Whittier 1894, xxi–xxii)

He is a poet worth reading.

Known as the Quaker poet, Whittier was born and spent his early life on his family's 120-year-old farmstead in Haverhill, Massachusetts. Whittier's formal education was limited to intermittent attendance at one of the local schools and only a year at the Haverhill Academy. It was there that Whittier was introduced to the poetry of Robert Burns. Burns's poetry, along with the New England landscape, his love for colonial legends and folktales, and the family's Quaker beliefs (i.e., pacifism, individual social responsibility, simple living, and equality) seeded Whittier's literary, journalistic, and political careers. Whittier worked as a farmer, cobbler, teacher, and newspaper editor, and also served in the Massachusetts state legislature in 1834 to 1835. Poetry, however, remained his vocation.

Whittier's first poem was published, at the urgings of his sister, in **William Lloyd Garrison's** *Newburyport Free Press* in 1826. This publication kindled Whittier's fiery and complex friendship with the burgeoning abolitionist editor—a friendship that would last until the emancipation of the slaves and beyond. Whittier delivered his first antislavery poem, "To William Lloyd Garrison" (1833), at the convention that formed the American Anti-Slavery Society, to which he later served as secretary. Shortly following with the prose tract *Justice and Expediency* (1833), Whittier wrote over one hundred poems in support of immediate emancipation of the slaves and warnings of an inevitable war between the states. These were collected in *Voices of Freedom* (1846), *Songs of Labor* (1850), and *In War Time* (1864). Many more poems were published in abolitionist newspapers such as Garrison's *The Liberator*.

In the 1888 edition of his completed poetical works, Whittier categorized his poetry under the following headings: Narrative and Legendary, Nature, Personal, Occasional, Antislavery, Songs of Labor and Reform, Poems Subjective and Reminiscent, and Religious. Almost one hundred poems have been used as hymns, including "Dear Lord and Father of Mankind" and "Immortal Love, Forever Full." Most anthologies focus on Whittier's popular ballads, such as "Cassandra Southwick," narrative poems such as "Barbara Fritchie," religious intimations such as "The Eternal Goodness," and the widely popular winter idyll "Snow-Bound." The latter is an example of Whittier's nostalgic power in poetry. It is a poem that explores the domestic space of home during a snow storm.

Must Read

"Snow-Bound: A Winter Idyl" by John Greenleaf Whittier. Anthologies vary widely on what they include of Whittier (if anything). Read this work and at least a couple of his anti-slavery poems. A few of his more famous poems are "Barbara Fritchie," "Thy Will Be Done," and "The Hunters of Men."

Edgar Allan Poe (1809–1849)

At the top of my teaching notes for Poe, I have written the word "troubled." Poe's life was very turbulent and complex; however, his imagination produced some of the most read stories of all time. He is best known for his gothic tales such as "The Cask of Amontillado" and "The Tell-Tale Heart," but Poe also wrote many poems and articles on literary criticism, and scholars point to him as the first detective-story writer.

By the age of three, Poe was an orphan—his father deserted the family and his mother died. He was unofficially adopted by a family named Allan of Richmond, Virginia. After an extended visit to England from 1815 to 1820, Poe returned to the United States and floundered at home until 1826 when he decided to study at the University of Virginia; however, his drinking and gambling ended his formal education early. Kicked out of the house and on his own, Poe migrated to Baltimore and then back to Richmond where he began writing poetry and joined the army. He was admitted to West Point in 1830, but his bad habits continued, ultimately resulting in his expulsion. The next several years of his life were marked by more writing, newspaper work, and the continuation of drinking and carousing. In 1836, he married his much, much younger cousin, Virginia Clemm. He continued to write feverishly and eventually published his earliest detective story, introducing Detective August Dupin. During this stage, Poe published "The Raven" (1845). Two years later, his wife died of tuberculosis. Then, Poe died a very mysterious death—his body was found on a Baltimore street—in 1849.

▶ *TRENDS* _____

Gothic novel: A term most frequently used to describe Edgar Allan Poe's work is "gothic." Gothic fiction is the literary precursor to horror fiction. These stories are mysterious, suspenseful, and terrifying. This genre's many conventions include dark castles or homes, storms, supernatural appearances, psychological issues, victimized women, and lots of screaming. Although gothic fiction was most prolific in England, Poe's stories and poems certainly imported its macabre conventions to America.

A professor who loves Poe may also require students to read Poe's most famous essay on literary criticism, "The Philosophy of Composition," which he wrote in 1846 for *Graham's Magazine*. In the essay, Poe explains his method for writing. Primarily, Poe was interested in exciting the senses—he coins the term "**effect**":

> I consider whether it can best be wrought by incident or tone—whether by ordinary incidents and peculiar tone, or the converse, or by peculiarity both of incident and tone—afterward looking about me for such combinations of event, or tone, as shall best aid me in the construction of the effect. (Baym et al. 2008, 725)

One of the most enduring comments in that article was that "there is a distinct limit, as regards length, to all works of literary art—the limit of a single sitting" (Baym et al., 726). This work is noteworthy for students because after he waxes eloquently on poetics, Poe explains many of the decisions behind composing "The Raven."

Must Read

Works by Edgar Allan Poe

"Ligeia"

"The Cask of Amontillado"

"The Fall of the House of Usher"

"The Tell-Tale Heart"

"The Purloined Letter"

Selected poems

"The Raven"

"To Helen"

"Annabel Lee"

Harriet Beecher Stowe (1811–1896)

Legend has it that upon meeting Stowe for the first time, President Abraham Lincoln remarked, "so this is the little woman who wrote the book that started this great war." *Uncle Tom's Cabin* (serialized in 1851) might be the single most important text published in the nineteenth century. There are many reports as to how well it sold (in book form) in 1852, but most publications agree that the novel sold more than 300,000 copies during its first year in print. Not only was it the most read book in America and England, but it also made Stowe an instant celebrity. Despite its popularity, *Uncle Tom's Cabin* was criticized by many southerners for overstating and embellishing slave life on plantations. In fact, Stowe also took some heat from northern abolitionists because some of her characters chose to immigrate back to Africa instead of staying and fighting for abolition. These sections seemed, to many, to support colonization—relocating free Blacks to western Africa. So in 1853, Stowe published *A Key to Uncle Tom's Cabin*. Each chapter is titled after one of the characters in the novel. The text is comprised of real stories and incidents that support the fictional depiction of that character. Her remarks in the first chapter sum up her feelings for both the novel and this work of nonfiction:

> At different times, doubt has been expressed whether the scenes and characters portrayed in "Uncle Tom's Cabin" convey a fair representation of slavery as it at present exists. This work, more, perhaps, than any other work of fiction that ever was written, has been a collection and arrangement of real incidents, of actions really performed, of words and expressions really uttered, grouped together with reference to a general result, in the same manner that the mosaic artist groups his fragments of various stones into one general picture. His is a mosaic of gems—this is a mosaic of facts.
>
> (Stowe 1853, 1)

To further discount her critics, and yet to stay current in the antislavery circles, Stowe published a second antislavery novel in 1856. *Dred: A Tale of the Great Dismal Swamp* is a complex, and at times convoluted, tale that follows many characters as they interact with slavery in the Deep South. Instead of colonization, Stowe uses Dred, an escaped slave who lives in the swamp, to introduce slave insurrection to the conversation. Unlike *Uncle Tom's Cabin*, *Dred* also gives credibility to the abolitionist movement through its character Edward Clayton. Again, in 1859, Stowe published still another antislavery novel. This time, she set the novel, *The Minister's Wooing*, in seventeenth-century America to satirize the Calvinist theology with which she was raised, while also exploring the slave trade that existed then.

Stowe also wrote regional literature depicting New England life and its complex relationship with Protestant Christianity, namely Calvinism: *The Pearl of Orr's Island* (1862), *Oldtown Folks* (1869), and *Poganuc People* (1878). What is most fascinating about Stowe's lifelong struggle with Calvinism was that she was a member of a powerful Protestant family. Her father, **Lyman Beecher**, was an influential minister. Her brother, **Henry Ward Beecher**, famously ministered the Plymouth Congregational Church in Brooklyn, New York, during the Civil War. Another brother, **Charles Beecher**, also became a minister in the Presbyterian and Congregational denominations. Her sister, **Catharine**, spent her life writing about education reform for children and women. And her half-sister, **Isabella Beecher**, spent her career fighting for women's suffrage. Although she struggled with the family religion, Stowe appropriated the family's willingness to engage fully in the heated social debates of the day.

Must Read

Uncle Tom's Cabin by Harriet Beecher Stowe: Anthologies vary on the excerpts of the novel they include. I suggest reading as many as possible; however, if time is short, read the Preface, as well as Chapter 1, "In Which the Reader is Introduced to a Man of Humanity," and Chapter 7, "The Mother's Struggle."

Harriet Jacobs (ca. 1813–1897)

Jacobs, along with Frederick Douglass, will help us explore another very popular genre of the time: the slave narrative. Both Jacobs and Douglass lived their lives as slaves and as free persons. Both were educated, and they both wrote narratives that changed the way nineteenth-century Americans viewed the institution of slavery.

Although *Incidents in the Life of a Slave Girl* is not as well-known or widely read as Douglass's timeless work, *The Narrative Life of Frederick Douglass*, Jacobs's memoir is arguably the first slave narrative published by a woman. And, more distinctly, her narrative is the first to expose white, northern readers to the horrors of sexual abuse and manipulation female slaves faced at the hands of their overseers and masters. Jacobs began writing the story of her life in 1853, but she did not publish the manuscript until 1861. Famous writer and abolitionist Lydia Maria Child helped edit the manuscript and added a preface to the work. Scholars still argue whether the text (or parts of the text, at least) should be read as a memoir or a piece of fiction.

Jacobs used the pseudonym **Linda Brent** (plus changed names in the novel) to protect all involved, especially her children. The primary conflict of the novel depicts Linda fighting off sexual advances from her master, Dr. Flint. Her only reprieve from such terror is her maternal grandmother's home, where she later hides for seven years in the attic. Before her escape, she falls in love with a white gentleman, Mr. Sands, and gives birth to two children. The narrative follows her struggles to fight for her freedom and the lives of her children with no help from her white lover. She eventually escapes to the North where she eventually attains her freedom and the guardianship of her children. My hope is that you will read the entire narrative to complement Frederick Douglass's work; however, a selection of some of the chapters will give you a sense of a female slave's perspective.

Must Read

Incidents in the Life of a Slave Girl by Harriet Jacobs

    Chapter 1, "Childhood"

    Chapter 7, "The Lover"

    Chapter 10, "A Perilous Passage in the Slave Girl's Life"

    Chapter 21, "The Loophole of Retreat"

    Chapter 41, "Free at Last"

Frederick Douglass (1818–1895)

Each major American literature anthology I use to create my college course includes *The Narrative Life of Frederick Douglass, An American Slave, Written by Himself* in its entirety. If you have not read this important slave narrative, then you should write a complaint letter to your high school history or English teacher. Along with the narrative, some anthologies include one of the many speeches he delivered to abolitionist groups in the North. One of the more popular is called "What to the Slave is the Fourth of July?" He gave this kind of speech several times. However, the primary theme is clear: how can we as a nation celebrate equality, freedom, and independence amidst the shadow of slavery?

Although Douglass's narrative was published in 1845, he spent much of his life editing, revising, and expanding his life's story. He published *My Bondage and My Freedom* in 1855; *The Heroic Slave*, a novella, in 1853; and *The Life and Times of Frederick Douglass* in 1881 and 1892. Beyond writing his memoir and touring the lecture circuit, Douglass also edited and helped found several abolitionist newspapers, most notably the *North Star* and the *New National Era*.

The *Narrative* itself was born of necessity, much like Stowe's *A Key to Uncle Tom's Cabin*. Many listeners of Douglass's speeches inquired about the authenticity of his stories. Take note that the two prefaces before the *Narrative* attempt to attach credibility to the text. The first is a note from the famous abolitionist and newspaper editor (*The Liberator*) William Lloyd Garrison. He heard one of Douglass's speeches and began to encourage the young orator to put his life's story in writing. The second piece is a letter from another noted Boston abolitionist, Wendell Phillips. At the time, testimonials like these were commonly included in writings by women and former slaves. Recall the letter of authenticity that was attached to Phillis Wheatley's poetry collection.

Slave narrative: What is interesting about this type of narrative is that its conventions are closely related to spiritual autobiographies and captivity narratives. Slave narratives contain religious themes and biblical allusions, stories of resistance and searches for freedom, the sins of religious hypocrisy and violence, and detailed description of life in the South. In most cases, these narratives were written with a white audience in mind in order to expose the atrocities of the slave system in the South to northern readers. Hundreds of these narratives were published between 1830 and 1865.

Frances Ellen Watkins Harper (1825–1911)

I am skipping over several important writers for the moment to introduce you to Frances Harper, simply because her writing was heavily influenced by Stowe, abolitionist newspapers, and the celebrity of Douglass. Frances Watkins was born to free Blacks in Baltimore and was known by that name until she married Fenton Harper in 1860. Harper is predominantly known for two key literary works: *Poems on Miscellaneous Subjects* (1854) and the novel *Iola Leroy; or, Shadows Uplifted* (1892). Most anthologies include a selection of her poems. Harper lectured for the Maine Anti-Slavery Society, and she aided slaves to safety on the **Underground Railroad**, but poetry was what made her famous. The fiery and famous abolitionist William Lloyd Garrison wrote a preface to the book, which sold thousands of copies in its first year of publication. Many of her poems use characters and themes from *Uncle Tom's Cabin* as their titles: "Eliza Harris," "Harriet Beecher Stowe," and "Uncle Tom's Cabin." Her poems uplift, encourage, and validate the Black experience in America—they contain strong and assertive language. Here is a brief excerpt from "Ethiopia":

> Yes! Ethiopia yet shall stretch
> Her bleeding hands abroad;
> Her cry of agony shall reach
> The burning throne of God.
>
> Redeemed from dust and freed from chains
> Her sons shall lift their eyes;
> From cloud-capt hills and verdant plains
> Shall shouts of triumph rise.

> (Harper 1988, 7)

Although she wrote many more stories, novels, and poetry collections, none were as well received as *Poems on Miscellaneous Subjects* and her novel, *Iola Leroy*. The narrative powerfully explores the life of a free mulatta as she interacts with racism, classism, and sexism in nineteenth-century America. Harper continued to publish throughout her life, as well as stay active in society and politics. She died in 1911.

Must Read

Poetry of Frances Ellen Watkins Harper

"Eliza Harris"

"Ethiopia"

"Bury Me in a Free Land"

Henry David Thoreau (1817–1862)

> When I wrote the following pages, or rather the bulk of them, I lived alone, in the woods, a mile from any neighbor, in a house which I had built myself, on the shore of Walden Pond, in Concord, Massachusetts, and earned my living by the labor of my hands only. I lived there two years and two months. At present I am a sojourner in civilized life again. (Thoreau 2008, 5)

Thus begins Thoreau's most heralded work, *Walden*. During a particular low period in his literary career, Thoreau decided to live in the woods (on property owned by Emerson) and begin writing a book and centering himself in the natural world. Thoreau moved into his temporary home during the summer of 1845. The proposed book was *A Week on the Concord and Merrimack Rivers*, which he published himself in 1849, and which met with little public appeal—it bombed. However, during that time at Walden Pond, Thoreau also began writing intimations on the self, reform, materialism, and civic life and its intersection with the natural world that would eventually become *Walden*. One of his themes starts with the premise that "the life which men praise and regard as successful is but one kind. Why should we exaggerate any one kind at the expense of the others?" Thoreau was very clear that this life in the woods was an "experiment" and not a complete lifestyle change. Most of Thoreau's works force readers to consider and examine their very existence and life choices. *Walden* was published in 1854 and met with relatively high praise and positive sales.

Walden's narrative structure is complex at best. It is not fiction, and it's not a spiritual autobiography or even an extended essay arguing a particular point. It is merely the record of life in the woods over a period of time. His thoughts are both pragmatic and idealistic. Thoreau tends to a bean field, takes walks in the woods, plays host to various visitors, and thinks. What organizes the book more than literary conventions are its concurrent themes and motifs: simplicity, freedom from society, the ills of materialism, industrial progress, and so on.

Keep in mind that Emerson and his transcendental idea played a very influential role in Thoreau's thinking and writing. Not only was Emerson friendly and hospitable to Thoreau, he also published many of Thoreau's essays in the *Dial*. Historians note that Thoreau even edited the transcendental newspaper for a short time.

The year 1846 was an important one in Thoreau's life as well. In an attempt to live out some of the ideologies he was writing about while living on Walden Pond, he ceased paying the poll tax. These monies were used to aid in the war against Mexico and, in Thoreau's mind, support a proslavery government. This decision landed the young idealist in jail in 1846 for one night until someone would pay the tax for him. After this event, Thoreau wrote and delivered an address in Concord called "The Rights and Duties of the Individual in Relation to the State" (1848). This address was published a year later as "Resistance to Civil Government." Later, the essay was published in a posthumous collection of Thoreau's writings titled *Civil Disobedience*. His primary question revolves around how an individual can remain such and still be a subject under a particular government. Thoreau writes:

> I think that we should be men first, and subjects afterward. It is not desirable to cultivate a respect for the law, so much as for the right. The only obligation which I have a right to assume is to do at any time what I think right. (Thoreau 2008, 228)

It is widely recognized that **Mahatma Gandhi** and **Martin Luther King Jr.** found inspiration in Thoreau's work for their own nonviolent approach to "civil" governments.

Must Read

Works by Henry David Thoreau

"Resistance to Civil Government"

From *Walden* (though if you have time, read all of it)

   1. "Economy"

   2. "Where I Lived, and What I Lived For"

   7. "The Bean-Field"

   8. "The Village"

   17. "Spring"

"Conclusion"

Walt Whitman (1819–1892)

Called **the father of free verse**, Whitman is arguably the most influential American poet of the nineteenth century. His poetry broke literary and social conventions, while maintaining a strong connection with, and for, the American people and the country's social landscape. Many scholars agree that Emerson's ideal poet in his essay "The Poet" is embodied in Walt Whitman. Emerson wrote

> The poet is the person . . . who sees and handles that which others dream
> of, traverses the whole scale of experience, and is representative of man,
> in virtue of being the largest power to receive and impart.
>
> (Emerson 2001, 184).

Later in the essay, Emerson suggests "Yet America is a poem in our eyes; its ample geography dazzles the imagination" (196). To many, Whitman answered the call for an American poet, writing about, for, and to Americans. In his preface to the 1855 edition of *Leaves of Grass*,Whitman echoes this call:

> The Americans of all nations at any time upon the earth have probably
> the fullest poetical nature. The United States themselves are essentially
> the greatest poem . . . but the genius of the United States is not best or
> most in its executives or legislatures, nor in its ambassadors or authors
> or colleges or churches or parlors, nor even in its newspapers or inven-
> tors . . . but always most in the common people.
>
> (Whitman 2001, 616–17)

Whitman personified this sentiment in the 1855 edition by using a picture of himself dressed in common attire as the title page, instead of a signature.

His seminal work, *Leaves of Grass*, was revised many times from its first publication (self-published) in 1855 to his death in 1892. The first edition contained only 12 untitled poems, while the "deathbed" edition in 1892, the one he preferred, included hundreds of poems under several headings, including "Inscriptions," "Children of Adam," "Calamus," and "Drum-Taps." This complex body of poetry has held many different shapes and variations: Whitman constantly revised individual poems, reorganized various sections of the text, and even re-titled particular poems. Studying a definitive *Leaves of Grass* is a difficult proposition. *Leaves of Grass* received a fair share of praise and ridicule through its many publications. Whitman sent a copy of the poems and an introductory letter to Emerson, who loved it and responded by saying, "I greet you at the beginning of a great career, which yet must have had a long foreground somewhere for such a start" (Whitman 2001, 637). However, there were many reviewers who found later revisions lewd, overtly sexual, subversive, and poetically inferior to the great British poets. The attack on Whitman's content refers to poems included under the sections "Calamus" and "The Children of Adam." In these, Whitman introduced readers, somewhat cryptically, to romantic relationships between men.

Another section of poetry that gained popular reception were those dedicated to President Abraham Lincoln and those that depicted Whitman's time as a nurse in a Union hospital in Washington City (now Washington, D.C.). During a search for his soldier brother, Whitman decided to stay in Washington and visit sick and injured soldiers. He wrote letters for them, told them stories, and took copious notes of his time there. The results are poems published under the heading "Drum-Taps" and a nonfiction book (some call a journal or diary) he titled *Memoranda During the War* (1872). These poems show a great love and admiration for Lincoln as well as a desire to tell the real story of the war—the individual sacrifice and suffering of each soldier on either side.

Whitman could also be called the first New Yorker. He was born in Long Island and spent much of his life in that city and in Brooklyn and Manhattan. Born into a Quaker family, Whitman was sensitive to the religion of his family; however, he denounced organized religion and orthodox Christianity. Along with creating a writing career, he worked as an editor on various newspapers, magazines, and journals, including the *Evening Post* and the *Brooklyn Eagle*.

Must Read

Works by Walt Whitman

Preface to *Leaves of Grass* (1855)

"One's Self I Sing"

"Song of Myself" (1881)

"Out of the Cradle Endlessly Rocking"

"When I Heard the Learn'd Astronomer"

"Beat! Beat! Drums!"

"The Wound-Dresser"

"When Lilacs Last in the Dooryard Bloom'd"

"Facing West from California's Shores"

"In Paths Untrodden"

Herman Melville (1819–1891)

Like Hawthorne's writings, Melville's work leans closer to the darker side of romanticism than do the works of Whitman, Thoreau, and Emerson. Books such as *Moby-Dick*, *Pierre*, *Benito Cereno*, and *The Confidence-Man* explore the struggles each individual faces with himself, God, the natural world, and his fellow man. To say that Melville focused on human depravity might be an understatement; however, his writing career did not begin this way. In the nineteenth century, Melville was popular and famous for his sea narratives. Combining high adventure with depictions of foreign islands and cultures, *Typee* (1846), *Omoo* (1847), *Redburn* (1849), and *White-Jacket* (1850) cemented his place as an important American writer. With this newfound celebrity, Melville began to inject into his work more philosophical angles, heavier metaphors and symbols, and greater narrative nuance, as well as socially objectionable content, that were not readily accepted by the reading public. In the middle of writing his four sea narratives, Melville published the very long sea narrative, *Mardi* (1849), which was lambasted by critics and ignored by readers.

However, all of these novels and public press gave Melville the encouragement and space to create his masterpiece, *Moby-Dick* (1851). Although not quite heralded as a masterpiece at its publication, it did receive various positive reviews. The novel begins with one of the most famous first lines in American fiction: "**Call me Ishmael**" (Melville 2001, 18). Ishmael, the narrator, tells his story of sailing on a wailing ship called the ***Pequod*** in search of a white sperm whale **Captain Ahab** refers to as Moby-Dick. Ahab's enigmatic presence begins with his wooden leg shaped from the jaw of a sperm whale, continues with his long monologues on the nature of evil, and ends with his tireless effort to exact his revenge on Moby-Dick, who caused the loss of Ahab's leg. The novel is complete with colorful minor characters: Pip, the cabin boy; **Queequeg**, the Polynesian harpooner; and Starbuck, the ship's first-mate. All die in their journey to kill the white whale except for Ishmael, who is left to tell the story. (*Note*: Whiteness is a peculiar metaphor in the novel; it is the color of evil as it represents absence.)

As Melville's novels became more ambitious, his readership and finances suffered. In 1852, Melville published *Pierre*, which received a devastating reception from readers and reviewers. Apparently, readers were not ready for a novel that explores incestuous romance, insanity, and religious hypocrisy. Feeling the financial hit of failing novels, Melville began to publish articles and stories in various magazines. His next novel, *Israel Potter* (1854), was first serialized in *Putnam's Monthly Magazine*. It was a satirical look at a Revolutionary War soldier who travels to Europe and meets various important American figures like Benjamin Franklin and Paul Jones.

A collection of his magazine stories was published in 1856 and given the name *The Piazza Tales*. Most anthologized works of Melville come from this publication. And the most notable among these is his complex and much debated short story, "Bartleby the Scrivener." In this tale, the Lawyer tells the story of one of his several scriveners, or copyists. Bartleby answers an ad for a job and is hired to join Turkey and Nippers as a copyist in the Lawyer's office. Conflict arises when the Lawyer asks Bartleby to complete a simple task, and his response is merely, "**I prefer not to**" (Melville 1984, 643). Thus begins a strange narrative exploring "passive resistance," authority, the definition and purpose of work, and life on the burgeoning New York Wall Street. Readers are given only a glimpse of Bartleby's motivation for such action when we learn at the very end of the story that he once worked for, and was fired from, the Dead Letter Office. The narrator presumes that this occupation caused his slippage into madness; however, readers and scholars have pondered whether Bartleby was mad, or whether he was the only sane one in an increasingly mad world.

In recent years, anthologies have begun to include Melville's novella regarding the slave trade (also published in *The Piazza Tales*) called *Benito Cereno*. What is fascinating about this work is that the source material comes from documents depicting a real slave insurrection aboard a Spanish slave ship. The novella follows Captain Amassa Delano's inspection of a ship along the coast of Chile. The narrator gives readers constant hints that all is not what it seems aboard the *San Dominick* captained by Benito Cereno. Not only are the slaves not securely fastened below the deck, but they also roam the boat freely and talk freely amongst themselves and their captain. Moreover, readers see only glimpses of other Spaniards, hiding in the corners of the boat. Most peculiar of all, Benito is constantly surrounded by a very short but assertive "servant" named Babo. Delano never discovers until late in the narrative that Babo is the leader of a major insurrection on board and that Benito Cereno has been held captive in order to get the slaves safely back to Africa. Benito Cereno was Melville's only direct attack on the American slave trade, as, many argue, Delano symbolizes America's ignorance and blindness to the atrocities of slavery.

Melville's last flop was an allegorical satire on American life, politics, and society called *The Confidence-Man*. Reviews were bad and sales were even worse. He swore never to write prose again. Turning to poetry, Melville wrote a collection of Civil War poems titled *Battle-Pieces: Aspects of the War* (1866). Although immediate reception and early twentieth-century criticism called it overly journalistic, detached, and forgettable, those poems are now considered, along with Whitman's "Drum-Taps," the most provocative and genuine poems to come out of that great American conflict. Anthologies typically include at least a couple of Melville's Civil War poems to complement "Bartleby the Scrivener." In 1876, Melville published a long (very long) religious pilgrimage poem called "Clarel" after a trip through Palestine and the Middle East.

Melville died in 1891, leaving an unfinished sea narrative, *Billy Budd*. The novel was not finished and published until 1924, ultimately reviving interest in Melville's previous work and literary career.

Must Read

Works by Herman Melville

"Bartleby the Scrivener"

Benito Cereno

"The Portent"

Emily Dickinson (1830–1886)

Melville, Whitman, and Thoreau are all examples of American writers who worked tirelessly to create a literary career. In contrast, though Dickinson is now regarded as one of America's greatest poets, her poems were hardly read in her lifetime. She published only a handful of poems, which obtained only a small readership. However, many of her poems were sent as gifts to friends, family, and neighbors. Historians note that Dickinson spent most of her life in her Amherst, Massachusetts, home and neighborhood. Her father, Edward, was a lawyer, state representative, and senator. They were strict Calvinists, and this religious upbringing became a poetic stimulus for young Dickinson. Many of her poems contain intimations on God, suffering, and human interaction with the divine. She wasn't always nice about it, either. Dickinson's formal education lasted less than a year at Mount Holyoke Female Seminary—a place where she began to question the religious faith of her family.

It is worth noting the people whom Dickinson both admired and grew close to during her lifetime. Her older brother, Austin, and her younger sister, Lavinia (who, like Dickinson herself, never married) remained Dickinson's closest relations. Austin eventually married a family friend, **Susan Gilbert**, and the couple moved into the Dickinson home. Scholars debate on the nature of Dickinson's relationship with Gilbert; ultimately, some argue that Dickinson certainly fell in love with her sister-in-law. Letters reveal that Dickinson intimately admired men as well.

R. W. Franklin, Harvard University's premier scholar on the works of Dickinson, noted in his exhaustive research, that 864 of Dickinson's 1,789 poems were composed during the four years between 1861 and 1865. Contemporary scholars have begun to locate what they call her war canon. Many poems, they argue, maintain images, metaphors, and direct references to the Civil War. In these poems, Dickinson continues her exploration of God, human existence, the natural world, and religious dogma.

The poetry itself is worth a few words. One of the reasons that Dickinson published only a handful of poems during her life was that they broke literary and social conventions in various ways. Place one of her poems next to one written by Longfellow, Whittier, or Bryant and you will immediately see the great differences between what nineteenth-century readers expected and what Dickinson delivered. Notice the short, fragmented lines, the many capitalized nouns, **her abundant use of dashes and spaces**, and her extended use of metaphor. You should immediately recognize an Emily Dickinson poem.

What is more fascinating than the details and speculations of her life is the way in which her poems became published. Just after Dickinson's death, her sister Lavinia and a family friend, **Mable Todd**, began transcribing and collecting Emily's many poems. Todd, with the help of **Thomas Wentworth Higginson**, published several volumes of her poetry from 1890 to 1896. Peculiarly, Higginson and Todd edited many of her poems, "correcting" sentence structure, punctuation, and capitalization to create a more "sound" poetic structure. At the same time, Susan Gilbert Dickinson and her daughter Martha Dickinson Bianchi began publishing Emily's poems in various literary magazines; and later in the early twentieth century, Bianchi collected and published many more volumes of Emily's poetry. Ultimately, these women are solely responsible for Dickinson's fame in the poetic world.

It's also important to note how the poems are organized. Because Dickinson did not title most of her poems, editors have numbered them. In 1955, Thomas Johnson produced a completed volume of Emily's poetry with corresponding numbers. However, in the late 1990s, R. W. Franklin renumbered Dickinson's poems in his three-volume collection, *The Poems of Emily Dickinson*. For convenience, please note which edition your anthology uses.

Must Read

Poetry of Emily Dickinson

First, read as many Dickinson poems as you can to get a sense of her style, structure, and thematic tendencies. Here are ten of my favorites. I've used the R. W. Franklin numbering:

> Number 112 "Success is counted sweetest"
>
> Number 207 "I taste a liquor never brewed—"
>
> Number 359 "A Bird came down the Walk"
>
> Number 372 "After great pain, a formal feeling comes"
>
> Number 409 "The Soul selects her own Society"
>
> Number 448 "I died for Beauty—but was scarce"
>
> Number 479 "Because I could not stop for Death"
>
> Number 591 "I heard a Fly buzz—when I died"
>
> Number 1263 "Tell all the Truth but tell it slant"
>
> Number 1773 "My life closed twice before its close"

REFERENCES

Baym et al. 2008. *The Norton Anthology of American Literature*, shorter 7th ed. New York: W. W. Norton.

Belasco, Susan, and Linck Johnson. 2008. *The Bedford Anthology of American Literature*, Vol. 1, *Beginnings to 1865*. Boston: Bedford/St. Martin's.

Emerson, Ralph Waldo. 2001. *Emerson's Prose and Poetry*. A Norton Critical Edition. Edited by Joel Porte and Saundra Morris. New York: W. W. Norton.

Harper, Frances Ellen Watkins. 1988. *Complete Poems of Frances E. W. Harper*. The Schomburg Library of Nineteenth-Century Black Women Writers. Edited by Maryemma Graham. New York: Oxford University Press.

Hollander, John. 1996. *American Poetry: The Nineteenth Century*. The Library of America. New York: Penguin Books.

Melville, Herman. 1984. *Pierre, Israel Potter, The Piazza Tales, The Confidence-Man, Uncollected Prose, and Billy Budd, Sailor*. The Library of America. New York: Library Classics of the United States.

———. 2001. *Moby-Dick*. A Norton Critical Edition, 2nd ed. Edited by Hershel Parker and Harrison Hayford.

Stowe, Harriet Beecher. 1853. *A Key to Uncle Tom's Cabin*. Boston: John P. Jewett.

Thoreau, Henry David. 2008. *Walden, Civil Disobedience, and Other Writings*. A Norton Critical Edition, 3rd ed. Edited by William Rossi. New York: W. W. Norton.

Wharton, Edith. 1994. *The Age of Innocence*. London: Wordsworth Editions.

Whitman, Walt. 2001. *Leaves of Grass and Other Writings*. A Norton Critical Edition. Edited by Michael Moon. New York: W. W. Norton.

Whittier, John Greenleaf. 1894. *The Complete Poetical Works of John Greenleaf Whittier*. Cambridge Edition. Boston: Houghton Mifflin.

Chapter 4

Realism and Naturalism (1865–1910)

REALISM

I am making a slight change to the dates that the College Board (creators of the CLEP tests) states in its literature. Some scholars believe that realism as a literary movement began closer to 1870, but many more scholars point to the beginning of the Civil War as the beginning of American literary realism. Bullets, bloodshed, and brotherly bickering ushered in a reality that reacted strongly to the idyllic existence American romanticism painted. Then, after the battles ended, America began to grow and to expand its urban areas at the expense of its rural areas. The Industrial Revolution and increased European immigration caused a boom in urban populations. Post–Civil War America found itself in an existence of disillusionment and cynicism. Major technological breakthroughs also occurred at the end of the nineteenth century: the invention of the telephone, the completion of the transcontinental railroad, and, of course, the introduction of the automobile. So literary realism is the label we give to those works that attempt to portray life as it actually is and not simply as the writer wishes (the latter being idealism). The brief historical information just mentioned is important because those incidents influenced writers who focused their plots and characters on the very immediate happenings of people in particular cultural moments. Realism is very interested in the mundane episodes of middle-class life; therefore, realist novels tended to lean towards social reform. Also, writers took it upon themselves to critically comment on America's politics, economics, industry, and social issues, as well as gender, class, and race issues.

Naturalism

Literary naturalism is said to be a product of scientific determinism. Here's a simple definition: You are controlled by your environment. There is no hope for you. Dreams come and dreams go. You are controlled by your gender, race, socioeconomic standing, and ethnicity. There is a glass ceiling and you will hit it every time you venture beyond your status. Depressing, huh? Yes, it is. There is more to the literary movement than that, of course. Naturalism was greatly influenced by the work of Charles Darwin, Isaac Newton, Karl Marx, and Emile Zola, and other naturalists who posited that humans are not that different from animals in that they merely respond to natural and environmental forces without fully understanding the forces or their reactions to them. What is also important about naturalist fiction is that the author and the narrator are amoral in their depictions of the characters and the plot: they do not judge or editorialize; they merely observe.

Regionalism

The end of the nineteenth century and the beginning of the twentieth century saw an increase in authors and works published outside of New England. It's not an understatement to assert that Boston was the cultural and intellectual center of America during the eighteenth and nineteenth centuries. However, westward expansion, the Civil War, the railroad, and a growing Union gave space for literature to be produced in the Middle West, the West, and the South. **"Regionalism"** is a literary term that refers to a work that connects itself to a particular geography: its history, culture, ways of speech, leisure activities, occupations, folklore, food, clothing, and so on. In fact, the setting of the story takes on the role of another character; the plot cannot take place just anywhere without suffering greatly. In this section, we will pay attention to regionalists such as Mark Twain, Kate Chopin, Willa Cather, and Jack London.

THE MAJOR WRITERS

Mark Twain (Samuel Langhorne Clemens; 1835–1910)

Twain is still one of the most recognizable names in American literature. Elementary students still read *The Adventures of Tom Sawyer* (1876), and many high school students are familiar with the highly comic story "The Notorious Jumping Frog of Calaveras County." Clemens chose the penname "Mark Twain," a steamboat term meaning "safe water," that both referred to his years as a steamboat pilot on the Mississippi River and to his years as a journalist and political humorist where pseudonyms were popular and necessary. Twain's writing has been praised and ridiculed for its strong denouncement of social ills. He constantly attacks and skewers American values that seem to contradict human decency and integrity: slavery and economics were two of his favorite topics. Twain wrote many articles and short tales for magazines and newspapers before he published *Innocence Abroad*, a satirical account of his traveling in Europe and the Holy Land, in 1869. Continuing his love for travel writing and satire, in 1872 Twain published *Roughing It*, which explored his adventures in the American West with his brother, Orion.

The Mississippi River and his boyhood home in Hannibal, Missouri, were never far from Twain's mind and imagination. The 1870s brought an increase in articles and stories that revolved around the lives of people in Missouri and along the Mississippi River. Although *The Adventures of Tom Sawyer* was published in 1876, Twain's first major collection of his regional tales, *Life on the Mississippi*, was published in 1883. And, his most famous work, *The Adventures of Huckleberry Finn*, was published in 1885. This novel, both much admired and criticized at its release, is the sequel (of sorts) to *Tom Sawyer*, which ends with Tom and Huck receiving a financial reward for having recovered a robber's stash of gold in a cave. *Huckleberry Finn* picks up with Huck living with the Widow Douglas and her sister Miss Watson in an effort to keep his drunken father, Pap, at a favorable distance. Huck quickly grows weary of "civilization," so he fakes his own death and runs away with one of Miss Watson's slaves, Jim. Trouble follows the two as they venture down the Mississippi River on a raft: they meet robbers, slave hunters, feuding southern families, and two con men (The Duke and the Dauphin) who eventually sell Jim to a farming family, to whom, as it turns out, Tom Sawyer is related. In an attempt to rescue Jim, Tom is shot in the leg, and Jim is returned to his owners. Later, it is revealed that Jim was a free man upon Miss Watson's death, and that the escape plan was a ruse to pay back Jim for running away. Huck discovers that Pap is dead, so the book ends with his desires to head west. If you have time, I recommend reading this incredibly important American novel, not only for its plot and social commentary, but also for Twain's use of southern vernacular and African-American dialect. Ernest Hemingway remarked that "all modern American literature comes from one book by Mark Twain called *Huckleberry Finn*" (Hemingway 1963, 22).

Twain continued with satirical writing and social commentary targeting American values and vices. In 1889, he published his Arthurian legend with an American twist titled *A Connecticut Yankee in King Arthur's Court*. It becomes a wonderful and tragic mix of cultures. *The Tragedy of Pudd'nhead Wilson* (1894) is also a satire in which Twain expands his exploration of the racial issues that continued to plague the United States almost thirty years after the Civil War. And although Twain continued to write and publish into the twentieth century, none of those works claimed the interest and intrigue of his earlier works.

Must Read

Works by Mark Twain

The Adventures of Huckleberry Finn

"The Notorious Jumping Frog of Calaveras County"

"A True Story"

Anthologies vary widely in their selections of Twain's nonfiction pieces. I recommend reading at least one essay so you get a sense of Twain's biting satire and poignant social commentary.

Henry James (1843–1916)

Many students who are first introduced to James initially assume him to be British. James's writing style is vastly different from the vernacular language Twain uses. His plots, characters, and settings exist in the upper echelons of society, both in America and abroad. This initial response is not entirely off base as James, along with his parents and siblings, spent considerable time in Europe when he was young. James was born into a wealthy New York family, and his brother, William, became one of America's most celebrated psychologists and philosophers. Like many authors of the nineteenth century, James tired quickly of formal education and dedicated his life to a literary career. For well over twenty years, James published plays, stories, novels, and literary criticism. His novels explored psychology, realism, naturalism, and connections between America and Europe.

Many of James's novels explore the adjustments Americans, especially women, face in European countries as they interact with different social structures and mores. These themes are paramount in *Daisy Miller: A Study* (1878), *The Portrait of a Lady* (1881), and *The Ambassadors* (1903). It was *Daisy Miller* that made James popular. This tale follows a young, naïve, and adventurous American girl as she bumbles socially through various European cities. She meets Winterbourne in Switzerland and dazzles him with her unorthodox and socially promiscuous ways. Later, Daisy scandalizes the American circles of Rome when she becomes romantically involved with an Italian named Giovanelli. Students should note here that one of the prevailing themes of the novella is the clash between the old, European aristocracy with its long-established traditions, and the new, American middle class with its developing traditions. One evening, Winterbourne, who goes to Rome knowing that he will see Daisy, discovers the lovers in the Coliseum. He asserts that Daisy will catch "Roman Fever" and quickly persuades Giovanelli to take her home. Daisy does become ill and eventually dies; however, she sends a note to Winterbourne telling him of the great and positive influence he had on her life. In some ways, *Daisy Miller* is a cautionary tale of American arrogance and naïveté in Europe, and in other ways, it is the story of a woman who is not afraid to live her life to the fullest. She is both hero and villain of her own story.

As I mentioned earlier, James wrote several novels using naturalism as a literary framework: *The Bostonians* (1886), one of his most popular, which depicted upper-class social life in America; *The Princess Casamassima* (1886); and *The Tragic Muse* (1889). Partly influenced by his brother's profession as a psychologist and partly due to the realist and naturalist movements of literature at the time, James spent a great amount of time exploring the psychology of his characters. James was more interested in *why* characters act the way they do instead of merely *what* they do. These themes are quite apparent in the widely anthologized *Beast of the Jungle* and his ghost story *Turn of the Screw*, the tale of a young governess who is given responsibility for two children on a rural estate. Tragedy strikes when the governess discovers apparitions of former estate employees lurking around the grounds searching for her children.

Most students will not know that Henry James was also an accomplished literary critic. His "Art of Fiction" (1884) is still read and studied in university English departments. The essay is a reaction to other literary critics who espoused to create strict rules for novel writing. James insisted "the only obligation to which in advance we may hold a novel, without incurring the accusation of being arbitrary, is that it be interesting" (James 2003, 380). James was also known to assert to writers that it was better "to show than to tell." It was better for the author to be completely absent from his texts, allowing the narrator, characters, and plot to do their job. At the end of his life, James became a British citizen, partly in disdain for America's initial refusal to enter World War I.

Must Read

Works by Henry James

Daisy Miller: A Study

The Beast in the Jungle

"The Real Thing"

"Art of Fiction"

Kate Chopin (1850–1904)

Chopin was not considered a major American writer after her death in 1904. She did not receive the recognition and praise she deserved until the latter part of the twentieth century when her work was rediscovered and added to college classrooms and literature anthologies. Chopin grew up in urban and upper-class St. Louis, Missouri. She married a southern businessman and spent several years in New Orleans until her husband's death. In 1884, she returned to St. Louis, only to suffer her mother's death and raise her six children on her own. It was at this time that Chopin began her literary career, especially targeting the lives of women (both in St. Louis and Louisiana) as they attempted to navigate the social mores of the waning nineteenth century. These themes brought her great approval and ridicule.

During her time, she published many regional tales of the Louisiana Cajuns and Creoles. These tales were eventually collected in *Bayou Folk* (1894) and made her a force in regional writing. These stories display the dichotomy between social conventions and a desire to stretch and resist those very conventions. Most anthologies include two stories from that collection: "At the 'Cadian Ball" and "The Storm."

Please note the differences in how Chopin handles the very delicate matters of sex, marital fidelity, and women's roles in high society. Students should note that "The Storm" was not even published during Chopin's lifetime.

In 1899, Chopin published her most controversial work, *The Awakening*. It damaged her literary career during her lifetime. *The Awakening* follows **Edna Pontellier** as she navigates the social conventions of her day, which centered on repressed emotional and sexual desires, with a certain aplomb. However, she befriends a married woman, Adele Ratignolle, and a young playboy, Robert Lebrun, during her family's summer vacation. On this vacation, and because of her burgeoning relationship with Robert, Edna begins to "awaken" to a life of freedom: she learns to swim, she picks up painting that she enjoyed as a youth, and she becomes aware of her sexual urges. She remains faithful to her husband but returns to New Orleans changed. At home, Mrs. Pontellier shirks her social obligations and gives herself completely to her painting. She moves out of her husband's home into a home of her own and begins a love affair with another playboy, Alcee Arobin. However, all the while she maintains a love correspondence with Robert. At this time, Edna is influenced and mentored by two women. Her friend, Adele, encourages her independent flair, but she also reminds her of her responsibilities to her husband, children, and social circles. Meanwhile, her artistic side is massaged by Mademoiselle Reisz, a pianist who encourages her to sacrifice to her art and seek out Robert and let him know of her true feelings. As the plot thickens, Edna finds herself all alone in a seemingly selfish world. With no other option in her mind, Edna walks out to sea never to return. Students will find Edna either incredibly selfish and self-serving or a tragic product of a sinister patriarchal culture.

Must Read

Works by Kate Chopin

The Awakening, if you have time

"Story of An Hour"

"Desiree's Baby"

"At the 'Cadian Ball"

"The Storm"

Edith Wharton (1862–1937)

Before Wharton and Chopin were added to American literature courses, Emily Dickinson was the only female representative. Like Chopin, young Wharton grew up in a socially mobile New York family and married a man equal in up-bringing. Her life centered on social affairs, balls, and fashion. Although she did publish a few poems and stories as a young girl and newly married woman, her life seemed preoccupied by the stresses of middle-class leisure life. In 1899, Wharton published a short story collection, *The Greater Inclination*, and several years later, her first novel, *The House of Mirth*. Her husband's continued infidelity finally gave Wharton the strength to divorce him and immigrate to France. There, she published many more novels, including her most famous and critically acclaimed: *Ethan Frome* (1911), *The Custom of the Country* (1913), and *The Age of Innocence* (1920). As did many writers of her day, Wharton used conventions of realism and naturalism to depict the trapped and controlled life of a woman in upper-class America. And like Chopin, many of her characters are faced with questions of true love and marital fidelity. What happens, she constantly asks, when society's pressures on human decisions becomes too much?

Due to the length of her most-read novels, *The House of Mirth* and *The Age of Innocence*, anthologies usually include a couple of short stories. However, if you have time, I recommend reading one of her novels. The famous New England novella, *Ethan Frome*, tells the story of a dutiful man, Ethan, his devotion to his invalid (and not so nice) wife, Zeena, and yet, his hidden affections for his wife's cousin Mattie Silver, who works and lives with the Fromes. The novel explores the sexual attraction between Ethan and Mattie. At the end of the novel, Zeena intends for Mattie to finally leave their home. Ethan offers to take her to the depot, and at a stop at the top of a hill, Mattie convinces Ethan to run their sled into a tree so they may spend their last moments on earth embraced. Unfortunately for them, they survive. The end of the novel shows Ethan entering the home, twenty years later, and quickly attending to two aging, crippled women. This novel is a great example of the naturalist underpinnings of many of Wharton's novels: characters are at the mercy of entities and events completely out of their control and beyond their understanding, so they are destined to sacrifice their dreams and heart's desires for a cold reality.

Wharton received many awards during her lifetime: The Pulitzer Prize for *The Age of Innocence*, the Chevalier of the Legion of Honor by the French government for her charity work during World War I, an honorary doctorate from Yale University, and the Gold Medal of the American Academy of Arts and Letters.

Must Read

Works by Edith Wharton

Ethan Frome, if you have time

"The Other Two"

"Roman Fever"

Theodore Dreiser (1871–1945)

Dreiser is one of many great writers that came out of the Midwest in the nineteenth century. Many of his novels are set in Chicago, although he was raised in a large, strict Indiana home. His siblings were rebellious and fiercely independent. One of his sisters actually ran away with a married man who embezzled money from his job. Dreiser used this true story to frame his first novel, *Sister Carrie* (1900). The novel follows a young country girl, Carrie Meeber, who moves to Chicago to live with her sister and brother-in-law in order to break away from small-town life. She quickly realizes the difficulty of finding full-time employment in Chicago's many factories; however, she does meet a quick-tongued and friendly salesman named Charles Drouet. He wines and dines her, and eventually, he puts her up in an apartment. At this time, she is introduced to one of Drouet's many social acquaintances, George Hurstwood. Hurstwood is a married, middle-class manager of a social club; he is socially mobile and financially stable. Both men fall in love with Carrie. Towards the plot's climax, George steals a large sum of money from the club's safe, kidnaps Carrie, and takes her to New York to live. It is there that George falls into a life of decrepitude and hopelessness, while Carrie gets a job as a stage dancer and finds her dreams fulfilled on stage. Eventually, George commits suicide out of despair, and Carrie discovers her own emptiness as a social celebrity. This novel represents Dreiser's compulsion toward naturalism: humans are not completely in control of their own decisions and fates. *Sister Carrie* was received as immoral and dangerous to readers, so much so that the publisher refused to market the book. Over the years, the novel has gained popularity and credibility within college classrooms and among scholars.

Many of Dreiser's novels focus on themes of social mobility, class differences, sexual empowerment, and the many issues that affect urban life. The early twentieth century proved very successful for Dreiser's novels: *Jennie Gerhardt* (1911), *The Financier* (1912), *The Titan* (1914), and his most celebrated and critically acclaimed novel, *An American Tragedy* (1925). This last great novel is a fictional account of a young upwardly mobile New York boy, Clyde Griffiths, who murders his pregnant girlfriend in order to chase his dreams of financial and social solidarity—the title kind of gives away the fact that Clyde is apprehended by the authorities and must pay for his crime. Overall, Dreiser was committed to exploring the social and sexual drives of urban Americans, especially as those drives conflicted with the social conventions of the day.

Must Read

Sister Carrie by Theodore Dreiser: Although this is a very long novel, I recommend reading the excerpts included in some anthologies. Note: Anthologies vary widely on Dreiser's short stories. One included "Butcher Rogaum's Door," and another included "The Second Choice."

Willa Cather (1873–1947)

Students could easily argue that Wharton, Dreiser, and Cather belong in the next chapter with those who published most of their work after 1910, and that argument would be valid. However, I place their work in this chapter because of their invaluable contribution to regionalism and realism. And, I like to discuss Dreiser, Wharton, and Cather among these other writers because they each began their writing careers and published at least one important novel before 1910.

With that apology out of the way, let's think about, arguably, the greatest female American novelist . . . ever, Willa Cather. Cather did for Nebraska what Dreiser did for Chicago, Jack London did for Alaska, Twain did for Missouri, and Wharton did for New Orleans. She gave it imaginary space in American minds, and she allowed readers to experience westward expansion in real and often painful terms. And, not only did Cather write about the Midwest experience, but she also wrote poignantly about the immigrant-Midwest experience. Her protagonists, usually female, must navigate not only the gender issues of the day but also the cultural clashes and conflicts many homesteaders faced.

Cather was born in Virginia, but her family moved to join other relatives in Nebraska. She was educated at the University of Nebraska, but she eventually headed east (Pittsburgh and New York) to work as an editor of *Home Monthly* and *McClure's*. Along the way, she published short stories in important newspapers and magazines. Cather's first collection of tales, *The Troll Garden*, was published in 1905. In it are two highly anthologized stories: "A Wagner Matinee" and "Paul's Case." After this publication and several years spent at *McClure's*, Cather decided on a life of full-time writing. These years proved to be her most successful. She published her first novel, *Alexander's Bridge* (1912), which was set in the East. Then, Cather returned to her childhood memories and set her most popular and critically acclaimed novels in the prairies of Nebraska: *O Pioneers* (1913), *The Song of the Lark* (1915), *My Antonia* (1918), and *A Lost Lady* (1923).

O Pioneers follows the life of a Swedish immigrant family attempting to prosper as homesteaders in Hanover, Nebraska. Alexandra Bergson is the only daughter, yet she is the toughest personality of the bunch. The beginning of the novel depicts the struggles and frustrations of farming in a desolate region, while introducing readers to various characters such as Alex's older brothers, Oscar and Lou; her younger brother, Emil; Carl Lindstrum, whose family moves away discouraged and beaten; Crazy Ivar, as he's called, who quotes Scripture and lives a very eccentric life; and a pretty little girl named Marie. The plot jumps 16 years later and shows the entanglement of all the characters. Alex has tamed the land and made quite a profit in farming. Her brothers have moved into town and raised families of their own on farms of their own. Marie has grown up and married a gloomy man named Frank Shabata. Emil leaves for studies at the state university and later for Mexico. Crazy Ivar now lives in Alex's barn and takes care of the horses, and Carl comes back to visit after seeking business ventures in the West. Subplots arise as Carl and Alex grow accustomed to each other, Emil and Marie fall in love under the watchful eye of Frank, and the brothers, Lou and Oscar, disapprove of Alex's relationship with Carl and her commitment to Crazy Ivar. The plot thickens: Carl is run out of town by the brothers, and Emil and Marie are shot and killed by a deranged Frank. Alex, however, seeks a pardon for Frank as he sits in a Lincoln jail, and Carl returns from Alaska to comfort Alex and seek her hand in marriage.

Must Read

Works by Willa Cather

O Pioneers or *My Antonia*

"Wagner Matinee"

"Neighbor Rosicky"

Stephen Crane (1871–1900)

Crane is most recognizable for his famous novel of the Civil War, *The Red Badge of Courage*. However, students forget that Crane was born several years after the war concluded. His Civil War novel was first serialized in many news-papers across the country before it was published in book form in 1895. *The Red Badge of Courage* is one of the first depictions of battles and soldiers from a realist perspective. The story follows a young Union soldier named Henry Fleming who desires the glory that he thinks battle provides. Readers are quick-ly introduced to Fleming's inner struggle with courage; he is not sure whether he will fight or run when conflict emerges. Henry manages enough courage to remain for the first battle, but he flees at the sign of a second attack by the Confederates. As he wanders through the forests, he runs into a dead corpse and eventually a group of wounded soldiers. Henry's romanticism towards war allows him to see wounds as "red badges of courage." He feels ashamed of his cowardice and his inability to show the other soldiers a wound of his own. Henry does get swept away in another regiment's retreat. As he tries to obtain information, a frightened soldier hits Henry over the head with a rifle. Note the irony here: Henry's only wound comes from retreat, not battle. Henry does re-turn to the ranks and fights like a man possessed, even taking up the flag when the color bearer falls. Ultimately, Henry finds courage and makes peace with his previous retreats, although readers are left to judge the degree to which Henry has matured and changed.

Although Crane died a young man, his life was filled with travel and writing success. His first novel, *Maggie: A Girl of the Streets*, was self-published in 1891 (a new edition was published in 1896 during his growing popularity). After *Red Badge of Courage*, Crane published a couple of collections of short stories, including more tales involving the Civil War, *The Little Regiment and Other Episodes of the Civil War* (1896). Crane's most famous short story, "The Open Boat," is the fictional account of how Crane survived a shipwreck on his way to Cuba as a war correspondent. This story, like many of his tales and poems, tends to utilize naturalist conventions, namely, the lack of control humans have over nature. An example of naturalism in Crane's poetry occurs in "A Man said to the Universe":

> A Man said to the universe:
> "Sir, I exist!"
> "however," replied the universe,
> "The fact has not created in me
> A sense of obligation."

> (Hollander 1996, 755)

Students will find this theme in much of Crane's writing. Humans are left on this world to fend for themselves without any help from a divine creator or the natural world. Crane's first collection of poetry (of which the above poem is a part), *The Black Riders and Other Lines*, was published in 1895. Four years later, Crane continued his fascination with war, publishing *War is Kind*. The title poem is a wonderful satire on the romantic notion of glory and war.

Must Read

Works by Stephen Crane

The Red Badge of Courage, if you have time

"The Open Boat"

"Do not weep, maiden, for war is kind"

THE MINOR WRITERS

Rebecca Harding Davis (1831–1910)

Although most anthologies place Davis among the authors of antebellum America, her work is largely a part of and a result of the Industrial Revolution. Her earliest and most famous work, *Life in the Iron-Mills* (1861), a novella published in the *Atlantic Monthly*, is certainly a precursor to the realistic fiction that would become more popular towards the end of the nineteenth century. This early success set the pattern for much magazine writing and many literary connections. Harding married L. Clark Davis while continuing to write romances and social reform novels. Her husband was a well-known editor, and their son, Richard Harding Davis, delighted in literary success as well.

Even though slavery was the issue of the day, young Harding used her literary energies to explore another group of oppressed and neglected: the immigrant laborer. Her novella begins with an epigraph from Alfred, Lord Tennyson's "In Memoriam": "O Life, as futile, then as frail! / What hope of answer or redress?" (Davis 1998, 39). This is not the language of American romanticism. In two brief lines, the reader is introduced to the primary themes of the story and to the themes of the life of a laborer: hopelessness, frailty, and futility. In the prose itself, the narrator introduces readers to a new literary movement based on the very real lives of real people:

> I know: only the outline of a dull life, that long since, with thousands of dull lives like its own, was vainly lived and lost: thousands of them, massed, vile, slimy lives, like those of the torpid lizards in yonder stagnant water-butt.
>
> (Davis 1998, 40–41)

The narrator of the novella is not described in any detail; however, some argue that the narrator is a female. What is certain is that the narrator plays an active (although somewhat detached) part in the plot. The story follows a Welsh immigrant ironworker by the name of Hugh Wolfe. He spends what free time he has at the mill sculpting figures out of scrap iron called korl. One evening, a group of businessmen walk through the factory and notice a beautiful korl sculpture of a woman. Hugh asks the men to help him financially with his sculpting and his artistic dreams. Deborah, Hugh's cousin, overhears the men reject Hugh's requests. In a desperate effort to help Hugh and herself, she takes one of the men's wallets and offers it to Hugh as a way out of poverty. Eventually, they both land in jail where they will be forgotten. Pretty sad story, actually. That's the point: to mirror the real lives of iron mill workers. *Life in the Iron-Mills* was revived in the early 1970s thanks to a reprinting and introductory essay by Tillie Olson. Most anthologies now include the entire novella.

Must Read

Life in the Iron-Mills by Rebecca Harding Davis

William Dean Howells (1837–1920)

Howells is known more for his social, literary, and political connections and acquaintances than he is his own writing. Although he published numerous works over his lifetime, students should be familiar with his work as a magazine editor and friend to authors. Howells was raised in a highly political Ohio family; his father espoused socialist ideas and was an ardent abolitionist. After publishing his first collection of poems, Howells was hired to write a party biography of Republican presidential candidate Abraham Lincoln. In New England, Howells became familiar with many popular writers of the day: Henry Wadsworth Longfellow, James Russell Lowell, Nathaniel Hawthorne, Ralph Waldo Emerson, Henry David Thoreau, and even Walt Whitman. His success prompted Lincoln to appoint Howells as American consul in Italy. On his return to the States, Howells worked as an editor of the *Atlantic Monthly* where he was assigned books by Twain and James. Then, in 1886, Howells began editing at *Harper's* where he became famous for his regular columns, "Editor's Study" and "Editor's Easy Chair." These columns aligned him with more and more popular writers of the day, including Crane, Wharton, Paul Laurence Dunbar, and Sarah Orne Jewett. During his time as editor and critic, Howells also found time to write fiction. Although his works are largely ignored today, *The Rise of Silas Lapham* (1885) continues to be his most famous effort. The novel is a classic rags-to-riches story that adds the moral and ethical dilemmas that accompany great wealth. Thereafter, Howells' works (criticism and fiction) became more sociopolitically minded as he continued to explore the moral failings caused by capitalism and economic corruption.

Must Read

"Edith" by William Dean Howells

Ambrose Bierce (1842–1914?)

Bierce follows suit with many nineteenth-century American writers: he did not have an interest in formal education and worked most of his life as a journalist and newspaper editor, namely for the *San Francisco Examiner*. In California, Bierce was a part of a small group of writers, including Mark Twain and Bret Harte, called the **San Francisco Circle**. As a newspaper man and social critic, Bierce was known for his biting satire and poignant criticism, sometimes given the moniker "Bitter Bierce" or "Almighty God Bierce." Beyond his vitriolic reputation, Bierce is unique, however, in his ability to tell stories of the Civil War because he actually served as a soldier in several of the war's most important and violent campaigns, including the Battle of Chickamauga and the Battle of Shiloh. These tales, specifically "Chickamauga" and "An Occurrence at Owl Creek Bridge," were greatly influenced by his time as a soldier, and are still widely read and anthologized. His collection of war stories was published as *Tales of Soldiers and Civilians* in 1891. Bierce's bitterness and acerbic wit and cynicism were major catalysts to his writing career. In 1911, Bierce published the still highly popular and widely quoted *The Devil's Dictionary*. In it, he offers alternative definitions for common words, ultimately satirizing human assumptions, the government, society in general, and common prejudices. He defines heaven as "a place where the wicked cease from troubling you with talk of their personal affairs, and the good listen with attention while you expound on your own" (Bierce 1993, 50). In an intriguing turn of events, Bierce, after a string of family tragedies, headed south for Mexico in 1913 to, supposedly, join Pancho Villa's revolution. He was never heard from again.

Must Read

Works by Ambrose Bierce

"Chickamauga"

"An Occurrence at Owl Creek Bridge"

Sarah Orne Jewett (1849–1909)

It would be rude to call Jewett a one-hit wonder, but it is clear that her story, "A White Heron," has kept her a part of the American literary canon since its publication in *A White Heron and Other Stories* in 1886. Jewett's ancestors were a part of the Puritan Great Migration of the 1630s, and her well-to-do family made their life in Maine, fully embracing the New England lifestyle. William Dean Howells proved helpful to Jewett's literary career as he both published her stories in the *Atlantic Monthly* and personally encouraged her to continue her literary pursuits. Like many writers of the time, she held strong acquaintances and friendships with local and national writers such as Harriet Beecher Stowe. The most intriguing stage of her life occurred after the death of one of her editor friends, James T. Fields. Jewett quickly connected with the grieving widow, Annie, which culminated into a long relationship between the two women. Historians point out that, at the time, two women sharing housing and intimate lives together was referred to as a "Boston marriage." Much ink has been spilled over the implications of such a marriage; however, the relationship became a major influence in her writing and social life. "A White Heron" is a wonderful example of regional writing, or what some call "local color" writing. Her young protagonist must make a decision between saving a beautiful bird or succumbing to the seemingly innocuous advances of a handsome hunter. Jewett's Maine, and especially the heron's nest, becomes a separate and important character in the story. Many of her novels and short story collections are read and taught today; however, "A White Heron" stands as exemplary of Jewett's work.

Must Read

"A White Heron" by Sarah Orne Jewett

Charlotte Perkins Gilman (1860–1935)

Most students do not know that Gilman was a tireless reformer and social activist. Most of her literary work was nonfiction, encompassing issues as far-ranging as children, domestic space for women, economics, socialism, and Christianity. Unfortunately, those many essays, articles, poems, and stories have fallen off the radar screen of most modern readers. However, Gilman's provocative and psychological tale, "The Yellow Wallpaper," is still widely read and anthologized. Historians tell us that Gilman was fiercely independent and struggled to reconcile a writer's life with the life of a wife and a mother. After the birth of her daughter, Katherine, Gilman suffered what is now called postpartum depression, a clinical condition many women experience after childbirth. However, in the late 1880s, she was treated for a "nervous condition" and put on bed rest. Gilman's doctor was Weir Mitchell, whose rest-cure treatment for women suffering what he often diagnosed as neurasthenia kept his patients isolated and inactive, and is now viewed as the misogyny it was. You can imagine what a life of physical and intellectual inactivity would do to a writer. Fortunately for us, this experience catapulted "The Yellow Wallpaper." The tale follows a young mother's decline into madness after childbirth and being placed on the "rest cure." During her stay in her room, she becomes obsessed with the patterns of the yellow wallpaper. Soon she notices a woman trying to escape from the wallpaper—a cage of sorts. Ultimately, she rips the paper, attempting to free the woman from the paper, only to discover that she is the trapped woman behind the wallpaper. Not only does the story verge on fantasy or horror, it is biting satire against nineteenth-century medical practices of male doctors toward female patients as well as a critique of the conventions of marriage and gender roles. Implicitly, the story makes an argument for the power of writing, especially by those oppressed by the majority. Gilman's life was filled with conflict, activism, and advocacy. Tragically, she committed suicide after being diagnosed with breast cancer.

Must Read

"The Yellow Wallpaper" by Charlotte Perkins Gilman

Edwin Arlington Robinson (1869–1935)

Robinson is another complex figure for anthologies. Although he wrote many poetry collections after World War I, his poetry was far from what other modernists were writing at the time. In fact, modernism is what helped kill his reputation as a poet until more recent scholarship. Robinson's poetry uses traditional forms, rhyme schemes, and structure; however, his wide-ranging use of **irony** is what sets him apart from other writers of his day. His poems are nostalgic, lyrical, ironic, and filled with human suffering and isolation. Robinson also delighted in short narratives and snapshots of New England characters; students will quickly recognize such famous Robinson poems as "Richard Cory," "Miniver Cheevy," "The Mill," "Mr. Flood's Party," and "Luke Havergal." Some consider Robinson a regional poet; he grew up in Maine and used those people, settings, and events to contextualize much of his poetry. Again, like many poets, Robinson flirted with higher education, his at Harvard, but yielded to financial difficulties and returned home. Robinson self-published two poetry collections in the 1890s but remained under the literary radar until President Teddy Roosevelt happened upon one of those collections, gave it a rave review, and eventually set up Robinson with gainful employment. With that encouragement, Robinson published critically acclaimed collections: *The Town Down the River* (1910), *The Man against the Sky* (1916), *The Three Taverns* (1920), *The Man Who Died Twice* (1924), and *Tristam* (1927). Most of his poems depict the Maine of his childhood; however, *Tristam* was one of several that sought to retell Arthurian legends in a long narrative form. Even during Robinson's lifetime, certain readers and scholars rejected his work as trite, too traditional, simple, and quite antiquated; however, recent scholarship celebrates Robinson's irony, character complexity, unique use of form and poetic structure, and his commitment to regional writing.

Must Read

Poetry by Edwin Arlington Robinson

"Richard Cory"

"Mr. Flood's Party"

"Miniver Cheevy"

"Luke Havergal"

"The Mill"

Jack London (1876–1916)

London's life and fiction was full of adventure. At this point in the study guide, we have left the cultural center of New England and ventured to the Midwest.

London represents major writers from the West Coast. He was born John Griffith Chaney, but his mother remarried, so the boy was then known as Jack London. The family lived in Oakland, California, for much of Jack's young life, and that city provided the young boy with lots of adventures and a myriad of jobs, including an illegal job hunting oysters in the Bay Area. Of course, London wasn't much for school. He traveled the country before attending Oakland High School, and then after graduation, attended the University of California at Berkeley for only a few months before heading out on adventures again. When the Alaskan Gold Rush hit in 1897, London was intrigued enough to go. When he returned, he began writing of his time in the Klondike. *The Son of the Wolf* (1900) was the first collection of these stories. Readers were astonished and mesmerized by these tales, so magazines began to publish London often and pay him handsomely. His popularity led him to novel writing, which resulted in *The Call of the Wild* (1903) and *The Sea Wolf* (1904). London's ideologies were quite complex, however. Though many scholars note that London wrote only for the financial rewards, he was also a known socialist and supporter of social Darwinism. Since his death, London's stories and novels have been relegated to high school classrooms and children's book editions, and yet, his narratives are important glimpses of a particular cultural moment. Anthologies vary widely on the stories they include, but they all seem to agree that London is not as important as other writers. Most works include only one of his many hundreds of tales.

Must Read

Works by Jack London

The Call of the Wild

"To Build a Fire," for its dedication to realism and naturalism

Also consider "The Law of Life" and "South of the Slot."

AFRICAN-AMERICAN LITERATURE AT THE TURN OF THE 20TH CENTURY

Forgive me for placing prominent African-American writers in a separate section. Obviously, these important writers should be read along with the many white writers of the nineteenth century. The primary reason for this section is that I want you to see how these African-American writers not only were responding to incidents and philosophies of the entire nation, but were also engaging in a heated and sophisticated conversation with each other. Life in post–Civil War America was not necessarily any easier for Black Americans than life during slavery. Although many Americans abhorred slavery, there still remained a racial prejudice against free Blacks. So these writers, as a precursor to the great Harlem Renaissance, began to ask the important questions about how Black Americans should engage in national politics, labor, religion, education, and literature. And they didn't always agree with each other.

Charles W. Chesnutt (1858–1932)

Chesnutt was the child of interracial parents and lived in Cleveland. The family moved back to Charles's father's hometown, Fayetteville, North Carolina, so Charles's father could take over his father's grocery business. The young Chesnutt enjoyed a life of formal education, later to become the principal of the State Colored Normal School. It was in this position that Chesnutt began to publicly question social prejudice and the glass ceiling many Blacks faced after the Civil War. He was always particularly interested in the unique issues facing interracial men and women. So back to Cleveland he went with his family in order to begin his socially influenced writing career. Chesnutt's fiction explores the particular problems Blacks and interracial people faced in America. His stories were first published in newspapers before his big break with the *Atlantic Monthly*, and later in two short story collections, *The Conjure Woman* (1899) and *The Wife of His Youth and Other Stories of the Color Line* (1899). Thereafter, he published many novels, including *The House behind the Cedars* (1900), *The Marrow of Tradition* (1901), and *The Colonel's Dream* (1905). American readers were ignorant of Chesnutt's racial makeup at first; however, historians are clear that Chesnutt never hid from his racial identity. In fact, he was heavily involved in organizations such as the National Association for the Advancement of Colored People (NAACP).

Must Read

"The Passing of Grandison" by Charles Chesnutt

Booker T. Washington (1856–1915)

Washington did not write novels, poetry, plays, or short stories. He didn't write political treatises or sermons. In 1901, Washington published his autobiography called *Up from Slavery*. This book was arguably the seminal work on the Black experience at the turn of the century. The title refers not only to Washington's progress from a son of a slave to a college president and internationally known writer and orator, but also to his ideals for all former slaves and their descendents. In fact, his book can be read as an argument for how free Blacks should interact with white-dominated America. His book was highly acclaimed, widely read, and hotly contested by other major Black thinkers, especially W.E.B. Du Bois. Washington's major premise was that African Americans must ignore racial segregation and political rejection in favor of good, honest hard work. He asserts that African-American products will be just as good as products manufactured by whites; therefore, they will experience financial gain, security, and possibly upward mobility. A famous line of Washington's was to "cast down the buckets where you are," which hopefully validated the individual's power to stay put and work hard (Belasco and Johnson 2008, 442). He urged his African-American listeners and readers to focus on individual success and not wait for the government or the white population to amend for past failings. Although his speeches and writings outraged some in the North, the majority of white audiences and poor Blacks applauded Washington for his efforts, which made him nationally famous and secured money for his burgeoning school, the Tuskegee Normal School and Industrial Institute in Alabama. He worked tirelessly to fund the school and created a vocational education for young southern Blacks. Students went to class, worked in school-owned industries, and lived in dormitories. *Up from Slavery* follows his stretched efforts to cut costs, raise money, give speeches, raise a family, attend to professors and students, deal with local and state officials, and maintain excellence in all of these affairs. Washington was honored for his work throughout his life and given an honorary doctorate by Harvard University. Before his death, he managed to publish more works about his life and educational work in Alabama: *Tuskegee and Its People* (1905) and *The Story of the Negro* (1909).

Must Read

Up from Slavery by Booker T. Washington

W.E.B. Du Bois (1868–1963)

Du Bois is usually taught as Booker T. Washington's antithesis. Unlike Washington, Du Bois was born to free parents in Massachusetts. Du Bois found his calling in the intellectual and educational world instead of the vocational world. He earned undergraduate degrees from Fisk University and Harvard, and was the first African American to receive a doctorate from Harvard. Continuing his intellectual calling, Du Bois taught and furthered his research on the slave trade and the plight of post–Civil War Blacks at various universities: Wilberforce University, the University of Pennsylvania, and Atlanta University. Before the turn of the century, Du Bois had already written and published important works on African American life, including his dissertation *The Suppression of the African Slave Trade to the United States of America, 1638–1870* (1896) and *The Philadelphia Negro* (1899).

In 1903, Du Bois published his most enduring book on African-American life, *The Souls of Black Folks.* The book is a miscellany of sorts: a collection of essays, stories, histories, revisions, spirituals, and sketches that summarize and propel Du

Bois's central teachings. The major premise of the book is that Blacks should engage in higher education, politics, intellectual occupations, and all that life has to offer. Du Bois praises Washington for his work and lectures, but he also challenges Washington's inability to see complete integration in America. Instead of merely working for freedom, Du Bois asserts that Blacks should demand voting rights and participation in elected office. Washington and Du Bois both agree that education is the key to liberation, but they disagree on the best type of education and how "liberation" should be defined. Du Bois also coins an important term for race studies, **"double-consciousness,"** which refers to the act of being aware of one's self only through the eyes of others. Basically, Du Bois argues that African-American identity is only defined by how whites see them. It is obvious that this work was just as controversial as Washington's. Southerners argued that Du Bois was a dangerous thinker; however, many young and aspiring African Americans were heavily influenced by his philosophies and writings.

After the publication of *The Souls of Black Folks*, Du Bois continued his lecturing, teaching, and journalistic work founding various Black advocacy newspapers. In 1909, Du Bois resigned from teaching and moved to New York where he continued his work with the NAACP and its journal, the *Crisis*. His relationship with the NAACP was turbulent and complex. On one hand, the organization became a mouthpiece for Du Bois and his philosophies, but on the other hand, he continually criticized the organization for neglecting the poor and for mismanagement. At this time, Du Bois became more interested in politics and joined the Communist Party in 1961. A couple of years later, Du Bois, fed up with American racism, immigrated to Ghana where he died in 1963.

Must Read

The Souls of Black Folks by W.E.B. Du Bois

Paul Laurence Dunbar (1872–1906)

Dunbar is most noted for his ability to use elevated poetic language in one poem and then use effective African-American dialect in the next. Here is the first stanza to "We Wear the Mask":

> We wear the mask that grins and lies,
> It hides our cheeks and shades our eyes,
> This debt we pay to human guile;
>
> With torn and bleeding hearts we smile,
> And mouth with myriad subtleties.

(Hunter 1996, 490)

Now compare those highly traditional lines to those of "An Ante-Bellum Sermon":

> We is gathahed hyeah, my brothahs,
> In dis howlin' wildaness,
> Fu' to speak some words of comfo't
> To each othah in distress.
>
> An' we chooses fu' ouah subjic'
> Dis—we'll splain it by an'by;
> "An de Lawd said, 'Moses, Moses,'
> An de man said, 'Hyeah am I.' "
>
> (Belasco and Johnson 2008, 374)

These poems show students an example of **poetic persona**. The poetic voice is not necessarily that of the author but that of a "second self" the poet uses to tell a particular story or to depict a particular event or person. Dunbar wrote both poems, but he used two very different personas to do so.

Dunbar was born in Kentucky to former slaves; his father escaped to Canada only to return to the United States to fight in the Civil War. Unlike many African Americans in post–Civil War America, Dunbar went to predominantly white schools and experienced a robust education. After graduation, however, Dunbar was relegated to the menial labors that awaited most Black men. Dunbar continued to write poetry and published several works in local magazines and newspapers. His big break occurred when he was invited to read one of his poems at the World's Colombian Exposition in Chicago in 1893. It was there that Dunbar met influential and financially secure admirers, like Frederick Douglass, who secured for him employment and helped him publish another book of poetry in 1895. His first major publication was *Lyrics of Lowly Life* (1896), which garnered much praise from readers and critics, including William Dean Howells. Dunbar also wrote plays, short stories, and novels. Late in life, he married Alice Nelson, who was an important writer of "local color" in her own right.

Must Read

Poetry of Paul Laurence Dunbar

"When Malindy Sings"

"Sympathy"

"We Wear the Masks"

"An Ante-Bellum Sermon"

REFERENCES

Baym et al. 2008. *The Norton Anthology of American Literature*, shorter 7th ed. New York: W. W. Norton.

Belasco, Susan, and Linck Johnson. 2008. *The Bedford Anthology of American Literature*, Vol. 2, *1865 to the Present*. Boston: Bedford/St. Martin's.

Bierce, Ambrose. 1993. *The Devil's Dictionary*. New York: Dover Publications.

Davis, Rebecca Harding. 1998. *Life in the Iron-Mills, A Bedford Cultural Edition*. Edited by Cecelia Tichi. Boston: Bedford/St. Martin's.

Hemingway, Ernest. 1963. *The Green Hills of Africa*. New York: Charles Scribner's Sons.

Hollander, John. 1996. *American Poetry: The Nineteenth Century*. The Library of America. New York: Penguin Books.

Hunter, J. Paul. 1996. *The Norton Introduction to Poetry*, 16th ed. New York: W. W. Norton.

James, Henry. 2003. *Tales of Henry James*. A Norton Critical Edition. New York: W. W. Norton.

Chapter 5

The Modernist Period (1910–1945)

This period of American history produced two world wars, the addition of the Nineteenth Amendment to the Constitution to give women voting privileges, a stock market crash causing the Great Depression, a growing African-American population, a decline in European immigration, popularity in psychoanalysis and all things Freud, and many advances in science and technology. As historians point out, America was still largely rural and agricultural, which caused a great distrust for progress and urban expansion. Many Americans sought the golden age—a time that was more simple and free. If you remember Nathaniel Hawthorne's definitions of romance, you understand that these "bygone days" didn't really exist in the first place. Each era is plagued with societal ills and shortcomings. However, after World War I, whether Americans liked it or not, the nation was entering a period of **modernity**. This term has very little to do with chronology and more to do with perspective. The modern era is any era that resists its past in a variety of ways. In other words, the writers, thinkers, artists, architects, and many others do not view the present as relatively aligned with its past. Their work is fundamentally different from work done in the past. As you read and explore authors of this period, pay attention to how different they are from American authors of the eighteenth and nineteenth centuries.

LITERARY MODERNISM

One of the driving questions of this literary period was, "What is the function of literature?" For the literary ancestors of modernist writers, the imaginative arts were produced "**to teach and to delight**" (Sidney 1998, 138). On one hand, literature maintained a didactic nature in which stories, poems, and even novels were written to teach a particular truth, or in the least, to be grounded in a central truth. Second, literature entertained its readers with exciting plots, familiar characters, domestic and exotic settings, and elevated language in very linear and traditional forms. This was the artist's job before literary modernism began asking questions.

Modernists found this description of literature too imitative and overly simplistic, partly because the nature of truth, according to modernists, was much more complex, detached, and multivocal than the Puritans and their descendants taught. Modernist writers found much of what the previous generations taught them about truth as suspect and simplistic, including social concerns, religion, politics, and art. According to Archibald MacLeish's modernist poem, "Ars Poetica," "A poem should not mean, / But be" (Hunter 1996, 254). In one sense, this passage could be the slogan for literary modernism. These writers resisted any moral or didactic leanings that could distract the reader from appreciating the aesthetic beauty of the poem itself. So poetry at this time dedicated itself to itself and neglected much of life outside of the poem. Good literature, according to the modernists, remained slightly beyond the grasp of general readers and became complex and abstract systems of art that preoccupied itself with its own meaning.

What is important to note about literary modernism is that not all of its literature sang the praises of the modern world. Although the literature's content and form break with tradition in many ways, some writers use these new forms and taboo issues actually to attack modernity, exploring the growing tension between freedom and loss. In fact, some could assert that the modern era is one of fragments. America was changing in many wonderful ways, but its changes were also in conflict with its past; therefore, its art reflects this time of tumult and fragmentation. No longer are novels linear and chronological in nature. No longer are poems strictly narrative or lyrical. No longer are any artistic works easily interpreted. No longer is the truth of a text easily determined. Basically, modern art and literature do not directly state what they are; meaning, as stated earlier, is less important than mere existence. Modernism is laced with suggestion, metaphor, irony, ambiguity, understatement and subtlety, tone and tense shifts, and sometimes impenetrable prose.

The common denominator for many of the modern poets is the literary journal *Poetry: A Magazine of Verse*. In 1912, Harriet Monroe founded and edited this poetry journal in Chicago that promised to introduce Americans to modern poetry. This "little magazine," still in influential existence today, helped produce major writers through publications and reviews. Monroe single-handedly aided in the careers of Robert Frost, Carl Sandburg, Ezra Pound, T. S. Eliot, and William Carlos Williams, just to name a few.

THE POETRY

Amy Lowell (1874–1925)

You should recognize this poet's last name as the same as popular nineteenth-century poet James Russell Lowell. In fact, Amy grew up in a wealthy, educated, and prominent Boston family. Although she did not pursue higher education, Lowell dedicated much of her life to reading and writing poetry, culminating in her first collection of poetry in 1912. This collection was filled with traditional poetry influenced by English romantics. Soon after this publication, Lowell began reading more experimental poems by Ezra Pound and Hilda Doolittle. These writers, who had by this time immigrated to Europe, called their new form "**imagism**." I will discuss this form later in the section on Pound; however, simply, imagism rejected long and elevated language in favor of crisp, clear language and precise images. After this conversion of sorts, Lowell began "preaching" the new poetry to whoever would listen. Her first collection of experimental poetry, *Sword Blades and Poppy Seeds*, was published in 1914. Lowell then edited several collections of imagist poetry and continued to write and publish several books of her own poetry: *Men, Women, and Ghosts* (1916), *Can Grande Castle* (1918), *Pictures of the Floating World* (1919), and *What's O'Clock* (1925). What separates Lowell's poetry from other imagists is that her poetry is still relatively accessible and easy to read. Many of her contemporaries denounced her poetry as too imitative and traditional; however, this mix of tradition and experiment helped keep Lowell popular and read.

Must Read

Poetry of Amy Lowell

"Venus Transiens"

"Madonna of the Evening Flowers"

"The Sisters"

"The Taxi"

Robert Frost (1874–1963)

Frost's early life and career were much like those of the authors of the previous chapter. His relationship with formal education was tenuous at best, and as he was committed to a life of poetry, Frost held many jobs—textile worker, journalist, teacher—in order to continue his passion for writing and provide for his family. Well into his thirties, Frost moved his family to England where he befriended Ezra Pound. This literary connection inspired Frost to continue writing poetry, which eventually resulted in *A Boy's Will* (1913) and *North of Boston* (1914). During his lifetime, Frost's poetry won four Pulitzer Prizes; he published numerous poetry collections, was given many honorary doctorates, and was asked to recite a poem at President John F. Kennedy's inauguration in 1961. Arguably, Frost is the most famous poet the United States has produced.

Frost resisted much of what literary modernism espoused. With regard to free verse, he is quoted as saying, "I'd just as soon play tennis with the net down" (*Newsweek* 1956, 56). Modernism enjoyed the difficulty and complexity of poetry, so Frost's colloquial language, simple themes, traditional lines, regional content, and simple images seem anachronistic. While much of Frost's poetry *is* traditional and conventional, his use of these conventions is what sets him apart and above from that tradition. Frost, in some ways, was the antithesis of literary modernism. Not only did his poetry reflect the ideas and landscape of New England (a very nineteenth-century thing to do), but his nature poetry was more aligned with the transcendentalists and his plain-folk rhythms and images more aligned with the regionalists like Mark Twain, Willa Cather, and Edwin Arlington Robinson.

His poetry is relatively simple to comprehend on the surface, but there are always many layers to Frost's poetry. Some scholars even call Frost a regional writer due to his preoccupation and love for New England and the ordinary people of that section of the nation. In the first four lines of "Mending Wall," notice how Frost manipulates the sound of the lines to reflect the content of the lines:

> Something there is that doesn't love a wall,
> That sends the frozen-ground-swell under it
> And spills the upper boulders in the sun,
> and makes gaps even two can pass abreast.
>
> (Kennedy and Gioia 2005, 480)

Literally, ground swells cause walls to crumble; however, notice that Frost, in a traditional iambic line, stresses the syllables "ground-swell" to accentuate the feeling of a moving ground. In poetics, we refer to this as a spondaic interruption. The **spondee** is a poetic foot with two stressed syllables that brings power and emphasis to that word. Frost doesn't just imitate traditional forms; he twists and stretches those conventions to create better, more complex poems.

Must Read

Poetry of Robert Frost

"Mending Wall"

"Birches"

"Design"

"The Road Not Taken"

"Desert Places"

"Out, Out—"

"Stopping by Woods on a Snowy Evening"

"After Apple-Picking"

"The Wood Pile"

"Fire and Ice"

Carl Sandburg (1878–1967)

Like his literary forbearers, Sandburg, too, had a disdain for formal education and a necessity to work menial jobs in order to help provide for his Swedish immigrant family. Sandburg worked as a common laborer, a soldier in the Spanish-American War, an agricultural worker, and even a railway hobo. After attending college for a few more years, Sandburg became more serious about writing. Infused with his progressive political tendencies, his writing landed him journalist and editing jobs in Chicago and Milwaukee. He also lectured extensively on various topics, including his political idol, Abraham Lincoln. In fact, Sandburg published voluminous biographies of Lincoln called *Abraham Lincoln: The Prairie Years* (1926) and *Abraham Lincoln: The War Years* (1939), which not only won him the Pulitzer Prize in History but also garnered him much credibility as a scholar and historian, and not just a regional poet. While he wrote poetry, Sandburg continued to work as a journalist with the *Chicago Daily News* where he penned an important story on the race riots of 1919. Sandburg continued to write in different genres for the rest of his life, yet his poetry has been his most enduring. In 1950, his *Complete Poems* was awarded a Pulitzer Prize.

Sandburg is most famous, however, for his first few poems that ended up in *Poetry* in 1914 and were later collected in *Chicago Poems* (1916). These poems were criticized by some for their raw content and highly experimental form. Now known as the Chicago Poet, Sandburg gave Chicago and its growing industry, increased immigrant population, blue-color population, and literary renaissance a voice and a place in American literary geography. Much like Walt Whitman's Manhattan, Twain's Mississippi River, and even Cather's Nebraska, Sandburg's regionalism was universal in scope—the Chicagoan's experience mirrored the human experience. Here are the opening lines of the title poem "Chicago":

> Hog Butcher for the World,
> Took Maker, Stacker of Wheat,
> Player with Railroads and the Nation's Freight Handler;
> Stormy, husky, brawling,
> City of Big Shoulders
>
> (Ellmann and O'Clair 1988, 270)

Not only do the lines break with traditional form, but the content is as industrious and raw as the city itself. Much like Whitman, Sandburg dedicated his poetic career to exploring new forms, lines, and images in an effort to elevate the working class people of the Midwest, namely Chicago.

Must Read

Poetry of Carl Sandburg

"Chicago"

"Fog"

"Grass"

Wallace Stevens (1879–1955)

Stevens is one of many poets during this era that had a "day job" beyond writing poetry, teaching, or newspaper reporting. At the advice and encouragement of his father, young Stevens worked very hard academically both at Harvard and at the New York Law School, which landed him a job as a legal advisor for a New York City insurance firm and eventually at the Hartford Accident and Indemnity Company in Connecticut. Although his literary life exploded in New York with increased literary acquaintances and the exciting cultural life, Stevens maintained a strict commitment to his occupation. Stevens did not begin seriously publishing poetry until he was in his mid-thirties and did not publish his first collected work, *Harmonium*, until 1923. Many critics claimed that this work was the essential modernist collection of the day. However, some critics felt his poems were not serious enough. It is true that Stevens pays a lot of attention to color, lively imagery, and even humor; however, each poem is an exercise in modernist ideology: truth is fleeting, poetic structure is subjective, and irony is prevalent. In his "Of Modern Poetry," Stevens defines the type of poetry that transformed much of his own work:

> The poem of the mind in the act of finding
> What will suffice. It has not always had
> to find: the scene as set; it repeated what
> Was in the script.
>
> (Ellmann and O'Clair 1988, 298)

Modernists like Stevens believed seriously that their poetry and literary style was unique and radically different from that of their predecessors.

And like many other modernists, Stevens placed the individual at the center of the world. For example, "Thirteen Ways of Looking at a Blackbird" focuses on individual observation and how that observation, although extremely subjective, helps define and interpret the world. Stanza VIII exemplifies this perfectly:

> I know noble accents
> And lucid, inescapable rhythms;
> But I know, too,
> That the blackbird is involved
> In what I know.
>
> (Ellmann and O'Clair 1988, 287)

Knowledge is the product of subjective observation. As time went on, Stevens's poetry became longer and more abstract; moreover, some critics assert that his poetry became much too difficult and convoluted, even by modernist standards. Overall, Stevens is noted for his desire to poetically depict the nature of poetry and the poet in twentieth-century America.

Must Read

Poetry of Wallace Stevens

"Sunday Morning"

"The Snow Man"

"Anecdote of the Jar"

"Disillusionment of Ten O'Clock"

"The Emperor of Ice-Cream"

"Thirteen Ways of Looking at a Blackbird"

"A High-Toned Old Christian Woman"

"Of Modern Poetry"

William Carlos Williams (1883–1963)

Williams represents another change in the "job" of the writer in the twentieth century. Unlike his predecessors, Williams did not want to make his money from writing. Instead, he studied medicine at the University of Pennsylvania and practiced medicine in his hometown of Paterson, New Jersey. Known as the "Doctor-Poet," Williams devoted as much time to his patients as he did American poetry. Like many modernists, Williams desired to change poetry and the way readers engaged with poetry. At the beginning of his literary career, Williams subscribed to the ideas of imagism. One of his most famous poems, "The Red Wheelbarrow," is a popular example of this type of poetry:

> so much depends
> upon
> a red wheel
> barrow
> glazed with rain
> water
> beside the white
> chickens.

> (Ellmann and O'Clair 1988, 318)

Notice that the poem does not use standard punctuation or capitalization, nor does it follow any conventional style of poetry. It is merely the image of a red wheelbarrow in the rain beside some chickens. That's it. Its poetic strength remains in the power of the object itself. Later, Williams rejected imagism as a mode of writing poetry and used the term "**objectivism**." Simply, the poet views the poem as an object, and that object allows the poet to see the world more critically, analytically, and clearly. There is much in common between imagism and objectivism. Some argue that the change in terms was highly arbitrary. Regardless, Williams constantly sought out new rhythms, idioms, and poetic structures to more perfectly match the American identity. These more vernacular verses became the antithesis to T. S. Eliot's and Ezra Pound's fascination with European intellect and culture. In 1923, Williams published *Spring and All*. His most experimental work, *Paterson*, was written from 1946 to 1958.

Must Read

Poetry of William Carlos Williams

"The Young Housewife"

"Danse Russe"

"To Elise"

"This Is Just to Say"

"The Red Wheelbarrow"

"Queen-Anne's-Lace"

"The Widow's Lament in Springtime"

"Spring and All"

Ezra Pound (1885–1972)

Ezra Pound was a friend, mentor, encourager, and inspiration to many modernist writers. Although he was born in the United States, Pound spent most of his life and poetic energies in Europe, mainly Venice, Paris, and London. It was during his years as a student at the University of Pennsylvania that he met Hilda Doolittle and William Carlos Williams. In his early twenties, Pound immigrated to Europe and eventually founded a group of modernist poets called the Imagists, which included Doolittle (later known as H. D.), Richard Aldington, and to some degree, Amy Lowell and Marianne Moore. As I've stated before, imagism defined the poem as an object, focusing intently on precise language and images. One of the most famous imagist poems is Pound's "In a Station of the Metro." Pound said that the poem was the result of seeing one beautiful face after another in the Paris subway system:

The apparition of these faces in the crowd;
Petals on a wet, black bough.

(Ellmann and O'Clair 1988, 381)

Students are not wrong if they compare these poems to Japanese haiku. Pound, among others, was heavily influenced by Asian culture and poetry. In 1915, he published a collection of Chinese translations called *Cathay*. During this time, Pound also moved away from the imagist movement toward a newer, avant-garde movement called **vorticism**. Pound coined the term to describe a particular type of art heavily influenced by cubism and futurism; however, the term is predominantly used to define visual art instead of poetry. Its work was highly abstract and modern, focusing on harsh lines and angles, as well as devoting its subject matter to urban areas and industry. Pound's most enduring work, however, is *The Cantos*, which took him nearly fifty years to complete. This long poem is made up of over one hundred poems, or "cantos," of varying lengths that provide many problems for readers. It is heavily allusive, political, multilinguistic, annotative, abstract, and sometimes impenetrable.

Pound worked tirelessly as a poet and as a promoter for modern poetry. He worked as foreign correspondent for Harriet Monroe's "little magazine" *Poetry* in Chicago. Pound also wrote many nonfiction works on economics, writing, politics, and issues pertaining to modernity. His political life was as radical as his artistic life. In Italy, Pound became fascinated with Benito Mussolini and Fascism, which ultimately landed him in Italian prison and in American court for treason. Eventually, charges were dropped and Pound returned to Italy where he lived until his death.

Must Read

Poetry of Ezra Pound

"In a Station of the Metro"

"The River-Merchant's Wife: A Letter"

"A Pact"

The Cantos: Read a variety of these poems to better understand the form and content.

H. D. (Hilda Doolittle; 1886–1961)

Hilda Doolittle was born into a Pennsylvania Moravian family. Moravians were a deeply religious people that believed in community, missions, and personal piety. Their roots are orthodox Christian, but their emphasis in ritual and mysticism set them apart from other mainline Protestant denominations. The

Moravian fascination with symbols and images must have had a great influence on the burgeoning modernist. As a student at Bryn Mawr College in Pennsylvania, Doolittle met and befriended other future poets, including Marianne Moore, William Carlos Williams, and her future fiancée, Ezra Pound. This love affair spanned two continents and much turmoil, including Pound's infidelity. Doolittle eventually fell in love with and married fellow imagist Richard Aldington. However, she still loved Pound and her work continued to be influenced by him. In 1913, he sent several of Doolittle's poems to Harriet Monroe, publisher and editor of *Poetry*, with the moniker "H.D., Imagiste." From then on, Hilda Doolittle wrote under the name H.D. Her first book of poems, *Sea Garden*, was published in 1916.

H.D. wrote many poetry collections, novels, and even plays throughout her life, even while her marriage collapsed, her daughter was stillborn, and society denounced her love affair with an affluent woman, Winifred Ellerman. Late in life, H.D. wrote her most celebrated and enigmatic poems, which departed quite deliberately at times from the imagism of her earlier work. From 1944 to 1946, she wrote three collections, *The Walls Do Not Fall*, *Tribute to the Angels*, and *The Flowering of the Road*, that became known as *Trilogy*. In a sense, the book attempts to create a religion, or at least create an amalgamation of other world religions, such as those of the ancient Greeks, Egyptians, and Hebrews, to create a separate religion. It is a religious, political, and personal epic that takes place during the bombing of London in World War II. It is noteworthy that H.D. studied under **Sigmund Freud** in Vienna for almost two years during the early stages of these manuscripts. Here is an excerpt from *The Walls Do Not Fall* that exemplifies imagism, allusion, and unconventional poetics:

> [3]
> Let us, however, recover the Sceptre,
> the rod of power:
> it is crowned with the lily-head
> Or the lily-bud:
> it is Caduceus; among the dying
> it bears healing:
> or evoking the dead,
> it brings life to the living.

(H.D. 1998, 7)

Much like other modernists, H.D. was fascinated by the past, but her poetry is anything but traditional. As I mentioned earlier, modern poetry is heavily allusive and dependent on historical works, images, and symbols; however, they are appropriated in very unconventional, and sometimes taboo, ways. In 1961, the year of her death, H.D. published the long, highly acclaimed feminist retelling of the Trojan War, *Helen in Egypt*. Some scholars consider her a minor poet, but her feminist participation in modern poetry should be included with Pound and Eliot.

Must Read

Poetry of H.D.

"Helen"

"Oread"

"Leda"

"Mid-day"

Marianne Moore (1887–1972)

In many ways, the modernists were a tight-knit community of writers, thinkers, and social activists. They read each other's work, promoted each other, critiqued each other, and ultimately propelled each other to literary success. It is no wonder that many of these writers were influenced by Thoreau, Whitman, Emerson, and transcendental thought; there are many similarities. Moore is another poet who was rewarded greatly for her poetic talent and her significant acquaintances. While studying at Bryn Mawr College, Moore met H.D., who helped her career by publishing several poems in the magazine *Egoist* in 1916. Like many poets, Moore worked ordinary jobs to provide for her family while she continually and tirelessly wrote and published her poetry. As a secretary at the New York Public Library, Moore became acquainted with Wallace Stevens and William Carlos Williams. It was several years later, before her first book of poems was published; H.D. helped compile a collection, titled simply *Poems*, and promoted it for publication in 1921. *Observations* was published in 1924 thanks to a generous relationship with and monetary award from the literary journal the *Dial*. Later, Moore edited the journal full time while working on her craft, promoting modern poetry, and socializing with other great writers and artists.

Most of Moore's imagery is drawn from the natural world, animals, people and art, and her poetry is also strikingly different from other modernist poets like Pound and H.D. Many of her poems utilize long, bumbling lines, as Whitman's works do, instead of the imagist techniques of her contemporaries. Second, she did not completely abandon poetic structure; her stanzas can be uniform and metric, while her use of rhyme can be traditional as well. Like other modernist poets, however, Moore broke many social and poetic conventions; she used allusions and quotations, and focused intently on the poetic object. As I mentioned in the introduction, these poets were also interested in poetry as a subject in their poems. Moore's most famous and anthologized poem is called "Poetry." Here is the original first line of that poem:

> I, too dislike it.
> Reading it, however, with a perfect contempt for it, one discovers in
> it, after all, a place for the genuine.
>
> (Ellmann and O'Clair 1988, 457)

Moore was a revisionist at heart. This poem is a good example of her undying effort to make a poem perfect. At the end of her life, Moore wrote essays and translations, won a Pulitzer Prize for her *Collected Poems*, and produced *Completed Poems* on her eightieth birthday.

Must Read

Poetry of Marianne Moore

"Poetry"

"To a Snail"

"The Mind Is an Enchanting Thing"

T.S. Eliot (1888–1965)

Eliot was born in St. Louis to a wealthy and very social family descended from prominent New England stock. His grandfather was Unitarian and a graduate of Harvard Divinity School, and he moved to the Midwest where he started a new church and a liberal arts university (Washington University, St. Louis). Eliot was formally educated at the best private schools and attended Harvard where he published poetry and other writings. His university education helped him craft a style of poetry very different from the British writers of his textbooks.

Eliot was also a famous expatriate, meaning he immigrated to Europe where he lived for much of his life. Before he turned forty, Eliot became a British citizen; however, we still claim him as an American poet. In 1910, Eliot studied at the Sorbonne in France and later moved to England where he began a friendship with other "expats" like Pound. His relationship with Pound proved to be incredibly beneficial to his literary career. Pound encouraged Eliot and, thanks to his involvement with the important literary magazine *Poetry*, persuaded Harriet Monroe to publish Eliot's first promising and famous long poem, "The Love Song of J. Alfred Prufrock" in 1915. The poem is a loose narrative about Prufrock's love for a woman. It is an internal monologue about the state of love, his doubts and moments of inferiority, and ultimately, his isolation as an individual from society. In a popular passage, Prufrock intimates on the dismal punishment of old age as he states, "I shall grow old ... I shall grow old ... / I shall wear the bottoms of my trousers rolled" (Ellmann and O'Clair 1988, 485). What is implied in much modernist writing is the youthful energy of change and rebellion; therefore, Prufrock represents the nightmare of modernism: getting old. Some scholars refer to the poem as *the* modernist poem.

In England, Eliot taught, worked at a bank, founded the literary journal *Criterion*, and continued to write poetry. Although Eliot began working on his most important poetic work in 1921, just after a brief stay in a mental hospital, "The Waste Land" was not published until 1922 in the *Criterion*. In this first edition, Eliot does not include the many footnotes that accompanied "The Waste Land" when he published it in book form. In a preface to the endnotes, he recommends two texts to help "elucidate" some of the problems his poem creates: Jessie L. Weston's *From Ritual to Romance* and *The Golden Bough*. These notes, which aid the reader in interpretation, have now become a very integral part of understanding and interpreting the poem itself. Many scholars also note how important Pound was to the editing and completion of this poem; he cut out many superfluous passages and helped Eliot rename the text, which Eliot had originally titled "He do the Police in different voices." Much like H.D.'s *Trilogy*, "The Waste Land" draws on many different religions and ancient cultures in an attempt to comment on the current state of the world. It is highly allusive, multilingual, and incredibly fragmented; it is a modern text. Some argue "The Waste Land" is, much like "Prufrock," a treatise against modernity and a tale of detachment, isolation, and fragmentation that leads only to demise.

Eliot continued to write profusely and represent modern poetry on the world's stage. Beyond poetry, Eliot also engaged in literary criticism. One highly anthologized essay, "Tradition and the Individual Talent," argued that each modern poet should weigh himself and his poetry with other poets and poems of the past. The world of poetry is a place unto itself; therefore, the past's history, politics, religion, and culture cannot inform the modern poet of his craft as can studying the actual poems of the past. This essay became an integral argument for a school of critics called the **New Critics** or **Formalists**.

Eliot's life was marked by a conversion from his family's Unitarianism to the Church of England in 1927. This spiritual epiphany influenced later works like *Murder in the Cathedral* (1935), *The Family Reunion* (1939), and *Four Quartets* (1943), which were all meditative and theological in nature. Still in midlife, Eliot received the Nobel Prize for Literature in 1948 and remains today one of the most celebrated poets of the United States and England.

Must Read

Poetry of T.S. Eliot

"The Love Song of J. Alfred Prufrock"

"Journey of the Magi"

"The Waste Land"

"Tradition and the Individual Talent"

Edna St. Vincent Millay (1892–1950)

Much like Marianne Moore, Millay did not shy from using traditional forms to frame her sometimes untraditional poetic subjects. The sonnet was her poetic form of choice; Millay used very patriarchal forms, the Shakespearean and Petrarchan sonnet, somewhat subversively to depict and explore women's issues and concerns. Millay also critiqued religious dogma and Christian traditions in her poems. The short "Second Fig" is a good example of Millay's poetic tone and gentle satire:

> "Safe upon the solid rock the ugly houses stand:
> Come and see my shining palace built upon the sand!"
>
> (Hunter 1996, 371)

What is most notable about this poem and most of her poetry, is Millay's poignant tone. Some call her cynical. Others refer to her as comical and satirical. Regardless, Millay poked fun at life taken seriously, especially love. Historians note that Millay had many love affairs during her life, so her poetry both reflects the sensuality of sex and promiscuous lust, but it also resonates loneliness and emptiness. Read "I, Being Born a Woman and Distressed" or "I Think I Should Have Loved You Presently" for good examples of this tension.

Millay grew up in a working-class family in Maine, yet her mother encouraged her to write poetry, enjoy music and drama, and read continuously. At a young age, Millay wrote and published poems in local magazines, but her first collection of poems did not surface until 1917 during her last year as a student at Vassar College. *Renascence and Other Poems* (1917) allowed her to live a bohemian poet's lifestyle in New York City. Later, Millay traveled through Europe and settled in upstate New York, but poetry remained her passion. *The Harp-Weaver and Other Poems* won her a Pulitzer Prize in 1922, the first ever awarded to a woman for poetry.

Like many of her contemporaries, Millay became more political in her later years. She is most famous for participating in a protest against the execution of two Italian anarchists, **Nicola Sacco and Bartolomeo Vanzetti**. Millay is aligned with Moore and H. D. as the most important women in modernism.

Must Read

Poetry of Edna St. Vincent Millay

"Euclid alone has looked on Beauty bare"

"I, Being Born a Woman and Distressed"

"First Fig" and "Second Fig"

"I Think I Should Have Loved You Presently"

---

e. e. cummings (1894–1962)

Cummings has the most distinct poetic style of any of his contemporaries. Students will immediately recognize a Cummings poem with its aversion to capitalization, punctuation, traditional poetic lines and forms, and spaces between words. Cummings was committed to the visual components of poetry, continually painting a picture with words. Cummings is also known for his paintings, which contained many conventions of modern art. Students will also recognize a Cummings poem for its common use of the vernacular; his poems read the way people talk. Read "in Just—," "Buffalo Bill's," and "anyone lived in a pretty how town" for good examples of Cummings' use of diction, poetic form, and vernacular voice.

Edward Estlin was raised in a relatively affluent Massachusetts home and enjoyed reading and writing at a young age. Like many families in the late nineteenth century, the Estlin family enjoyed parlor readings that revolved around the Fireside Poets, like Henry Wadsworth Longfellow and William Cullen Bryant. Later, however, Cummings was inspired by the experimental poetry of Amy Lowell and Ezra Pound. This fascination with modernism was also propelled by his hate for war, even though he served in the Army during World War I. Like many writers, Cummings found a home in the *Dial*, the fledgling literary journal dedicated to modern poetry. His association with the journal eventually led to an affair with the senior editor's wife, Elaine Thayer, whom he soon married and divorced. After several years of painting, writing, and publishing, Cummings published his first collection, *Tulips and Chimneys*, in 1923. Throughout his life, Cummings published many collections of experimental poetry that continually pushed the definition of "poetry" and "modernism." Humorously, in 1935 Cummings published *No Thanks*, which he dedicated to the numerous publishers that refused to buy the work.

Must Read

Poetry of e. e. cummings

"in Just—"

"Buffalo Bill's"

"next to of course god america I"

"i sing of Olaf glad and big"

"anyone lived in a pretty how town"

"i thank You God for most this amazing"

Hart Crane (1899–1932)

Crane committed suicide just a few months before his thirty-third birthday. His life was filled with broken relationships, inner turmoil, alcohol, and poetry. Crane spent his childhood moving back and forth from Cleveland to New York to the West Indies as his parents split and reconciled numerous times. One fun fact is that his father established candy stores in Cleveland and invented the Life Saver. In

New York, Crane met and befriended several emerging writers such as e. e. cummings. He also published a few poems in modern "little magazines" like *Pagan* and the *Dial*; he became associate editor of the *Dial* in 1918. Crane's poetry can be categorized as traditional because he does utilize traditional forms, meter, and rhyme; however, the urban setting that grounds many of his poems leads Crane's poetry away from the imitative and simple. Some scholars assert that Crane's poetry is overly abstract and dense.

Must Read

Poetry of Hart Crane

"To Brooklyn Bridge"

"The Broken Tower"

"Chaplinesque"

THE FICTION

Gertrude Stein (1874–1946)

No other author in the twentieth century was as influenced by painting as Stein. As an American expatriate, Stein lived most of her adult life in Paris where she met, befriended, and worked with famous European artists like Pablo Picasso and Henri Matisse. She and her brother collected art, and Stein even posed for Picasso. As I mentioned earlier in this chapter, the period between the two world wars was a time of great literary experimentation. One of the products of such experimentation was the **sketch**. Unlike the short story that is preoccupied with plot, character, setting, and conflict, the sketch is heavily influenced by the visual arts in that it is preoccupied with a single scene, moment, character, or image. Much like imagist poetry, the sketch is grounded in precise language and sensory detail. Some scholars call Stein's work "still-life studies" or "word portraits." You should recognize her writing as incredibly experimental, paying close attention to images and wordplay.

Although Stein grew up in the United States, after her parents' death, she and her brother moved to Paris where they began to mingle with and influence other artistic and literary expatriates: Ernest Hemingway, F. Scott Fitzgerald, and Sherwood Anderson. In Paris, she wrote and published many collections of sketches, memoirs, and essays. Her most famous were *Tender Buttons: Objects, Food, Rooms* (1914), a collection of word portraits about mundane objects and everyday life; *The Autobiography of Alice B. Toklas* (1933), a memoir told from the perspective of Stein's longtime companion, lover, and secretary; and *Ida, a Novel* (1941), a grand modernist and feminist novel about a woman "whose life," according to the inside flap of the novel, "consists mainly of resting, because she is always tired; of talking to herself; and of getting married, time after time."

Must Read

Works by Gertrude Stein

Anthologies vary widely on what they include. Here are my recommendations:

"Objects" or another selection from *Tender Buttons: Objects, Food, Rooms*

"Ada"

Sherwood Anderson (1876–1941)

Anderson's *Winesburg, Ohio* (1919) is still considered one of the most influential collections of short stories of the American twentieth century. Both experimental and modern, Anderson introduces readers to an underbelly of American small-town life, wiping away the romantic nostalgia that sometimes plagued American ideals and visions.

Unlike the expatriates and wealthy children of New England, Anderson lived a life much like his nineteenth-century American literary ancestors: hard work and financial hardship that sent him to Chicago as a laborer and to Cuba as a soldier in the Spanish-American War. After working many different jobs, Anderson relocated his family to Cleveland where he lived a life filled with tension and stress between work, family, and his intense desire to be a writer. In 1912, he abandoned his family and headed for Chicago, which was a burgeoning literary and artistic center at the time. Anderson's literary career took off there, spanning several decades, cities, and even continents. Some scholars and historians argue that Stein's *Tender Buttons* greatly influenced Anderson's writing style and subject choice; Anderson met and befriended Stein when he traveled to Paris. Although Anderson published many collections of stories, novels, and even an autobiography, he could never imitate or duplicate the literary influence of *Winesburg, Ohio*.

What you will notice right away is that the book is a collection of short stories or sketches; however, they are loosely tied together by recurring characters, especially the young, small-town journalist George Willard. The book is not a simple annotation of small-town life. In each sketch it is clear that Anderson explores psychology, sexuality, and the suggestion of moral decay in this American small town. The book begins with a sketch called "The Book of the Grotesque." In it, he writes

> You see the interest in all this lies in the figures that went before the eyes of the writer. They were all grotesques. All of the men and women the writer had ever known had become grotesques.
>
> (Anderson 1993, 5)

To Anderson, these characters—these **grotesques**—"took the truth to himself, called it his truth, and tried to live his life by it, he became a grotesque and the truth he embraced became a falsehood" (Anderson 1993, 6). The term originally referred to art and sculpture that was bizarre, fantastic, abnormal, and that symbolized the horror of being human in a very inhumane and distrustful world. Anderson's characters are sad, tragic, comic, and endearing all at the same time. Readers are mesmerized by these characters' inability to act and react effectively and appropriately in a world that doesn't see much use in their existence.

Must Read

From *Winesburg, Ohio* by Sherwood Anderson

"The Book of the Grotesque"

"Mother"

"Hands"

Katherine Anne Porter (1890–1980)

Porter is the first writer, thus far in our review, who spent many years living in Texas. She lived a very nomadic life and was married many times. Her travels took her to New York, Mexico, Paris, and even Berlin. Porter's literary career started when she moved to Greenwich Village in New York City, which was another burgeoning literary and artistic community. In Mexico, Porter dabbled in politics and social reform, which ultimately resulted in her returning to New York.

What is also peculiar about Porter is that her first collected and acclaimed work was not published until she was forty. *Flowering Judas and Other Stories* (1930) was the culmination of many years of fiction writing; it solidified her reputation as a serious writer and allowed her to continue to publish. She wrote much about her days in Texas: *Pale Horse, Pale Rider* (1939) and *The Leaning Tower and Other Stories* (1944). In 1962, Porter wrote the novel *Ship of Fools*, which became a successful movie in 1965 starring Vivien Leigh. That same year the *Collected Stories of Katherine Anne Porter* received the Pulitzer Prize for Fiction.

Porter's fiction has been praised for its craft and clear writing; her use of language not only paints pictures but also allows readers to experience the incidents of the story. In one of her most famous and highly anthologized stories, "The Jilting of Granny Weatherall," she writes, "What does a woman do when she has put on the white veil and set out the white cake for a man and he doesn't come" (Porter 2008, 422). Her simplicity of language carries immense emotional weight. Her stories depict real people experiencing real life; subsequently, most of her characters are woman who must navigate a very male world.

Must Read

Works by Katherine Anne Porter

"Flowering Judas"

"The Jilting of Granny Weatherall"

F. Scott Fitzgerald (1896–1940)

Fitzgerald is heralded as the writer of the **Jazz Age**, a term he coined in his short story collection *Tales of the Jazz Age* (1922) to describe and define the years between World War I and the Great Depression. This era was marked by an increase in youthful abandonment and characterized by flappers, gangsters, speakeasies, riotous parties, sexual infidelity, and racial and sexual tolerance. Given these factors, it is not surprising that the Jazz Age also marked a great conflict between the traditions of the American past and the nontraditional sensibilities of the youthful future. Fitzgerald's stories and novels explore this tension between "old" and "new." During the **Roaring Twenties**, Fitzgerald wrote many highly profitable stories for the *Saturday Evening Post*, as well as collections of stories such as *Flappers and Philosophers* (1920) and *All the Sad Young Men* (1926), and the semiautobiographical novel *This Side of Paradise* (1920), which begins to explore the youthful socialite's plight in postwar America. In 1925, during an expanded time in Europe with other expatriates like Hemingway and Stein, Fitzgerald published his most celebrated novel, *The Great Gatsby*.

The narrator of *Gatsby* is a young Minnesota man named Nick Carraway who has moved to Long Island, New York, to make it in business. There, he lives in the West Egg district that is commonly associated with "new money." His neighbor is Jay Gatsby, who lives in a large mansion and is known for hosting lavish weekly parties. Nick also has connections with East Egg, the upper-class "old money" section of Long Island. His cousin Daisy Buchanan lives there with her husband Tom; they have a tense marriage due to Tom's infidelities with Myrtle Wilson, who lives in a lower-class industrial section of the area. The plot intensifies when Nick is eventually invited to one of Gatsby's parties. It is there that Nick learns of Gatsby's dying love for Daisy; Nick reunites them and the two begin a love affair. Tom discovers the affair and, at a heated conversation with Daisy and Gatsby in New York City, divulges to Daisy information about Gatsby's illegal and unethical manner of making money. Returning together to West Egg, Daisy and Gatsby's car strikes and kills Myrtle in "the valley of ashes" where Myrtle lived. Daisy was driving the car, but Gatsby takes the blame. Tom tells George, Myrtle's husband, that Gatsby killed Myrtle, so George shoots and kills Gatsby in Gatsby's own swimming pool. After the funeral, Nick leaves New York in a fit of disgust and bewilderment. The novel is a wonderful testament to the power and obsession with wealth and social status. Dreams of individual success and monetary security outweigh and demolish moral and ethical responsibility. Greed, cynicism, and the hedonistic impulses of young, rich Americans plague the characters, conflicts, and entire plot. To some critics, this novel is the story of 1920s America.

Fitzgerald's life mirrored, in many ways, the life of Gatsby and Nick Carraway. He grew up in Minnesota, but he spent his life in New York and in Europe trying to grasp and maintain a life of success, social glamour, and pleasure. His marriage was plagued by his wife Zelda's mental and emotional instabilities and his alcoholism. After the 1920s, Fitzgerald never regained his earlier popularity, but he continued to write novels and stories, including *Tender is the Night* (1934), *Taps at Reveille* (1935), and the posthumously published novel *The Last Tycoon* (1941). Fitzgerald finished his career writing Hollywood screenplays with other aging, and sometimes broke, authors like William Faulkner.

Must Read

Works by F. Scott Fitzgerald

The Great Gatsby

"Babylon Revisited"

"Winter Dreams"

William Faulkner (1897–1962)

Faulkner is most well-known for his fictional Mississippi County, **Yoknapa-tawpha**. He writes of the families there in an attempt to address the compelling issues of southern identity: race, class, sex, gender, and how those elements are in constant tension with each other. Faulkner's novels, much like Fitzgerald's, explore the tension between the old antebellum South and the progressive nature of post–World War I social and economic leanings. Influenced by Sherwood Anderson to write about the place and people of his youth, Faulkner began his obsession with that "little postage stamp of native soil" called Mississippi (Belasco and Johnson 2008, 949). Thereafter, Faulkner established the Compson family as the symbolic tragic, southern family. In the novels *The Sound and the Fury* (1929) and *Absalom, Absalom!* (1936), Faulkner not only addresses social taboos such as interracial sexuality and incest, but he also plays with narrative form. In the following passage from the conclusion of *Absalom, Absalom!*, one of the narrators, Quentin Compson, reveals a symbolic tension between telling stories of the South and living out their meaning when he attempts to answer his roommate Shreve's question about why Quentin hates the South so much:

> "I don't hate it," Quentin said, quickly, at once, immediately; "I don't hate it," he said *I don't hate it* he thought, panting in the cold air, the iron New England dark: *I don't. I don't! I don't hate it! I don't hate it!*
>
> (Faulkner 1951, 378)

Faulkner used **stream of consciousness** (made famous by James Joyce's *Ulysses*), which focused on the mental-emotional life of the characters instead of the external. Simply, the narrative mimics what a character thinks and not just what he says. Students will recognize stream-of-consciousness writing because of its lack of standard spelling, punctuation, dialogue tags, and sentence structure. For example, Quentin, in *The Sound and the Fury*, thinks

> Why shouldn't you I want my boys to be more than friends yes Candace and Quentin more than friends *Father I have committed* what a pity you had no brother or sister *No sister no sister had no sister*.
>
> (Faulkner 1990, 95).

Later, Faulkner focused his attention to the poor whites of Yoknapatawpha in a trilogy commonly referred to as the Snopes Trilogy: *The Hamlet* (1940), *The Town* (1957), and *The Mansion* (1959). Many of the characters, plots, and settings of these novels were introduced in earlier short stories like the highly anthologized "Barn Burning," which was published by *Harper's* magazine in 1939. As I stated earlier, many of Faulkner's novels and stories addressed the racial tensions of the day, and although critics lambasted Faulkner for his seemingly moderate stance on integration, his novels certainly explored taboo topics and exposed narrow southern thinking. *Light in August*'s Joe Christmas (1932), *Intruders in the Dust*'s Lucas Beauchamp (1948), and even selected stories in *Go Down, Moses* (1942) present readers with interracial characters and African Americans attempting to adjust and survive in the Depression-era South. In his final years, Faulkner won two Pulitzer Prizes for Fiction and the Nobel Prize for Literature in 1949.

Faulkner was not necessarily liked or respected in his hometown of Oxford, Mississippi. He attended the University of Mississippi off and on while maintaining menial jobs in and around town. He was once fired from a position at the local post office for losing too much mail. In another strange episode, Faulkner returned from military training in Canada with the British Royal Air Force during World War I with grand stories of war and capture. He even carried a cane and walked with a limp. However, his training in Canada was not even completed when the war ended. Legend also has it that Faulkner would commence a long drinking binge in his antebellum mansion, Rowan Oak, after he finished each novel.

Must Read

Works of William Faulkner

The Sound and the Fury, As I Lay Dying, or *A Light in August,* if you have the time—and the energy

"That Evening Sun"

"Barn Burning"

"A Rose for Emily"

Ernest Hemingway (1899–1961)

It is commonly attributed to Ernest Hemingway that he said, "My aim is to put down on paper what I see and what I feel in the best and simplest way." This is a far cry from the highly modernist stream-of-consciousness writing found in Faulkner's stories. Hemingway's sentences were short and crisp, his paragraphs were contained and tight, and adjectives were used sparingly. You will recognize a Hemingway story for its tight dialogue with spare narration and editorializing, as well as the short, descriptive sentences. Note this first line from *The Old Man and the Sea*: "He was an old man who fished alone in a skiff in the Gulf Stream and he had gone eighty-four days now without taking a fish" (Hemingway 1952, 9). There are no adjectives or colorful descriptors. Hemingway simply reports what he sees; that is his brilliance.

One of Hemingway's biggest writing influences was his time spent as a reporter and journalist for the *Kansas City Star*. At the beginning of World War I, Hemingway worked as a junior reporter writing short pieces on politics and society. In 1918, Hemingway finally succeeded in participating in the war. Although the Army rejected him because of his poor vision, the Red Cross enlisted him as an ambulance driver in Italy. It was there that he sustained shrapnel wounds in his leg and spent many months recovering in an Italian hospital. This period of his life was later fictionally portrayed in *A Farewell to Arms* (1929). The novel follows an American soldier, Henry, and a British nurse, Catherine, as they navigate a complex love affair during wartime. Before Hemingway published this best-selling novel, he wrote several books depicting his time in Paris with other expatriates like Sherwood Anderson, Ezra Pound, and Gertrude Stein: *In Our Time* (1925), *The Sun Also Rises* (1926), and *Men without Women* (1927). The impotent, yet very masculine wine-loving narrator of *The Sun Also Rises*, Jake Barnes, introduces readers to the raucous and vibrant lives of expatriates living in Europe; however, this novel also revealed Hemingway's burgeoning passion and admiration for bullfighting. He noted once that "bullfighting is the only art in which the artist is in danger of death and in which the degree of brilliance in the performance is left to the fighter's honor" (Hemingway 1932).

Like many other authors of his generation, Hemingway became increasingly aware of international politics, especially concerning communism and the Spanish civil war. Although he was criticized by some for telling too much in *For Whom the Bell Tolls* (1940), it was also bought and produced as a film by Paramount Studios. During and after these events, Hemingway struggled with depression, alcoholism, and failing marriages. He still wrote and published, but he did not receive high praise until he wrote *The Old Man and the Sea* in 1952. It is the very simple story of a lowly elderly fisherman, Santiago, who epically battles a giant marlin out at sea. What is common to Hemingway's writing is the moral and physical courage displayed during the great sea battle. What is peculiar is that Santiago is not charged with youthful machismo, arrogance, and ignorance. In his old age, he is a man. This book, along with his earlier work, helped Hemingway win the Nobel Prize of Literature in 1954. Unfortunately, Hemingway committed suicide in 1961 in the same manner as his father had more than thirty years prior.

Must Read

Works by Ernest Hemingway

A Farewell to Arms or *The Sun Also Rises*, if you have time

The Snows of Kilimanjaro (the whole collection)

Old Man and the Sea

John Steinbeck (1902–1968)

Steinbeck should be recognized for two key literary concepts: regionalism and naturalism. Most of Steinbeck's stories and novels take place in the California valleys, hills, and plains of his childhood in Monterey County (south of San Francisco). The Salinas Valley became a literary canvas for Steinbeck to express his disdain for economic and social corruption, as well as his compassion for common laborers and migrant workers. During his career, he wrote *Tortilla Flat* (1935), *In Dubious Battle* (1936), and *East of Eden* (1952), which all took place in California. Second, his compassion for his characters was not overshadowed by the overwhelming power of elements beyond their control. His use of literary naturalism exposed the inability of characters to rise above their social standing, whether it be due to gender, race, socioeconomic status, or even mental capabilities. His characters have dreams, aspirations, and desires; however, they are trapped in a universe that cares nothing for them.

One of his most read novels, *Of Mice and Men* (1937), is exemplary of the conflation of regionalism and naturalism. George and Lenny are two California migrant workers who are traveling from ranch to ranch trying to save enough money to buy their own land to raise crops and rabbits. Due to Lenny's mental limitations and his affinity for soft things, they are run out of town after town. In their current employment, George pleads with Lenny not to talk to the boss's son's wife (strictly called Curley's wife) and stay focused on work. Although they befriend many of the workers, and even include the crippled, old farmhand Candy in their dreams, misfortunes are inevitable. In the climactic scene, Lenny inadvertently kills Curley's wife and is forced to run from the ranch. George eventually catches up with Lenny, but instead of running to the next job, George mercifully shoots Lenny in the back of the head as Lenny daydreams about the land, garden, and rabbits he will get to tend. None of the characters realize their dreams. Steinbeck also introduces readers to gender and racial tensions in this novel.

The Grapes of Wrath (1939) remains Steinbeck's masterpiece. Although he continued to write about poverty and socioeconomic unrest, Steinbeck left the valleys of California for the dustbowls of Oklahoma. In this truly American **epic**, Tom Joad is a recently released convict who returns to his family farm only to realize that many families are heading to California to look for promised jobs picking fruit as migrant workers. Tom meets his family and begins an arduous trip west—one that is not free from death and much strife. Once they arrive in California, they realize that the promised land is filled with too many migrants looking for jobs, overcrowded camps, corrupt police, and crooked farmers. Tom befriends an ex-preacher, Jim Casey, who provides the novel a space to explore worker's unions, religion, and the corruption of industry. Casey is killed by the police as he tries to unionize the workers against corrupt leadership. Tom witnesses the murder and kills one of the policemen in defense. The rest of the novel follows Tom's escape into hiding and his family's journey from one farm to the next in order to survive. Some critics called it a pack of lies, but overall, the novel was heralded for its realism and depiction of a very dark time in American history.

Steinbeck finished his literary career with a New England tale of materialism and greed called *The Winter of Our Discontent* (1961) and a travel memoir, *Travels with Charley in Search of America* (1962), that recollected the author's journey across the country with his poodle, Charley. He won the Nobel Prize for Literature in 1961.

Must Read

Works by John Steinbeck

The Grapes of Wrath, if you have time

Of Mice and Men

"The Leader of the People"

THE DRAMA

Susan Glaspell (1876–1948)

Glaspell is most widely known for founding a theater group with her husband in New York called the **Provincetown Players**. This group later included Eugene O'Neill and Edna St. Vincent Millay. They produced socially conscious, feminist, and satirical pieces. After the death of her husband, Glaspell continued to write plays and novels, many of which became best sellers and award winners: *The Comic Artist* (1927), *Brook Evans* (1928), and a play based on the life of Emily Dickinson that won a Pulitzer called *Alison's House* (1930). Widely anthologized, however, is Glaspell's feminist critique drama titled *Trifles* (1916).

Glaspell was born in Davenport, Iowa, and became a reporter and journalist in Des Moines. She wrote funny, satirical columns and investigated various cases and stories particular to Iowa current events. One of those investigations led to the writing of *Trifles*. In 1901, Margaret Hossack was accused, tried, and convicted of killing her sleeping husband with an axe. This real-life event influenced the young reporter to fictionalize the case in a drama and later in a short story renamed "A Jury of Her Peers." The plot revolves around Minnie Wright who has been arrested for the murder of her distant and abusive husband; however, the audience never meets Minnie. The play takes place in the Wright's kitchen. The men are investigating the crime scene while their wives discuss the horrible act and Minnie's depressive life with the deceased man. The play is a wonderful depiction of irony as the audience is led to believe that the women have a much better idea about who actually killed the husband and why than the men do. The play was originally staged by the Provincetown Players in 1916 and transformed to prose in 1917.

Must Read

Trifles by Susan Glaspell

Eugene O'Neill (1888–1953)

Many scholars refer to O'Neill as the father of modern American drama. His plays were heavily influenced by Greek tragedies, his personal and family traumas, American realism, and German expressionism. During his career as a playwright, O'Neill won four Pulitzer awards for his dramas, including *Beyond the Horizon* (1920) and *Long Day's Journey into Night* (1940). The latter, a widely anthologized, semiautobiographical play, was not performed on stage until after O'Neill's death; the playwright requested this due to the play's autobiographical nature. The drama follows the turmoil of one Connecticut family in the time span of one day. All the men are addicted to alcohol, and the mother is addicted to morphine. The play is filled with deceit, love, hate, confusion, and emotional abandonment.

O'Neill's life was as problematic and traumatic as the lives of his characters. He was born into a family troubled by drug and alcohol abuse, and infidelity. The young O'Neill spent most of his time at his boarding school away from his family until he became a young father himself. Fearful of fatherhood and boredom, O'Neill traveled the world as a sailor. His writing career was supported and encouraged by his actor father. Ultimately, he was discovered and mentored by Susan Glaspell and the Provincetown Players. They produced several of his one-act plays before his full-length dramas garnered public and critical attention. He won the Nobel Prize in 1936.

Must Read

Long Day's Journey into Night by Eugene O'Neill

THE HARLEM RENAISSANCE

As I stated in the previous chapter, the African-American writers of this literary era deserve their own section, partly because their involvement in modernity was as much about race as it was about economics, religion, and art. Like W.E.B. Du Bois and Booker T. Washington years before, African-American writers of this era did not agree on how African Americans should advance, so the literature is best read as a conversation. Simply put, the **Harlem Renaissance** was a boom of art, social commentary, and even politics centered in Harlem, New York, but stretching to other major northern urban areas. These writers largely denied any European influence on their works and dedicated their art to upholding Black dignity, history, and experiences. Many writers created literature to expose white audiences to Black life; however, others refused to pander to audiences that oppressed them. Many of these writers were showcased in important African-American literary anthologies: *The Book of American Negro Poetry* (1922), *The Book of American Negro Spirituals* (1925), *The New Negro* (1925), and *The Second Book of American Negro Spirituals* (1926).

James Weldon Johnson (1871–1938)

Best known for his songwriting, Johnson spent a career writing stories, essays, songs, novels, poems, and memoirs depicting the struggles of Black Americans during the 1920s and 1930s. Johnson was born and raised in a cultured and educated Florida home. He was educated at one of the few integrated schools in Jacksonville and later Atlanta University where he began his career as a writer and activist. As a songwriter, Johnson collaborated with his brother to pen many famous songs used for Broadway and published in song anthologies. Their most famous song, "Lift Ev'ry Voice and Sing" was chosen by the National Association for the Advancement of Colored People (NAACP) as the "Negro National Anthem." His songwriting skills certainly influenced his poetry. In 1927, Johnson published the highly acclaimed poetic revision of biblical narratives called *God's Trombones: Seven Negro Sermons in Verse*. "The Creation" is highly anthologized. Below are the first two stanzas:

> And god stepped out on space,
> And he looked around and said:
> I'm lonely—
> I'll make me a world.

> And far as the eye of God could see
> Darkness covered everything,
> Blacker than a hundred midnights
> Down I a cypress swamp.

(Belasco and Johnson 2008, 572)

It has been written that the title for this collection came to Johnson after comparing a preacher's voice to the sounds of a trombone. What the reader will notice right away is Johnson's lack of Black dialect. In an effort to resist cultural stereotypes, Johnson utilized elevated speech and traditional poetic metaphors to advance Black issues. Note the difference between "The Creation" and poems in the last chapter by Paul Laurence Dunbar.

In 1912, Johnson wrote a semiautobiographical novel about the life of a young interracial man passing for "white" in New York. The narrator is born in a white, cultured world; however, he "learns" that he is Black and chooses the cowardly track of becoming white in order to resist prejudice and scorn. Although *The Autobiography of an Ex-Colored Man* was not received well, scholars now declare it as the bridge between the slave narrative and the Black novel. Johnson was a pioneering member of the Harlem Renaissance and a prolific writer and activist.

 Must Read

Works by James Weldon Johnson

The Autobiography of an Ex-Colored Man, if you have time

"The Creation"

Claude McKay (1889–1948)

McKay was born and educated in Jamaica in a highly educated farming family. After meeting the English literary editor Walter Jekyll, McKay began writing dialect verse. This influence took McKay to the United States where he began his education at Booker T. Washington's Tuskegee Institute but transferred to Kansas State College and eventually dropped out of school to further his literary career in Harlem. McKay's first collection of poetry, *Harlem Shadows* (1922), is considered the collection that began the Harlem Renaissance. Dropping dialect verse for more elevated poetic language, McKay published highly acclaimed and controversial poetry about the Black experience. Here is an excerpt from an early, important poem called "If We Must Die":

> If we must die, let it not be like hogs
> Hunted and penned in an inglorious spot,
> While round us bark the mad and hungry dogs,
> Making their mock at our accurse lot.
> If we must die, O let us nobly die.
>
> (Ellmann and O'Clair 1988, 517)

Later, McKay turned to prose and published the first and only best-selling book by an African American, *Home to Harlem* (1928), which became one of the last enduring works of the Harlem Renaissance. In it, McKay explored the artistic, philosophical, and political figures and theories of the movement, as well as the many complexities of living in Harlem during the Renaissance.

Like many writers of his generation, McKay became increasingly frustrated by American social structures and politics; this took him to Europe, Africa, and the Soviet Union where he leaned heavily on socialist thinkers and politicians. Towards the end of his career, McKay wrote many more memoirs and novels, and he finally became an American citizen in 1940 and a converted Roman Catholic in 1944.

Must Read

Poetry of Claude McKay

"If We Must Die"

"The Harlem Dancer"

"America"

"The Lynching"

Zora Neale Hurston (1891–1960)

A key and controversial figure of the Harlem Renaissance, Zora Neale Hurston lived a life as complex and tragic as her characters. She was educated at Howard University and Barnard College where she began a career as a writer and an anthropologist. Under the direction of Franz Boas, Hurston studied Black southern culture as it pertained to speech, dance, art, religion, and folklore in her hometown of Eatonville, Florida (one of the first intentional all-Black communities). This study produced a highly successful book, *Mules and Men* (1935), that helped earn her a Guggenheim Fellowship to continue anthropological work. However, a year earlier, Hurston had published her first novel, *Jonah's Gourd Vine*, and it was such a literary work that it garnered the most attention from her fellow Harlem writers. Hurston did not believe that Black writers should write to white audiences, yet her contemporaries like Richard Wright and Langston Hughes accused her of pandering to whites' stereotypes of Blacks. Drawing upon her knowledge of Black southern culture, Hurston created complex and complicated characters, and she used dialect and colloquial speech in books that contained raw discussions of the Black experience. Sadly, though, Hurston wrote several more books that were rejected by publishers, and she moved back to Florida where she worked as a maid. She died destitute and forgotten in 1960 in a welfare home; her body was buried in an unmarked grave. Some historians argue that if it were not for author Alice Walker, who helped revitalize interest in her work, Hurston might still be a forgotten literary figure.

Hurston's most acclaimed work, *Their Eyes Were Watching God* (1937), is one of the most important and controversial novels of the Harlem Renaissance. The story of Janie Crawford and her return to Eatonville, Fla., the novel explores themes that include gender, sexuality and self-identity as well as race. An author who died in near obscurity, Hurston is now recognized as an uncompromising and inspirational figure in American literature.

Must Read

Works by Zora Neale Hurston

Their Eyes Were Watching God

"Sweat"

"The Gilded Six-Bits"

Jean Toomer (1894–1967)

Toomer did not learn of his own interracial heritage until he was in his early teens. His early education occurred at all-white schools in New York; however, he chose to attend an all-Black high school when he moved to Washington, D.C., to live with his grandparents. Toomer's resistance to claim one cultural identity over the other became his mantra as he enrolled in and dropped out of several colleges and moved from town to town. After an influential trip to the Deep South, Toomer began writing stories, sketches, essays, and poems that were collected and formed the genre-resistant *Cane* (1923). This example of high modernism was incredibly influential to Harlem Renaissance writers. The book became central to African-American literature; therefore, fearing being pigeonholed as a "Black" writer, Toomer refused to include his writings in Black anthologies and spent his literary energies on spirituality and philosophy. Controversially, Toomer married two white women in the 1930s and converted to Quakerism.

Must Read

From *Cane* by Jean Toomer

"Portrait in Georgia"

"Blood-Burning Moon"

"Seventh Street"

Sterling Brown (1901–1989)

The Harlem Renaissance is usually characterized by its fascination and commitment to the Black urban experience. Brown, however, spent his literary career exploring the rural experiences and lives of African Americans. Like Hurston, Brown commonly used dialect and colloquial speech to depict southern life. His first collection of poetry, *Southern Road* (1932), caused much discussion among fellow Harlem Renaissance writers due to its setting, use of dialect, and exploration of Black folklore and music. For many, it was more of an anthropological study than a collection of poetry. The first stanza of "Tin Roof Blues" is a great example of Brown's poetry influenced by African-American song and dialect:

> I'm goin' where d Southern crosses top de C.&O.
> I'm goin' where d Southern crosses top de C.&O.
> I'm goin' down de country cause I cain't stay here no mo'.
> (Belasco and Johnson 2008, 751)

Not only did Brown write poetry, but he also published several works of literary criticism, *The Negro in American Fiction* (1937) and *Negro Poetry and Drama* (1937), and a very important anthology of African-American writing titled *The Negro Caravan* (1941). Brown's commitment to African-American studies and literary criticism earned him much praise from whites and Blacks in the 1930s. Brown earned degrees from Williams College and Harvard, and then began teaching at various colleges. Later in life, Brown published another collection of poetry and continued to write and lecture on African-American issues such as folklore, music, and racial tensions.

Must Read

Poetry of Sterling Brown

Anthologies vary widely on what they include, but here are my suggestions:

"Ma Rainey"

"Tin Roof Blues"

"Master and Man"

Langston Hughes (1902–1967)

Hughes is recognized as the most influential and important writer during the Harlem Renaissance. His fascination with and commitment to urban, Black life and to jazz and the blues marked his poetry and his differences with other Harlem writers. Your will recognize a Hughes poem because of its use of dialect, Black speech patterns, urban content, use of jazz patterns, and the use of **open verse**. Although *The Weary Blues* (1926) was Hughes's first published collection of poems, individual poems were published in some of the most important African-American magazines and anthologies, including *The New Negro*, *Crisis*, and *Opportunity*.

Although Hughes was clear that his poetry was an attempt to advance the culture, art, and lives of African Americans, he was also clear that his poetry was a part of the national literature, which also included white poets like Walt Whitman and Carl Sandburg. Hughes's poem "I, Too" is a direct response to Whitman's "I hear America Singing."

Hughes's interracial childhood certainly fueled his poetry. He was born in Missouri; however, due to his parents' divorce, Hughes lived with his grandmother in Kansas (that side of the family contained many abolitionists during the Civil War). Hughes created many personas that speak to the interracial life. "Cross" is a well-known example:

My old man's a white old man
And my old mother's black.
If ever I cursed my white old man
I take my curses back.

If ever I cursed my black old mother
And wished she were in hell,
I'm sorry for that evil wish
And now I wish her well.

My old man died in a fine big house.
My ma died in a shack.
I wonder where I'm gonna die,
Being neither white nor black?

(Hughes 2004, 16–17)

Hughes's father became disenchanted with America and racism, so he moved to Mexico where Langston lived with him periodically. Like many poets of his generation, Hughes bounced around from job to job and from college to college; he traveled to Mexico, Africa, Cuba, and spent much time in Harlem. The publication of his first collection ignited his poetry career and his life in politics.

You should take note of the pattern in African-American artists' affinity for progressive politics, especially socialism and communism. In the 1930s, the American Communist Party campaigned heavily for economic and racial equality; these ideas persuaded many important Harlem writers and artists to support that political party. For Hughes, a visit to the Soviet Union in the early 1930s spawned many political essays, screenplays, and poems. Hughes also worked as a reporter during the Spanish Civil War and continued to speak out against American racism and for communist ideals.

Must Read

Poetry of Langston Hughes

"The Negro Speaks of Rivers"

"Mother to Son"

"I, Too"

"Theme for English B"

"The Weary Blues"

"Harlem"

"Mulatto"

Countee Cullen (1903–1946)

Cullen's philosophies regarding Black writing in America were quite complex but important to the Harlem Renaissance. You will recognize a Cullen poem right away by its adherence to traditional poetic form, rhyme, and meter, and its content's strict focus on the African American experience. This was a very controversial move for the young Cullen because, in an effort to elevate African American literature and advance the race, he conflated the important issues of the day with the forms of the oppressive power structures. His influences were not blues, jazz, or southern folklore. Instead, Cullen read the British romantics and American formalists. One of the most famous examples of Cullen's poetry is called "Incident":

> Once riding in old Baltimore,
> Heart-filled, head-filled with glee,
> I saw a Baltimorean
> Keep looking straight at me.
>
> Now I was eight and very small,
> And he was no whit bigger,
> And so I smiled, but he poked out
> His tongue, and called me, "Nigger."
>
> I saw the whole of Baltimore
> From May until December;
> Of all the things that happened there
> That's all that I remember.
>
> (Ellmann and O'Clair 1988, 662)

Much like Sterling Brown, Cullen was highly educated and intellectually engaged. He received college degrees from New York University and Harvard. Cullen's first collection of poetry, *Color* (1925), was published before he graduated from college. His popularity soared as he continued to write poetry and win literary awards. In 1947, *On These I Stand: The Best Poems of Countee Cullen* was published to honor a career and a life of literature and Black activism.

Cullen's fiction, essays, short stories, plays, and memoirs are also important parts of the Harlem Renaissance. He created a character named Jesse B. Semple (also called Simple) for a Chicago newspaper (later, the columns were collected in a multivolume edition) that poked fun at social injustice and racism. Probably because Black anthologies helped start Cullen's career, he spent much of his later life in the 1960s editing and promoting contemporary Black writers and anthologies like *New Negro Poets USA* and *The Best Short Stories by Negro Writers*.

Must Read

Poetry of Countee Cullen

"Yet Do I Marvel"

"Incident"

"Heritage"

Richard Wright (1908–1960)

Wright is most well-known for his unapologetic and uncompromising novel *Native Son* (1940), which was an indictment of the institution of racial segregation and racism in America; however, Wright published many short stories and essays that not only tried to advance the lives of Black Americans but also indicted white America for its part in racial segregation and injustice. *Uncle Tom's Children* (1938) and *Black Boy* (1945) are representative of Wright's disgust of racism and the harsh and often brutal realities of life in Black America. Many scholars refer to Wright's work as part of American realism and naturalism. The following synopsis of *Native Son* establishes Wright's sensibilities of African-Americans' reality and their inability to rise above that stark reality.

Native Son

The provocative title implies that the violent, bitter, and isolated Black man is a product of his own country. Bigger Thomas, the main character, embodies everything that white America fears about Black Americans; however, Wright makes the genius claim that white America created Bigger Thomas. Bigger is a twenty-year-old kid living in segregated Chicago in the 1930s. In the opening scene of the novel, Bigger wakes up in his small family apartment and kills a rat with a frying pan. His mother pesters him to take a job with a rich white family, but he leaves to join his friends to roam the city and plan a robbery of a white man's store. Readers get a clear picture early of Bigger's plight: he lives a hopeless life that is given to him by the white power structure. He cannot transcend his place in life no matter what he does. Bigger sabotages his own robbery by beating up one of his friends, so without that social support, he takes a job as a chauffeur with the Dalton family. The Dalton family subplot is interesting because Mr. Dalton is a "philanthropist" in the sense that he hires poor, Black people to work for him, and he donates money to Black schools and organizations; however, he is also a slum lord. Dalton owns and operates the filthy apartments that house so many destitute Blacks on the South Side of Chicago.

The plot escalates when Bigger takes this job. One evening, he secretly escorts Mary Dalton and her communist boyfriend, Jan, around town and eventually to a South Side diner where the three of them get drunk. Bigger is pressed into joining them because of their pushy tolerance and progressive politics; however, Bigger is all too aware of the social taboos that they are breaking. In the middle of the night, Bigger carries a drunken Mary to her bedroom where he is slightly and briefly sexually aroused by being in close proximity with a beautiful white girl. Mary's blind mother enters the room because she hears a noise. Frightened and angered, Bigger covers Mary's mouth to keep her from yelling, which suffocates her. Bigger attempts to hide the body by shoving it into the house's furnace, but it doesn't quite fit, so Bigger must decapitate it so all of the body will burn and leave no trace of evidence. This is the gruesome beginning of Wright's condemnation on the country and racial ideologies that cause brutal violence.

Bigger attempts to play the "ignorant Black servant" in order to defer any blame, while he also writes anonymous ransom notes that lead back to Jan and his communist friends. Bigger runs from the law as long as he can; however, after he rapes and murders his own girlfriend and Mary's bones are found in the furnace, Bigger is arrested and tried for murder. His case becomes wildly popular, and Jan encourages his friend, Max, to defend Bigger for free. Although Max rebukes Bigger for his actions, he reminds the court that Bigger is a product of American racism and that there will be more "Biggers" if racism does not end. It is clear that Bigger begins to see Max and Jan as humans; however, after Bigger's death sentence, he claims that his murderous actions must be for good because it was only then that he started to feel. At this point, Bigger completely and fully embodies the murderous Black stereotype that white America has created. The novel ends with Max leaving Bigger's cell and the narrator focusing on Bigger: "Then he smiled a faint, wry, bitter smile. He heard the ring of steel against steel as a far door clanged shut" (Wright 2005, 430).

Must Read

Works by Richard Wright

"The Man Who Was Almost a Man"

Native Son

REFERENCES

Anderson, Sherwood. 1993. *Winesburg, Ohio*. New York: Penguin.

Baym, Nina, et al. 2008. *The Norton Anthology of American Literature*, shorter 7th ed. New York: W. W. Norton.

Belasco, Susan, and Linck Johnson. 2008. *The Bedford Anthology of American Literature*, Vol. 2, *1865 to the Present*. Boston: Bedford/St. Martin's.

Ellmann, Richard, and Robert O'Clair. 1988. *The Norton Anthology of Modern Poetry*, 2nd ed. New York: W. W. Norton.

Faulkner, William. 1951. *Absalom, Absalom!* New York: The Modern Library.

———. 1990. *The Sound and the Fury*. New York: Vintage.

H. D. 1998. *Trilogy*. Edited by Aliki Barnstone. New York: New Directions.

Hemingway, Ernest. 1932. *Death in the Afternoon*. New York: Charles Scribner's Sons.

———. 1952. *The Old Man and the Sea*. New York: Charles Scribner's Sons.

Hughes, Langston. 2004. *Vintage Hughes*. New York: Vintage.

Hunter, J. Paul. 1996. *The Norton Introduction to Poetry*, 6th ed. New York: W. W. Norton.

Kennedy, X. J., and Dana Gioia. 2005. *An Introduction to Poetry*, 11th ed. New York: Pearson/Longman.

Newsweek. "Match Point." January 30, 1956.

Porter, Katherine Anne. 2008. "The Jilting of Granny Weatherall." *The Seagull Readers: Stories*, 2nd ed. Edited by Joseph Kelly. New York: W. W. Norton.

Sidney, Philip. 1998. "An Apology for Poetry." *The Critical Tradition: Classic Texts and Contemporary Trends*, 2nd ed. Edited by David H. Richter. New York: Bedford/St. Martin's.

Wright, Richard. 2005. *Native Son*. New York: Harper Perennial.

Chapter 6

The Contemporary Period (1945–Present)

I am using a different angle in this chapter than in previous chapters. Instead of a chronological approach, I want to introduce you to different pockets, communities, and cultures of writers in postwar America. World War II was a triumphant time of community and patriotism, but it also produced many fears about the future, cultural integration, the economy, gender and sex relations, and the role of government in individual lives. The literature of this time mirrors the growing skepticism of the American dream as well as the importance of each individual story in the overall American story. The constructs I have created for this section are fairly arbitrary (and arguable); however, they should give you a sense of the literary conversations that occurred after World War II and still continue today. One caveat: This is the hardest chapter to write because the contemporary authors and texts are always changing. A contemporary author like Sherman Alexie or Jhumpa Lahiri included in many 2008 anthologies may not be included five or ten years from now. Obviously, I cannot write about authors who have not yet gained public popularity but who may in five or ten years. My aim is to introduce you to the provocative and enduring literary voices of postwar America. At the end of this chapter, I've included a list of contemporary authors and their works that I recommend reading.

THE EARLIER GENERATION

Eudora Welty (1909–2001)

Welty is among many southern writers such as William Faulkner and Flannery O'Connor who created characters commonly referred to as the **grotesque**. As I mentioned in the last chapter, the grotesque usually describes the very real and very horrible aspects of being human. Many of her characters are physically and mentally challenged, racist, sexist, eccentric, and ultimately and completely immersed in their cultural moment. With this in mind, Welty allowed her characters to walk, talk, and act as they felt, which can create much humor for the reader. Like many of her characters, Welty rarely left her hometown. She was born and raised in Jackson, Mississippi, and left the South only for educational purposes: to attend the University of Wisconsin and then to study advertising at Columbia University in New York. Welty's life and fiction revolve around the individual and the complex and complicated culture of the American South. Students should also note that Welty was an accomplished photographer as well as a fiction writer. Her most famous pictures were taken while she worked for the Works Progress Administration in the 1930s. Welty's depiction of the effects of the Great Depression on Americans is as real and as raw as her fiction. She once said about her pictures that "[my snapshots] were taken spontaneously—to catch something as I came upon it, something that spoke of life going on around me" (Marrs 2005). Her ideas about photography parallel her short stories. On the surface, they are mere snapshots of individuals merely living their lives; however, they also speak of life around them in profound and universal ways.

Anthologies vary on which Welty stories they include, so I recommend that you read "Why I Live at the P.O.," "A Worn Path," or "Petrified Man." Each of these stories was first published in Welty's first collection, *A Curtain of Green and Other Stories* (1941). This collection is also important because fellow writer Katherine Anne Porter wrote the introduction to the collection, which helped Welty begin her career as a fiction writer. Her stories earned her many awards, including the O. Henry Prize and the Pulitzer (both for *The Optimist's Daughter* in 1972). Other important works include *Delta Wedding* (1946), *The Golden Apples* (1949), and her very popular autobiography, *One Writer's Beginnings* (1984).

The Optimist's Daughter

This short, award-winning novel tells the story of Judge McKelva; his daughter, Laurel; and his rather young new wife, Fay. Judge's failing eyesight sends him to New Orleans for surgery, and Laurel travels from Chicago to be with him during the recovery. The surgery is a success; however, Judge does not respond well to the rigors of surgery and suffers greatly during the recovery. Eventually he dies, so the two women must take Judge's body to Mount Salus, Mississippi, for the funeral. Laurel must deal not only with the loss (compounded with the distant loss of her mother and husband) but also with Fay (and her family) in the McKelva family home. As reviewers often note, not much happens in this novel; however, Welty is able to show readers the immense value of being human: the selfishness and vulgarity of Fay, Laurel's growing ability to feel and cope with loss, and the complex tensions between classes in the South. The prominent theme explored in the novel is the ability to and necessity of coming to grips with one's past in order to understand one's future.

Must Read

Works of Eudora Welty

"Petrified Man"

"A Worn Path"

"Why I Live at the P.O."

Flannery O'Connor (1925–1964)

O'Connor died before she turned forty of complications attributed to lupus. She rarely left Georgia, let alone the South. On the surface, O'Connor's life looks as isolated and confined as that of Emily Dickinson; however, like Dickinson and Welty, O'Connor's stories and characters are filled with great complexity and depth that explore what it means to be southern, what it means to be male and female, and ultimately what it means to be human. O'Connor resisted the claim that she, like Welty and Sherwood Anderson, wrote about the grotesque. Her characters were real, although they were at times absurd, ridiculous, and horrible. Ultimately, they were real. In "Good Country People," Manly Pointer convinces Joy Hopewell (who calls herself Hulga), in a quasi-romantic scene, to remove her prosthetic leg and then runs off with it, leaving her alone in the attic of a barn in the woods. Readers laugh and cringe at the audacity of the act. That feeling is very typical when engaged with an O'Connor story. We are amused and bewildered by the grotesque, but very real, nature of her characters. Readers are very rarely allowed inside the head and heart of these characters. Merely, we are allowed to hear them and watch them act, which results in our false and pretentious judgment of these characters.

O'Connor is also known for her devout Christian faith. She was committed to Roman Catholicism her entire life, and her stories and novels are laced with religious allusions, themes, and symbols. Her collection of essays, *Mystery and Manners* (1969), reflects a particular worldview that influenced the way in which she created characters, developed plot, and constructed meaning:

> I see from the standpoint of Christian orthodoxy. This means that for me the meaning of life is centered in our Redemption by Christ and what I see in the world I see in its relation to that. I don't think that this is a position that can be taken halfway or one that is particularly easy in these times to make transparent in fiction.
>
> (O'Connor 1997, 32)

What is telling about this quotation is that O'Connor reveals the difficulty in making a truth claim in a culture (and a genre) that tends to lean heavily towards religious ambivalence and skepticism. I recommend "Revelation" for an exemplary story that intersects culture and religion.

O'Connor's stories were published in *A Good Man is Hard to Find* (1955) and *Everything That Rises Must Converge* (1965). She also wrote two novels: *Wise Blood* (1952) and *The Violent Bear It Away* (1960). *The Complete Stories of Flannery O'Connor* won the National Book Award in 1972.

Must Read

Works by Flannery O'Connor

"A Good Man is Hard to Find"

"Good Country People"

"Revelation"

Theodore Roethke (1908–1963)

In the last chapter, you learned that modernist poetry tended to focus on the poem or the actual writing of poetry. What you will discover in this chapter is that many poets returned to the self as the primary subject of their poetry. These poets were heavily influenced by the British and American romantic poets like William Wordsworth and Walt Whitman. What also separates this generation of poets from the modernists was their desire to return to traditional poetic forms (as well as take on new forms) like the sonnet and the villanelle. Roethke's poems can be intensely personal and autobiographical; however, he uses traditional poetic forms and strict meter to trap or encapsulate the moment for poetic reflection. In one of his most famous poems, "My Papa's Waltz," the speaker depicts a child dancing with his drunken father. The structure of the lines and rhyme of the poem signify the waltz; however, the dark word choice forces the reader to take pause and closely analyze the scene. Many student readers debate whether it is a poem about a dance or about abuse. Take a look at the first stanza:

> The whiskey on your breath
> Could make a small boy dizzy;
> But I hung on like death:
> Such waltzing was not easy.
>
> (Ellmann and O'Clair 1988, 778)

Written in iambic trimeter (three beats), the poem takes on the physical nature of a waltz, but words like "death" and "whiskey" create wonderful ambiguity and tension. Many scholars compare Roethke's poems to those of Robert Frost in this regard. Concomitantly, Roethke, like Frost, is sometimes considered a regional writer. He grew up on a large plot of land in upper Michigan where his family ran many greenhouses. Many of his poems depict the harsh and wonderful childhood he experienced under the guidance of German-born grandparents and a hard-working (and a hard-drinking) father. Roethke's life was also troubled with bouts of depression (later diagnosed as bipolar disorder), alcoholism, and marital infidelity.

Roethke taught at many colleges and universities and wrote award-winning poetry collections such as *Open House* (1941), *The Lost Son and Other Poems* (1948), *The Waking, Poems* (1953), and *Words for the Wind* (1958).

Must Read

Poetry of Theodore Roethke

"My Papa's Waltz"

"I Knew a Woman"

"Cuttings"

"Root Cellar"

"Elegy for Jane"

Elizabeth Bishop (1911–1979)

The two themes that are most prevalent in Bishop's poems are loss and geography. Some historians point to her father's tragic death and her mother's mental collapse and subsequent removal to an institution when Bishop was a very young child as the impetus for much of her poetry on loss. In her most famous poem on this topic, "One Art," she poignantly and humorously discusses the ease and pain of losing:

> The art of losing isn't hard to master;
> So many things seem filled with the intent
> To be lost that their loss is no disaster.
>
> Lose something every day. Accept the fluster
> Of lost door keys, the hour badly spent.
> The art of losing isn't hard to master.
>
> (Ellmann and O'Clair 1988, 829)

Like Roethke's, Bishop's poetry is very personal and intimate; however, it is quite often bounded and shaped by traditional poetic forms. This poem, for instance, is a **villanelle**. This form usually includes 19 lines, which are broken up into five triplets and a quatrain. The first line is repeated in the sixth, twelfth, and eighteenth lines, while the third line is repeated in the ninth, fifteenth, and nineteenth lines. What makes this poetic form remarkably difficult to write well is that the poem is driven by only two rhymes. The use of traditional forms (structure) allows Bishop to construct her intensely personal and intimate feelings without sounding like mere confession or complaint.

In 1976, Bishop published her final volume of poems, *Geography III*. This work is notable not only because it contains some of her best, and most anthologized, work, but also because the title mirrors her life's and work's commitment to place and location. Bishop spent her childhood with one set of grandparents in Worcester, Massachusetts, and the other set of grandparents in Nova Scotia. Bishop moved to New York and then to Key West, Florida, before spending more than 15 years in Brazil. The landscape and minute setting of place became incredibly important to Bishop's poetry, especially as she used that particular location to explore deeper, universal truths. For example, in her poem "In the Waiting Room," she recalls a time when she waited for her aunt in a dentist's waiting room in Worcester. This small, seemingly insignificant place fosters a moment of great maturation and change for the young speaker as she discovers a *National Geographic* magazine on the seat next to her and begins to recognize her own humanity.

Note also that Bishop had a long-standing poetic relationship with the Confessional poet Robert Lowell. This relationship produced many wonderful poems that could be read as a conversation between the two. I recommend Bishop's "The Armadillo" and Lowell's "Skunk Hour." Bishop's *North & South and A Cold Spring* won the Pulitzer Prize in 1955 and *The Complete Poems* won the National Book Award in 1969.

Must Read

Poetry by Elizabeth Bishop

"One Art"

"In the Waiting Room"

"The Fish"

"The Armadillo"

"Sestina"

"The Man-Moth"

John Updike (1932–2009)

Although Updike may not be considered a contemporary of the previously mentioned writers, his stories were certainly influenced by earlier generations, and his fiction has become quite influential for many writers today; therefore, he fits quite appropriately between generations. I have always thought that Updike was the master at describing, exploring, and analyzing white, middle-class American life. His characters get married, buy houses, have affairs, work at jobs, dialogue with children and parents, eat meals, play games, go to parties, pray, and eventually come to grips with their own inability to deal with that white, middle-class American existence.

Updike grew up in Pennsylvania, which became the canvas for many of his stories and novels, including *The Centaur* (1963), set in the fictional town of Olinger. Many of his stories are loosely based on his relationships with his parents, wives, and children. And, like O'Connor's Catholicism, Updike's religious faith (orthodox Protestant Christianity) plays an important role in his character's lives and the structure of the novel. I suggest reading "Pigeon Feathers" and "Lifeguard" for excellent examples of the intersection between faith and fiction.

After graduating from Harvard and studying art in England, Updike took a job as a staff writer at *The New Yorker*. That very famous magazine became the home for his nonfiction and fiction work for many years, even after he resigned as a staff writer in 1957. After that, Updike devoted his life to full-time writing, producing a large volume of essays, poems, plays, short stories, and novels. Updike's most famous portrayal of white, middle-class, suburban American life is found in the four-novel serious revolving around Harry "Rabbit" Angstrom: *Rabbit, Run* (1960), *Rabbit Redux* (1971), *Rabbit is Rich* (1981), and *Rabbit at Rest* (1990). Rabbit is a former high school basketball standout whose obsessions with his past glories undermine his ability to effectively live in the present. Readers watch Rabbit make incredibly deplorable decisions; however, we empathize with his human frailty and inability to act with grace and direction. A short story in memory of Rabbit called "Rabbit Remembered," told by his son and daughter, was published in *Licks of Love* (2000).

Must Read

Works by John Updike

"A & P"

"Separating"

"Pigeon Feathers"

Rabbit, Run, if you have time

POSTWAR DRAMA

Tennessee Williams (1911–1983)

Many critics point to Williams's turbulent and conflicted life as an impetus for the violence, isolation, and confusion viewed in his plays. Both he and his sister, Rose, experienced times of depression and mental angst; however, as Rose was institutionalized after undergoing a frontal lobotomy, Williams turned to writing, drinking, and using drugs to anesthetize his growing angst and fear of failure. As a child, his family left Mississippi and settled in St. Louis where young Thomas (his given name) explored literature to escape increasing family tension. Like many writers, he attended and dropped out of college and also took several menial jobs while writing at night. In college, he was given the moniker "Tennessee" because of his southern accent and thus used it as his penname thereafter. In the late 1930s, Williams moved to New Orleans and began to write and produce one-act plays. It was there that Williams began to take ownership of his burgeoning genius and his homosexuality. *The Glass Menagerie* (1945) was Williams's first success. Labeled by many scholars as semiautobiographical, the play is introduced by the protagonist and narrator, Tom, as a "memory play." The plot is merely Tom's recollections about his mother, Amanda, and his sister, Laura, who is disabled and constantly occupied by her little glass animal collection. The father is absent from the plot, and the mother simply lives to recall her childhood. Tom recalls trying to find a suitor for his sister, but his attempts fail, and he eventually leaves home never to return.

The year 1947, however, proved to be Williams's most successful year on Broadway. *A Streetcar Named Desire* was not only critically acclaimed and popular with general playgoers, but the play also made Williams rich when it became a movie starring Vivien Leigh and Marlon Brando. The plot of the play revolves around the relationship between Blanche DuBois, a Mississippi schoolteacher who has left her ancestral home to live in New Orleans; Blanche's sister, Stella Kowalski, who left the pretensions of her past for the working-class, yet romantic, existence that her husband provides; and Stella's husband, Stanley, who works for an auto-supply dealer. Mystery, deception, and cruelty plague the lives of these characters and the life of the drama. Stanley detests Blanche, Stella and Stanley's marriage is deteriorating, and Blanche tries desperately to escape a past that continually catches up to her. In the end, Stanley rapes Blanche, yet no one believes her accusations, and Stanley and Stella ultimately institutionalize her. The themes of the play mirror this generation's critique of the American dream. It is no accident that Blanche takes a streetcar route called "Desire" to her sister's apartment on Elysian Fields Avenue. Readers quickly discover that this place is not idyllic or peaceful; the America of this play is filled with animalistic desires, psychosis, failed dreams, and much confusion. The Kowalskis' apartment becomes a final resting place for Blanche, but it is not the peaceful reward that the ancient Greeks had in mind.

The plays Williams wrote in the latter part of his life never received the public and critical acclaim of *Streetcar*; however, he continued to write and produce plays up until his death, including *Cat on a Hot Tin Roof* (1955), *Sweet Bird of My Youth* (1959), and *The Night of the Iguana* (1961).

Must Read

Plays by Tennessee Williams

Streetcar Named Desire

The Glass Menagerie

Arthur Miller (1915–2005)

Miller's life is almost as dramatic and famous as his plays. In 1956, after divorcing his first wife, Miller married Marilyn Monroe. During that time, because of Miller's radical political views, he was summoned to appear before the House Un-American Activities Committee to answer questions about his possible affiliation with communist organizations. This period of our history, known as the Red Scare, was headed by Wisconsin Senator Joseph McCarthy. Ultimately, this frenzy of ignorance, prejudice, and fear encouraged and inspired Miller to pen his retelling of the seventeenth-century Salem Witch Trials called *The Crucible* (1953), which won a Tony Award for best play.

Before this rather tumultuous time in Miller's life, he was known for writing riveting plays about American family life and, like many other writers, the individual's struggle in an ever-changing and sometimes unforgiving society. His first breakthrough play was called *All My Sons* (1947), which explored the life of a father and businessman who makes his money sending damaged military equipment to the Army during World War II.

It was 1949, however, that proved to be Miller's biggest year. *Death of a Salesman* was incredibly popular with Broadway theatergoers. The play won Miller a Pulitzer Prize as well. The plot follows the life of a Brooklyn traveling salesman, Willy Loman, and his family: his wife, Linda, and his visiting sons, Biff and Happy. Minor characters also include the Lomans' neighbor, Charley, and his son, Bernard; Willy's brother, Ben; Willy's boss, Howard Wagner; and The Woman, Willy's daydream mistress. Readers should also note that the Loman family home is surrounded by looming high-rise buildings; this comes to symbolize the passing away of the traditional American dream. The play begins with Willy returning from a failed business trip. At home, Willy journeys through several flashbacks and daydreams that introduce the viewers to the past when life was manageable and the boys were young, energetic, and optimistic. These daydreams and flashbacks also become central to the plot. It becomes clear to the viewer that the realities of the present and of the past are beginning to mix with fictional daydreams in Willy's mind. In the midst of present stresses, characters from Willy's past enter the stage to talk sense into him. For example, Willy's brother, Ben, continues to enter Willy's psyche, persuading Willy to join him in Alaska. Ultimately, Willy's daydreaming, fake optimism, and disillusionment drive him away from his family and eventually to his own death. The play is a wonderful comment on the stresses of American capitalism, but it is also the story of a struggling family in a time when every family desires (yet also questions) the American dream.

Must Read

Death of a Salesman by Arthur Miller

THE CONFESSIONAL POETS

The confessional poets were a group of poets writing in the 1950s and 1960s who took personal poetry to a completely different level. In some ways influenced by the British romantic poets like William Wordsworth and Samuel Taylor Coleridge and especially by Walt Whitman, the confessional poets wrote very personal, sometimes startling, poems about their own struggles and experiences with family members, drugs and alcohol, sexuality, politics, and mental illness. The poems certainly react to a previous generation of poets who maintained that the poem's author and its speaker are entirely two different personas; confessional poems seek to blur that line between author and speaker. In this way, the poems treat very private matters quite publicly.

John Berryman (1914–1972)

Like many confessional poets, Berryman used his poetry to explore his own battle with personal demons. Berryman's father committed suicide when Berryman was a young child. This tragedy caused the family to move to New York; from there, Berryman was sent to attend a private boarding school in Connecticut where he began to immerse himself in writing and literary studies. After graduation from Columbia and Cambridge universities, Berryman made a life for himself in academics, teaching at various prestigious universities such as Harvard and Princeton, and eventually finishing his career at the University of Minnesota. It was there, in 1972, that Berryman committed suicide by jumping off a bridge into the Mississippi River. He was plagued with depression, signs of mental illness, and an addiction to alcohol.

Berryman's most influential poems are two very different works. First, in 1953, after many years of study and research, Berryman published "Homage to Mistress Bradstreet," which is a 57-stanza poem about the life and writing of the Puritan poet. It is predominantly a first-person account of Bradstreet's passionate, dangerous, and complicated life as it lies in contrast to her traditional and conventional poetry. Berryman explores the tension between Miss Bradstreet, the poet, and

Anne, the Puritan woman. However, there are parts of the poem where Berryman inserts his own voice to take on the style of a dialogue. This poem, as is the case in most of Berryman's later work, is a mixture of **lyric** and **narrative**, using separate stanzas to narrate her life.

The Dream Songs was published in 1969; however, this collection was many years in the making. First, *77 Dream Songs* was published in 1964; *His Toy, His Dream, His Rest* was written in 1968; and still other "Dream" poems were published post-humously. In all, 385 poems were written with "dreams" in mind. The protagonist is the semiautobiographical Berryman here called Henry. Berryman's now famous introduction to *The Dream Songs* explores the tension, frequently found in confessional poetry, between the persona of the speaker and that of the poet:

> The poem then whatever its wide cast of characters, is essentially about an imaginary character (not the poet, not me) named Henry, a white American in early middle age sometimes in blackface, who has suffered an irreversible loss and talks about himself sometimes in the first person, sometimes in the third, sometimes even in the second; he has a friend, never named, who addresses him as Mr. Bones and variants thereof.
>
> (Berryman 1988, vi)

The poem's style, voice, length, and tension pay homage to other long, American poems like T.S. Eliot's *The Wasteland*, Ezra Pound's *Cantos*, and especially Walt Whitman's "Song of Myself." Berryman's work won him a Pulitzer Prize, the Bollinger Prize, and a National Book Award.

Must Read

The Dream Songs and "Homage to Mistress Bradstreet" by John Berryman: I recommend reading excerpts from these two works. Many poetry anthologies include selections from these texts.

Robert Lowell (1917–1977)

Some scholars point to Lowell's *Life Studies* (1959) as the beginning of the confessional movement in American poetry. However, this departure from conventional poetry deeply contrasts Lowell's family history and early life and work. Lowell is descended from Puritan stock on his mother's side (an ancestor traveled on the *Mayflower*) and American literary stock on his father's side (James Russell Lowell and Amy Lowell were relatives). He was educated at fine schools in New England and began college at Harvard. Lowell, however, was also quite contentious and rebellious; this personality trait sent him eventually to Ohio where he studied and wrote poetry under Allen Tate and John Crowe Ransom at Kenyon

College. After college, Lowell continued to shock his family by officially converting to Roman Catholicism in 1940 and moved further south to study under Robert Penn Warren at Louisiana State University. These literary influences are important to mention because they make up what literary theory refers to as **New Critics or formalists**. These critics paid little attention to the author's background, cultural influences, or any social influence on poem. What was crucial to the New Critics was the self-contained, individual poem itself. New Critics are famous for paying sole attention to the poem's form, or makeup, and its level of irony, metaphor, and ambiguity. These literary theories heavily influenced Lowell's first, and critically acclaimed, collection of poems called *Lord Weary's Castle* (1946). This work, written by Lowell while he was still in his twenties, won the poet many awards and fellowships, including the national poet laureate position in 1947.

Lowell's later work is usually studied in stark contrast to his earlier work influenced by New Criticism. *Life Studies, For the Union Dead* (1964) and *Notebook* (1970) are intensely personal works that explore not only Lowell's personal struggles and ideologies, but they also posit themselves in a particular cultural moment. Lowell continually attacks, makes amends, and attacks again the New England of his childhood: its past failings and how those moments translate to the present. For example, the title poem "For the Union Dead" is a poem about the Civil War memorial in Boston that portrays the white union officer, Robert Gould Shaw, as he leads his all-Black regiment to battle. The poem explores the complexities and contradictions of the Union (and its racial tensions) one hundred years after the war. These years were heavily influenced by the poems of the Beat poets in San Francisco and New York and Lowell's growing need for his poetry to grow organically out of his own struggles and desires. Lowell did publish several collections in the late 1960s and 1970s; however, they did not receive the critical acclaim of his earlier formalist work and his more confessional poems.

Must Read

Poetry of Robert Lowell

"Skunk Hour"

"For the Union Dead"

"Memories of West Street and Lepke"

"The Quaker Graveyard in Nantucket"

Anne Sexton (1928–1974)

Sexton is not considered the most popular confessional poet today, but she did create a more complex and appealing public persona during her writing career.

Sexton was known to be attractive, vivacious, and quite compelling. Her first and most famous collection, *To Bedlam and Part Way Back* (1960), was very much in the confessional vein. These poems poignantly explore her mental breakdowns and time spent in psychiatric hospitals. Later collections like *All My Pretty Ones* (1962) and *Live or Die* (1966), which earned her a Pulitzer, continued to explore issues surrounding madness, women in contemporary America, family struggles, death, beauty, and suicide. Sadly, Sexton took her own life before she turned fifty.

What is also intriguing about Sexton was her relationship with other confessional poets. In 1957, Sexton began attending writing seminars at Boston University and other writing groups where she met Robert Lowell and befriended Sylvia Plath and Maxine Kumin. These relationships encouraged her confessional-style writing. She is also a part of a large group of poets who began writing at the encouragement of a health professional or psychiatrist. Here are the first six lines of a greatly emotional and personal poem "Sylvia's Death," which she wrote about Plath's suicide:

> Oh Sylvia, Sylvia
> with a dead box of stones and spoons,
> with two children, two meteors
> wandering loose in the tiny playroom,
> with your mouth into the sheet,
> into the roofbeam, into the dumb prayer

(Baym et al. 2008, 2615)

Must Read

Poetry of Anne Sexton

"Her Kind"

"Housewife"

Sylvia Plath (1932–1963)

Although Plath died tragically by her own hand at a young age, she is arguably the most famous poet from the confessional movement. Lowell referred to this generation of Americans as the "tranquilized fifties." This moniker was very true of Plath's early life. She was born and raised in New England, educated at the finest schools, including Smith College and Cambridge, and enjoyed a life filled with culture and affluence. In England, she met and married the English poet **Ted Hughes**. They had two children and both began their poetic careers with increasing success. Plath wrote and published her first collection, *The Colossus*, in 1960; however, the power of her poetic energies did not surface until *Ariel* was published shortly after her death in 1965. Historians tell us that Hughes, who had separated from Plath and their children just prior to her suicide, reorganized her poems and even refused to publish several poems because of their content. As executor of Plath's will, Hughes published several more collections of her poems: *Crossing the Water* (1971), *Winter Trees* (1972), and *Collected Poems* (1981).

The style and structure of Plath's early work is, like Lowell's, characterized by relatively conventional forms, structures, and rhyming; however, her later work, like Lowell's *Life Studies*, is purely confessional in mode, tone, and structure. Plath's lines become looser, her language becomes stronger and intimate, and her subject manner contains public demonstrations of private thoughts and struggles. For examples of her early, more formal poetry, read "Mirror" and "Morning Song." "Daddy" and "Lady Lazarus" are two examples of Plath's confessional style that dominated the last few years of her life.

Plath is also known for a semiautobiographical novel, *The Bell Jar*, which was probably written in the late 1950s but did not see publication until the year of Plath's death. Because of its personal nature, the book was published under the pseudonym Victoria Lucas. It is the story of a young Massachusetts college student named Esther Greenwood who moves to New York to work as an editor for a magazine. She befriends and lives with many girls and finds herself torn between rebellion and conformity. Her attempts at rebellion almost cost Esther her virginity (once at her choice and another by force). Her return to Boston turns disastrous as she breaks up with her college boyfriend, learns she has been denied participation in a writing class, and spends too much time dwelling on the rough life lessons she learned in New York. Ultimately, she tries to commit suicide. After several attempts and continued electric therapy at her mother's suggestion, she is sent to a private hospital by a famous novelist (a woman who also provided Esther with college scholarships). There, Esther meets Dr. Nolan, whose demeanor and alternative methods are quite effective in helping Esther. She also meets and befriends a like-minded girl named Joan who ultimately makes sexual advances towards Esther. The novel ends quite ambiguously. Joan commits suicide, and Esther loses her virginity to a math professor during one of her visits away from the hospital. She starts the next semester with hesitant optimism, knowing that her emotional stability is always quite tenuous.

Must Read

Works by Sylvia Plath

"Mirror"

"Lady Lazarus"

"Daddy"

"Morning Song"

The Bell Jar (her autobiographical novel), if you have time

Adrienne Rich (1929–2012)

The essential component of most confessional poetry is its dedication and pre-occupation with **the self**. What sets Rich's poetry apart from that of other confessional poets is her ability to connect the self with the larger world. Students will get the feeling that reading poets such as Plath, Sexton, and Lowell is like looking at someone's diary without their permission. This is not, however, the feeling one gets after reading Rich's poems. Her poetic use of structure, metaphor, language, and persona give much depth to very personal, and sometimes private, material. For a remarkable example of **post-confessional personal poetry**, read Rich's "Diving in to a Wreck." On the surface, the poem is about a scuba-diving adventure:

> First having read the book of myths,
> and loaded the camera,
> and checked the edge of the knife-blade,
> I put on
> the body-armor of black rubber
> the absurd flippers
> the grave and awkward mask.
>
> (Ellmann and O'Clair 1988, 1327)

After subsequent readings, students should come to the realization that this "dive" is much more than an undersea adventure and the "wreck" is much more than a sunken ship. This narrative is as much about relationships and living life in communion with other people than it is about exploring life under the ocean. Toward the end of the poem, Rich writes, "I came to explore the wreck / . . . I came to see the damage that was done / and the treasures that prevail" (Ellmann and Johnson). Her poems explore the intimate and universal at the same time.

Like the confessional poets, Rich did begin her career writing formal verse influenced by traditional male poets. Her first collection, *A Change of World* (1951), contains more traditional and conventional verse, in contrast to later works such as *Snapshots of a Daughter-in-Law* (1963) and *Necessities of Life* (1966) in which she begins to play with line breaks, more intimate content, and increasingly sociopolitically charged issues. These collections were also published at a time of great personal and national turmoil. Rich became more involved in social protest (the Vietnam War) and social justice (education equality in the inner cities). These cultural moments heavily influenced the collections *The Will to Change* (1971) and *Diving into the Wreck* (1973). Several years after her husband's death in 1970, Rich began a love affair with writer Michelle Cliff and also began to write about lesbian issues and American sexual culture. Her poetry, at this time, aligned itself with the critique and exploration of patriarchal culture and of conventional roles for women. Take note that Rich is also an accomplished essayist and prose writer. Her varied subjects include poetics, Jewish identity, sexuality, and feminism. These essays were collected in several volumes including *Of Woman Born; On Lies, Secrets, and Silences: Selected Prose 1966–1978* and *Blood, Bread, and Poetry: Selected Prose 1979–1985*. Ultimately, Rich wrote and continues to write volumes and volumes of poetry and prose that explore the intersection between the individual self and the culture and environment around that self.

Must Read

Poetry of Adrienne Rich

"Storm Warnings"

"Diving into the Wreck"

"Snapshots of a Daughter-in-Law"

"Power"

"A Valediction Forbidding Mourning"

THE BEAT GENERATION

During the "tranquilized fifties," as coined by Lowell, there were a group of writers and artists in New York who wrote socially and politically subversive literature that rejected American mainstream values. Topics included drug experimentation, homosexuality and promiscuity, socialism and radical politics, and Eastern religions. These writers later emigrated to San Francisco where they influenced a new generation of "hippies" and antiestablishment thinkers, artists, and writers. Although the term "beatnik" was said to have been used by a journalist who criticized these poets for their "counterculture," the term **"beat"** is often associated with Jack Kerouac as a shortened form of "deadbeats," "beaten down" or "beatified." Beyond Allen Ginsberg and Kerouac, many of the important beatniks in New York were William S. Burroughs, Gregory Corso, and Neal Cassady. In San Francisco, Lawrence Ferlinghetti, Gary Snyder, and Kenneth Rexroth were among many who increased the Beat movement. You will recognize a poem from this era because of its **open-verse form**, its oftentimes objectionable or controversial subject matter, and its use of the confessional first-person voice.

Allen Ginsberg (1926–1997)

On the night of October 7, 1955, at the Six Gallery in San Francisco, Ginsberg read "Howl" for the first time. This reading ushered in a new era for poetry: one of open-verse, taboo issues, and social protest. Soon after the reading, fellow poet and owner of City Lights Bookstore, Lawrence Ferlinghetti, offered to publish the work, later along with several other Ginsberg poems, in his Pocket Poets series. This publication caused such a public outcry that Ferlinghetti was even tried for publishing obscenity.

In the introduction, William Carlos Williams writes, "Hold back the edges of your gowns, Ladies, we are going through hell" (1959, 8). "Howl" is aptly titled: the poem is a raging scream for the loss and madness of the poet's generation, much like Whitman's "barbaric yawp" in "Song of Myself." Ginsberg wrote long, bumbling lines that tried to mimic human thought, and he also used the catalog and first-person voice, much like Whitman, to create an intimacy and connection between the reader and the subject matter. Here is the beginning of "Howl":

> I saw the best minds of my generation destroyed by
> madness, starving hysterical naked,
> dragging themselves thought the negro streets at dawn
> looking for an angry fix,
> angelheaded hipsters burning for the ancient heavenly
> connection to the starry dynamo in the machinery of night,
> who poverty and tatters and hollow-eyed and high sat
> up smoking in the supernatural darkness of
> cold-water flats floating across the tops of cities
> contemplating jazz.
>
> (Ginsberg 1959, 9)

Most lines in the rest of the poem begin with "who" as the poem continues to catalog those "best minds of [Ginsberg's] generation." Although Ginsberg continued to write poems for almost forty more years, no poem amounted to the critical, public, and literary appeal and attention as "Howl."

Ginsberg's background is as mythic as the persona he creates in his poetry. He was born to a poet–English teacher father and a mentally ill, communist mother in Paterson, New Jersey. He graduated from Columbia University; however, he was arrested as an accomplice for robbery when police found stolen goods in his apartment. As part of a plea-bargain agreement, Ginsberg was committed to a mental hospital where he met the artist and writer Carl Solomon (Ginsberg dedicated "Howl" to this young man). After his release, Ginsberg spent time at home where he met and befriended the popular poet William Carlos Williams. His encouragement, along with the encouragement he received from English professors at Columbia, persuaded Ginsberg to continue writing poetry. His relationships with Burroughs, Kerouac, Corso, Peter Orlovsky, and other Beat writers have become legendary.

Must Read

Poetry of Allen Ginsberg

"A Supermarket in California"

"Howl"

"America"

Jack Kerouac and *On the Road*

Another important piece of Beat literature is Kerouac's travel narrative published in 1957. The narrative is a loosely based and semiautobiographical story about Kerouac's (Sal Paradise's) cross-country journeys with his pal Neal Cassady (Dean Moriarty). Essentially, *On the Road* is Sal's story as he travels with Dean (and leaves him on several occasions) during a three-year period. Along the way, the two characters meet several odd, strange, and eccentric characters. Some of these characters were influenced by other Beat writers: Allen Ginsberg (Carlo Marx) and William S. Burroughs (Bull Lee). The plot is less important than the strange, plotless journey. Kerouac's writing style also mirrors the content quite explicitly. An initial draft was written on a 120-foot scroll and includes stream-of-consciousness and paragraph-long sentences. Just as the work's subject matter questions American ideals and values, the narrative structure questions and resists common literary practices of the day.

THE AGE OF MULTICULTURAL LITERATURE

AFTER THE HARLEM RENAISSANCE

Ralph Ellison (1913–1994)

Ellison wrote one novel during his lifetime. *Invisible Man* (1952) tells the story of an unnamed character who attempts to navigate American racism during the 1930s. Ultimately, it is the story of African Americans during the first half of the twentieth century. Our narrator/protagonist, now living underground, beneath a manhole, in New York, explains his invisibility in the prologue of the novel:

> I am an invisible man. No, I am not a spook like those who haunted Edgar Allan Poe; nor am I one of your Hollywood-movie ectoplasms. I am a man of substance, of flesh and bone, fiber and liquids—and I might even be said to possess a mind. I am invisible, understand, simply because people refuse to see me.
>
> (Ellison 1990, 3)

The narrator tells the story of his life: his humble but promising beginnings at a college scholarship event, his experiences at a Black college, life in Harlem, work with a Black nationalist organization, and the eventual disintegration of that organization and his life above ground. *Invisible Man* still remains one of the great American novels.

Ellison grew up in Oklahoma City where his parents moved to distance themselves from the racist South. Historians tell us that, in the hopes that the young boy would grow to be a poet, Ellison's father named him Ralph Waldo after the great nineteenth-century poet/essayist Ralph Waldo Emerson. As a young child, Ellison was influenced by jazz and blues music, the works of Harlem Renaissance writers like Countee Cullen and Langston Hughes, and the radical socialist politics of his mother. After high school, Ellison attended Booker T. Washington's Tuskegee Institute in Alabama; however, he left before graduating and found his literary career in New York. There, Ellison was encouraged by Richard Wright to publish essays and stories for various magazines and literary journals. Ellison spent most of his adult life writing essays and teaching literature at various colleges and universities both in the United States and abroad. Unfortunately, he failed to produce a second novel during his lifetime. In 1999, *Juneteenth* was published as a much-edited version of a voluminous second novel Ellison never completed.

Must Read

Invisible Man by Ralph Ellison: At minimum, read the first chapter, "Battle Royal"; read the entire novel if you have time.

Gwendolyn Brooks (1917–2000)

Brooks is easily one of the most celebrated poets of the twentieth century. Brooks represents, in many ways, the product of essential debate during the Harlem Renaissance. During the 1920s and 1930s, Black artists argued vehemently about the target audience and ultimate purpose of their work. As I stated in the last chapter, many writers like Hughes wrote for a largely white audience, while other writers like Hurston refused to pander to an oppressive white audience. The year 1967, scholars tell us, proved to be a turning point for the literary life of Gwendolyn Brooks. Before that date, her poetry, much like that of Hughes, Cullen, and Paul Laurence Dunbar, revolved around Black urban life in an attempt to bring national (white) awareness to the urban experience. These poems were published in the critically acclaimed and awarded collections *A Street in Bronzeville* (1945) and *The Bean Eaters* (1960), and the novel *Annie Allen* (1949). In these collections, Brooks utilized various traditional forms, dialects, and poetic structures to encapsulate the Black urban experience. Below are the first few lines of "kitchenette building":

> We are things of dry hours and the involuntary plan,
> Grayed in, and gray. 'Dram' makes a giddy sound, not strong
> Like 'rent,' 'feeding a wife,' 'satisfying a man.'
> (Baym et al. 1995, 2503)

In 1967, however, scholars note a particular change in both the tone of and target audience for her work. That was the year that Brooks met and befriended Amiri Baraka, James Baldwin, and writers involved in the **Black arts movement**. This movement was the literary arm of the Black power movement that swept urban centers in the 1960s and 1970s. At this point, her essays and poems were dedicated and directed to African Americans. Instead of merely observing Black urban life, Brooks's poetry turned more political and revolutionary. *In the Mecca* (1968) is her collection that is most representative of this shift in her literary career. Brooks even left her publishing company to be represented by smaller African-American publishers.

For the rest of her life, Brooks toured the country giving readings, leading workshops, and bringing poetry and art to the forgotten places of America. In 1985, she was named to the position now called poet laureate.

Must Read

Poetry of Gwendolyn Brooks

"kitchenette building"

"We Real Cool"

"The Bean Eaters"

"The Mother"

"The Last Quatrain of the Ballad of Emmett Till"

James Baldwin (1924–1987)

Baldwin grew up in Harlem and was actually taught by Countee Cullen in junior high school. His love for books and reading was, at times, a reaction and an escape from his abusive and oppressive home life. Although his stepfather was a preacher, he was also a violent man. His influence on Baldwin was far-reaching. On one hand, Baldwin used literature to reject his stepfather, but on the other hand, Baldwin became a preacher himself during his teenage years. After his father's death, Baldwin left the ministry and moved to the artistic neighborhood of Greenwich Village where he met Richard Wright. Later he moved to Paris to flee American racism and focus on his literary career. Baldwin wrote many collections of essays and novels that attacked and explored race, gender, class, and sexuality. In 1953,

Baldwin wrote an autobiographical novel called *Go Tell It on the Mountain*, and in 1955, he wrote his first promising essay collection (heavily influenced by Wright) called *Notes of a Native Son*.

What makes Baldwin's work so fascinating and important to the American literary landscape, however, was his preoccupation with race and sexuality in America. Not only do his stories and novels explore racial tensions, but they also explore another taboo subject of the 1950s and 1960s: homosexuality. These works include *Giovanni's Room* (1956) and *Another Country* (1962). Baldwin continued to lecture and read in the United States, and write more stories and essays about race relations. *Nobody Knows My Name* (essays) and *Going to Meet the Man* (stories) became his most celebrated works in the 1960s. His stories are fused with religious language and allusions, sociopolitical commentary, and representative characters. Baldwin never considered himself an expatriate like Wright; however, he lived most of his life in Paris.

Must Read

Works by James Baldwin

"Sonny's Blues"

"The Rockpile"

Notes of a Native Son

Toni Morrison (1931–2019)

Morrison was born and raised in northern Ohio within the family-like community of Lorain. She, like many of her contemporaries, was encouraged by her parents to participate in education and the arts. Morrison graduated from Howard University and then received a master's degree from Cornell in 1955. After graduation, she taught writing, married, and mothered two children. Her divorce sent her into the workforce and more directly into the literary life. Morrison began working as an editor for Random House, where she stayed from 1967 to 1983, writing at night while raising her two sons. Her first novel, *The Bluest Eye* (1970), is set in her hometown of Lorain. The story revolves around young Pecola Breedlove who wants nothing more than to have blue eyes (the symbol of white beauty) just like Shirley Temple. The novel is told by several narrators and begins to explore the eventual madness that Pecola suffers due to her search for genuine love. The themes of love, betrayal, identity, and societal pressures in this initial novel permeate many of Morrison's novels to date. Although Morrison's work has a Midwestern feel, the novels share with the southern writers like Faulkner a need and desire to explore the grotesque and to explore the late twentieth-century Black experience. Morrison's novels include *Sula* (1973), *Song of Solomon* (1977), *Tar Baby* (1981), the Pulitzer Prize-winning

Beloved (1987), *Jazz* (1992), *Paradise* (1997), *Love* (2003), and *A Mercy* (2008). Morrison now teaches creative writing at Princeton University.

Morrison's most celebrated and critically acclaimed novel is *Beloved*. The novel takes place in post–Civil War Ohio and explores the life of Sethe, a former slave from Kentucky now living with her daughter, Denver, in the home previously owned by her mother-in-law, Baby Suggs. A domestic ghost is said to haunt the home. Paul D., a former slave who worked with Sethe, shows up one day and with him comes years of suppressed tales and tragedies. The novel travels from past to present in an attempt to reconcile the past, especially Sethe's murder of one of her daughters, whose headstone simply states "Beloved." During Paul D.'s stay at Sethe's home, called 124, a young woman named Beloved shows up. It is believed that she is the reincarnation of Sethe's dead daughter. This is just another example of the supernatural presence in the novel, and it also perpetuates the novel's exploration of sanity, mourning, and identity.

Must Read

Works by Toni Morrison

The Bluest Eye, Song of Solomon, or *Beloved*

"Recitatif"

THE JEWISH INFLUENCE ON THE AMERICAN NOVEL

Bernard Malamud (1914–1986)

Although Malamud disliked the label "Jewish-American writer," many of his stories and novels explore the lives of Jews in America and elsewhere. His stories are universal in the sense that they pit the individual against his/her own society, yet Malamud pays close attention to how the character's faith/culture play a role in how that character responds and reacts to that particular society. Many of his characters are middle-class, middle-age Jews working and navigating America and finding much success and much failure. His critically acclaimed early fiction demonstrated this tension: *The Assistant* (1957); *The Magic Barrel* (1958), a collection of stories that won the National Book Award; and *The Fixer* (1966), which won the National Book Award and a Pulitzer Prize. Malamud continued to write fiction well into the 1980s. His most popular novel, however, had little to do with Jewish America. In 1952, he wrote a baseball novel called *The Natural*.

Roy Hobbs is a rural kid who also happens to be a baseball prodigy. The story begins on a train headed to Chicago where Roy will begin a major league career. On the train, he meets a woman named Harriet Bird. Hobbs also meets a big-time, big-league slugger named Whammer (a Babe Ruth figure). During one of the stops, the scout who is bringing Roy to Chicago claims that the young kid can strike out the Whammer with just three pitches. Hobbs does just that and wins the affection of Ms. Bird. At a Chicago hotel room, Harriet asks Hobbs, "Roy, will you be the best there ever was in the game?" When Hobbs answers, "That's right," she shoots him (Malamud 1980, 33). Fifteen years later, Hobbs attempts a comeback with the New York Knights. After a slow start, Hobbs becomes a hero at the plate. He also tries to steal the girl (Memo Paris) from the team's star (Bump Baily), who ultimately dies after chasing a fly ball into the outfield wall. The plot of the novel thickens when the corrupt owner of the team, Judge Banner, offers Hobbs a lot of money to throw the next game. Hobbs reluctantly agrees, but certain outside forces encourage him to change his mind at the last minute. In terrific tragic fashion, however, Hobbs still strikes out and the public discovers the bribe, leaving Hobbs in shame.

The novel's popularity rose considerably when it was made into a movie starring Robert Redford, Glenn Close, Kim Basinger, Barbara Hershey, and Wilfred Brimley. What also made the movie so popular was the drastic change at the end. Instead of striking out and leaving in shame, Hobbs, before the game, throws the money back at the Judge and refuses to take the bribe. At the plate, Hobbs hits a homerun that shatters the outfield lights, creating a firework display as he rounds the bases in true heroic fashion. So don't see the movie and think that you've read the book, too.

Must Read

"The First Seven Years" by Bernard Malamud

Saul Bellow (1915–2005)

Much of Bellow's work explores the Jewish-American experience amidst the long shadow of World War II and the Holocaust. Although, like Malamud, Bellow did explore the very mundane aspects of Jewish-American life, the tragedies and effects of the war became an important canvas for Bellow's work and art. Bellow was born in Canada, but his family immigrated to Chicago when he was young. There, Bellow found books and writing as an escape from the burdens of post-Depression America and the sometimes fiery exchanges with his father. Like many authors, Bellow bounced around menial jobs and colleges before finally graduating at Northwestern University. He seriously began his writing career while teaching at the University of Minnesota. *The Victim* (1947), his first critically acclaimed novel, follows Asa Leventhal's journey into mental illness as he moves to Staten Island to attend to his sick nephew. Anti-Semitism, inner turmoil, and external burdens become too much for the protagonist.

In 1956, Bellow published *Seize the Day*, a story that follows the very sad life of Tommy Wilhelm. In midlife, Tommy has lost his job, his wife, much contact with his children, his support and encouragement from his father, and most of his money. The plot follows Tommy's last-ditch attempts to put his life back together, which eventually fail. However, at the end of the novel, Tommy cleanses his pent-up emotions through three important confrontations: another rejection by his father, a raucous argument with his wife, and, finally, a tearful deluge at a stranger's funeral.

What is central to most of Bellow's fiction is the individual's fight and journey through society. How can individuals find happiness in a prejudiced, oppressive, and unforgiving world? Often called the Great American novel by contemporary writers, *The Adventures of Augie March* (1953) follows the **eponymous** character through the trials, tribulations, and undulations of life. Many scholars refer to Augie as the **Everyman**: he experiences poverty, wealth, love, loss, education, and ignorance. It is the quintessential story of man versus society. Note that this novel is often referred to as a **picaresque**: a genre of fiction that uses elements of satire and realism to explore the adventures of a lower-class citizen in a corrupt or jaded society. The novel won Bellow a National Book Award and much popularity among writers and readers. Bellow wrote many more novels, including *Herzog* (1964); *Humboldt's Gift* (1975), which won the Pulitzer; and *The Dean's December* (1982).

Must Read

"Looking for Mister Green" by Saul Bellow

MORE MODERN AND CONTEMPORARY AUTHORS

As I stated earlier in the introduction of this chapter, anthologies vary on what contemporary authors they include. Below is a long list of authors and texts that are worth reading. There is a chance that these works and their authors could show up on the exam, so make sure you familiarize yourself with them.

Short Fiction

"I Stand Here Ironing" by Tillie Olson

"Everyday Use" by Alice Walker

"What We Talk about When We Talk about Love," "Cathedral," by Raymond Carver

"Defender of the Faith" by Philip Roth

"The Swimmer" by John Cheever

"The Things They Carried" by Tim O'Brien

"Lullaby" and "Yellow Woman" by Leslie Marmon Silko

The Lone Ranger and Tonto Fistfight in Heaven by Sherman Alexie

"No Name Woman" by Maxine Hong Kingston

Novels

House on Mango Street by Sandra Cisneros

The Joy Luck Club by Amy Tan

Poetry

"Still I Rise" by Maya Angelou

"Myrtle" and "Farm Implements and Rutabagas in a Landscape" by John Ashberry

"Riprap" by Gary Snyder

"Coal" and "The Woman Thing" by Audre Lorde

"Those Winter Sundays" by Robert Hayden

"Dear John, Dear Coltrane" and "Martin's Blues" by Michael S. Harper

"This Land is a Poem" and "Call It Fear" by Joy Harjo

"The White Porch" and "Lost Sister" by Cathy Song

"Persimmons," "My Father, In Heaven, Is Reading Out Loud," and "Eating Alone" by Li-Young Lee

Drama

A Raisin in the Sun by Lorraine Hansberry

The Little Foxes by Lillian Hellman

Nonfiction

Excerpts from *The Way to Rainy Mountain* by N. Scott Momaday

REFERENCES

Baym et al. 2008. *The Norton Anthology of American Literature*, shorter 7th ed. New York: W. W. Norton.

———. 1995. *The Norton Anthology of American Literature*, shorter 4th ed. New York: W. W. Norton.

Belasco, Susan, and Linck Johnson. 2008. *The Bedford Anthology of American Literature*, Vol. 2, *1865 to the Present*. Boston: Bedford/St. Martin's.

Berryman, John. 1988. *The Dream Songs*. New York: Farrar, Straus and Giroux.

Ellison, Ralph. 1990. *Invisible Man*. New York: Vintage.

Ellmann, Richard, and Robert O'Clair. 1988. *The Norton Anthology of Modern Poetry*, 2nd ed. New York: W. W. Norton.

Ginsberg, Allen. 1959. *Howl and Other Poems*. San Francisco: City Lights Bookstore.

Hunter, J. Paul. 1996. *The Norton Introduction to Poetry*, 6th ed. New York: W. W. Norton.

Kennedy, X. J., and Dana Gioia. 2005. *An Introduction to Poetry*, 11th ed. New York: Pearson/Longman.

Malamud, Bernard. 1980. *The Natural*. New York: Avon Books.

Marrs, Suzanne. 2005. *Eudora Welty: A Biography*. New York: Harcourt.

O'Connor, Flannery. 1997. *Mystery and Manners: Occasional Prose*. New York: The Noonday Press.

Williams, William Carlos. 1959. "Introduction." *Howl and Other Poems* by Allen Ginsberg. San Francisco: City Lights Bookstore.

PRACTICE TEST 1

CLEP American Literature

Also available at the REA Study Center (*www.rea.com/studycenter*)

This practice test is also offered online at the REA Study Center. Since all CLEP exams are administered on computer, we recommend that you take the online version of the test to receive these added benefits:

- **Timed testing conditions** – Gauge how much time you can spend on each question.
- **Automatic scoring** – Find out how you did on the test, instantly.
- **On-screen detailed explanations of answers** – Learn not just the correct answers, but why the other answer choices are incorrect.
- **Diagnostic score reports** – Pinpoint where you're strongest and where you need to focus your study.

Practice Test 1

CLEP American Literature

Answer Sheet

1. Ⓐ Ⓑ Ⓒ Ⓓ Ⓔ	35. Ⓐ Ⓑ Ⓒ Ⓓ Ⓔ	69. Ⓐ Ⓑ Ⓒ Ⓓ Ⓔ
2. Ⓐ Ⓑ Ⓒ Ⓓ Ⓔ	36. Ⓐ Ⓑ Ⓒ Ⓓ Ⓔ	70. Ⓐ Ⓑ Ⓒ Ⓓ Ⓔ
3. Ⓐ Ⓑ Ⓒ Ⓓ Ⓔ	37. Ⓐ Ⓑ Ⓒ Ⓓ Ⓔ	71. Ⓐ Ⓑ Ⓒ Ⓓ Ⓔ
4. Ⓐ Ⓑ Ⓒ Ⓓ Ⓔ	38. Ⓐ Ⓑ Ⓒ Ⓓ Ⓔ	72. Ⓐ Ⓑ Ⓒ Ⓓ Ⓔ
5. Ⓐ Ⓑ Ⓒ Ⓓ Ⓔ	39. Ⓐ Ⓑ Ⓒ Ⓓ Ⓔ	73. Ⓐ Ⓑ Ⓒ Ⓓ Ⓔ
6. Ⓐ Ⓑ Ⓒ Ⓓ Ⓔ	40. Ⓐ Ⓑ Ⓒ Ⓓ Ⓔ	74. Ⓐ Ⓑ Ⓒ Ⓓ Ⓔ
7. Ⓐ Ⓑ Ⓒ Ⓓ Ⓔ	41. Ⓐ Ⓑ Ⓒ Ⓓ Ⓔ	75. Ⓐ Ⓑ Ⓒ Ⓓ Ⓔ
8. Ⓐ Ⓑ Ⓒ Ⓓ Ⓔ	42. Ⓐ Ⓑ Ⓒ Ⓓ Ⓔ	76. Ⓐ Ⓑ Ⓒ Ⓓ Ⓔ
9. Ⓐ Ⓑ Ⓒ Ⓓ Ⓔ	43. Ⓐ Ⓑ Ⓒ Ⓓ Ⓔ	77. Ⓐ Ⓑ Ⓒ Ⓓ Ⓔ
10. Ⓐ Ⓑ Ⓒ Ⓓ Ⓔ	44. Ⓐ Ⓑ Ⓒ Ⓓ Ⓔ	78. Ⓐ Ⓑ Ⓒ Ⓓ Ⓔ
11. Ⓐ Ⓑ Ⓒ Ⓓ Ⓔ	45. Ⓐ Ⓑ Ⓒ Ⓓ Ⓔ	79. Ⓐ Ⓑ Ⓒ Ⓓ Ⓔ
12. Ⓐ Ⓑ Ⓒ Ⓓ Ⓔ	46. Ⓐ Ⓑ Ⓒ Ⓓ Ⓔ	80. Ⓐ Ⓑ Ⓒ Ⓓ Ⓔ
13. Ⓐ Ⓑ Ⓒ Ⓓ Ⓔ	47. Ⓐ Ⓑ Ⓒ Ⓓ Ⓔ	81. Ⓐ Ⓑ Ⓒ Ⓓ Ⓔ
14. Ⓐ Ⓑ Ⓒ Ⓓ Ⓔ	48. Ⓐ Ⓑ Ⓒ Ⓓ Ⓔ	82. Ⓐ Ⓑ Ⓒ Ⓓ Ⓔ
15. Ⓐ Ⓑ Ⓒ Ⓓ Ⓔ	49. Ⓐ Ⓑ Ⓒ Ⓓ Ⓔ	83. Ⓐ Ⓑ Ⓒ Ⓓ Ⓔ
16. Ⓐ Ⓑ Ⓒ Ⓓ Ⓔ	50. Ⓐ Ⓑ Ⓒ Ⓓ Ⓔ	84. Ⓐ Ⓑ Ⓒ Ⓓ Ⓔ
17. Ⓐ Ⓑ Ⓒ Ⓓ Ⓔ	51. Ⓐ Ⓑ Ⓒ Ⓓ Ⓔ	85. Ⓐ Ⓑ Ⓒ Ⓓ Ⓔ
18. Ⓐ Ⓑ Ⓒ Ⓓ Ⓔ	52. Ⓐ Ⓑ Ⓒ Ⓓ Ⓔ	86. Ⓐ Ⓑ Ⓒ Ⓓ Ⓔ
19. Ⓐ Ⓑ Ⓒ Ⓓ Ⓔ	53. Ⓐ Ⓑ Ⓒ Ⓓ Ⓔ	87. Ⓐ Ⓑ Ⓒ Ⓓ Ⓔ
20. Ⓐ Ⓑ Ⓒ Ⓓ Ⓔ	54. Ⓐ Ⓑ Ⓒ Ⓓ Ⓔ	88. Ⓐ Ⓑ Ⓒ Ⓓ Ⓔ
21. Ⓐ Ⓑ Ⓒ Ⓓ Ⓔ	55. Ⓐ Ⓑ Ⓒ Ⓓ Ⓔ	89. Ⓐ Ⓑ Ⓒ Ⓓ Ⓔ
22. Ⓐ Ⓑ Ⓒ Ⓓ Ⓔ	56. Ⓐ Ⓑ Ⓒ Ⓓ Ⓔ	90. Ⓐ Ⓑ Ⓒ Ⓓ Ⓔ
23. Ⓐ Ⓑ Ⓒ Ⓓ Ⓔ	57. Ⓐ Ⓑ Ⓒ Ⓓ Ⓔ	91. Ⓐ Ⓑ Ⓒ Ⓓ Ⓔ
24. Ⓐ Ⓑ Ⓒ Ⓓ Ⓔ	58. Ⓐ Ⓑ Ⓒ Ⓓ Ⓔ	92. Ⓐ Ⓑ Ⓒ Ⓓ Ⓔ
25. Ⓐ Ⓑ Ⓒ Ⓓ Ⓔ	59. Ⓐ Ⓑ Ⓒ Ⓓ Ⓔ	93. Ⓐ Ⓑ Ⓒ Ⓓ Ⓔ
26. Ⓐ Ⓑ Ⓒ Ⓓ Ⓔ	60. Ⓐ Ⓑ Ⓒ Ⓓ Ⓔ	94. Ⓐ Ⓑ Ⓒ Ⓓ Ⓔ
27. Ⓐ Ⓑ Ⓒ Ⓓ Ⓔ	61. Ⓐ Ⓑ Ⓒ Ⓓ Ⓔ	95. Ⓐ Ⓑ Ⓒ Ⓓ Ⓔ
28. Ⓐ Ⓑ Ⓒ Ⓓ Ⓔ	62. Ⓐ Ⓑ Ⓒ Ⓓ Ⓔ	96. Ⓐ Ⓑ Ⓒ Ⓓ Ⓔ
29. Ⓐ Ⓑ Ⓒ Ⓓ Ⓔ	63. Ⓐ Ⓑ Ⓒ Ⓓ Ⓔ	97. Ⓐ Ⓑ Ⓒ Ⓓ Ⓔ
30. Ⓐ Ⓑ Ⓒ Ⓓ Ⓔ	64. Ⓐ Ⓑ Ⓒ Ⓓ Ⓔ	98. Ⓐ Ⓑ Ⓒ Ⓓ Ⓔ
31. Ⓐ Ⓑ Ⓒ Ⓓ Ⓔ	65. Ⓐ Ⓑ Ⓒ Ⓓ Ⓔ	99. Ⓐ Ⓑ Ⓒ Ⓓ Ⓔ
32. Ⓐ Ⓑ Ⓒ Ⓓ Ⓔ	66. Ⓐ Ⓑ Ⓒ Ⓓ Ⓔ	100. Ⓐ Ⓑ Ⓒ Ⓓ Ⓔ
33. Ⓐ Ⓑ Ⓒ Ⓓ Ⓔ	67. Ⓐ Ⓑ Ⓒ Ⓓ Ⓔ	
34. Ⓐ Ⓑ Ⓒ Ⓓ Ⓔ	68. Ⓐ Ⓑ Ⓒ Ⓓ Ⓔ	

Practice Test 1

CLEP American Literature

(Answer sheet on facing page.)

TIME: 90 Minutes
100 Questions

DIRECTIONS: Each of the questions or incomplete statements below is followed by five possible answers or completions. Select the best choice in each case and fill in the corresponding oval on the answer sheet. Some questions will ask you to match terms with one another or to put a list in chronological order.

Questions 1–2

You don't know about me, without you have read a book by the name of "The Adventures of Tom Sawyer," but that ain't no matter. That book was made by Mr. Mark Twain, and told the truth mainly. There was things which he stretched, but mainly he told the truth.

1. The last line infers what literary device?

   (A) Simile   (D) Synecdoche

   (B) Metaphor   (E) Metonym

   (C) Hyperbole

2. Who is the narrator of this passage?

   (A) Samuel Clemens   (D) Jim

   (B) Omniscient narrator (E) Mark Twain

   (C) Huck Finn

3.   Modernist writers resisted any moral or didactic leanings that could distract the reader from appreciating the aesthetic beauty of the poem itself. According to Archibald MacLeish's modernist poem "Ars Poetica,"

"A poem should not mean, / But ___."

(A)   be   (D)   die

(B)   live   (E)   sing

(C)   rest

4.   What term is often associated with Jack Kerouac, Allen Ginsberg, William S. Burroughs, and Neal Cassady to describe a group of writers and artists who lived in New York and wrote socially and politically subversive literature that rejected American mainstream values?

(A)   Hippies

(B)   Yuppies

(C)   Surrealists

(D)   Post-modernists

(E)   The Beats

5.   This book by Cotton Mather is very nostalgic in its attempt to recall a time of ecclesiastical order and church authority, so contemporaries will not forget the people and ideologies that first settled America. The book is entitled

(A)   *The American Jeremiad*

(B)   *Sinners in the Hands of an Angry God*

(C)   *The Wonders of the Invisible World*

(D)   *Magnalia Christi Americana*

(E)   *Personal Narrative*

6.   Writers and poets, such as Ernest Hemingway, Ezra Pound, and T.S. Eliot, who moved to Europe to write, live, and meet other writers are commonly referred to as

(A)   immigrants   (D)   traitors

(B)   emigrants   (E)   enemies of the state

(C)   expatriates

7.   Match the following literary periods with the dates listed below:

      The Modernist Period

      The Romantic Period

      The Period of Realism and Naturalism

      _____ 1830–1870

      _____ 1870–1910

      _____ 1910–1945

Questions 8–10

      Something there is that doesn't love a wall,
      That sends the frozen-ground-swell under it
      And spills the upper boulders in the sun,
      and makes gaps even two can pass abreast.

8.   Literally, ground swells cause walls to crumble. Notice, however, that the poet in a traditional iambic line, stresses the syllables "ground-swell" to accentuate the feeling of moving ground. In poetics, we refer to this as a spondaic interruption. The **spondee** is a poetic foot defined as

      (A)   a stressed syllable followed by an unstressed syllable

      (B)   an unstressed syllable followed by a stressed syllable

      (C)   two stressed syllables

      (D)   two unstressed syllables followed by a stressed syllable

      (E)   a stressed syllable followed by two unstressed syllables

9.   This poem, "Mending Wall," explores the relationship between neighbors. However, the speaker of the poem is not clear whether walls/barriers are good or bad for relationships. This type of tension found inside a literary work is usually referred to as

      (A)   ambivalence   (D)   allegory

      (B)   ambiguity   (E)   conflict

      (C)   sarcasm

10. Who wrote "Mending Wall"?

    (A) Robert Service   (D) Jack London

    (B) T.S. Eliot   (E) Robert Frost

    (C) Henry David Thoreau

11. Washington Irving's "Rip Van Winkle" is set before and after which period in United States history?

    (A) The Civil War   (D) World War I

    (B) The War of 1812   (E) World War II

    (C) The Revolutionary War

12. What is the name of the literary journal that was founded by Harriet Monroe in 1912 and aided in the careers of many poets like Robert Frost, Carl Sandburg, Ezra Pound, T.S. Eliot, and William Carlos Williams?

    (A) *The Atlantic Monthly*

    (B) *Harper's Magazine*

    (C) *The New Yorker*

    (D) *Poetry: A Magazine of Verse*

    (E) *The Dial*

Questions 13–15

> We is gathahed hyeah, my brothahs,
> In dis howlin' wildaness,
> Fu' to speak some words of comfo't
> To each othah in distress. / An' we chooses fu' ouah subjic'
> Dis—we'll splain it by an'by;
> "An de Lawd said, 'Moses, Moses,'
> An de man said, 'Hyeah am I.'"

13. This poem, titled "An Ante-bellum Sermon," is an example of

    (A) ventriloquism   (D) allegory

    (B) poetic persona   (E) narrative

    (C) heroic line

14.   What literary device does the poet utilize in this poem to accentuate the vernacular of Blacks in nineteenth-century America?

(A)   Poetic persona   (D)   Allegory

(B)   Narrative   (E)   Realism

(C)   Dialect

15.   The poem was written by

(A)   Langston Hughes   (D)   Gwendolyn Brooks

(B)   Paul Laurence Dunbar   (E)   Sterling Brown

(C)   Countee Cullen

16.   "Reason is the basis of all authority" is a major tenet of

(A)   romanticism   (D)   puritanism

(B)   realism   (E)   the Age of Enlightenment

(C)   transcendentalism

17.   According to Ernest Hemingway, "All modern American literature comes from one book by Mark Twain..." What is the name of the book to which Hemingway was referring?

(A)   *The Adventures of Tom Sawyer*

(B)   *Huckleberry Finn*

(C)   *Roughing It*

(D)   *A Connecticut Yankee in King Arthur's Court*

(E)   *The Great Gatsby*

18.   Many scholars appropriately link William Cullen Bryant, John Greenleaf Whittier, and Henry Wadsworth Longfellow to a group of famous poets known as the

(A)   Fireside Poets   (D)   Beats

(B)   Metaphysical Poets   (E)   Transcendentalists

(C)   Romantics

19. Carl Sandburg is most noted for his poetry about Chicago. However, he is also famous for writing a biography of what American president?

    (A) George Washington   (D) Abraham Lincoln

    (B) Ulysses S. Grant   (E) William Taft

    (C) Andrew Jackson

20. Which essay was NOT written by Ralph Waldo Emerson?

    (A) "The Great Lawsuit: Man versus Men, Woman versus Women"

    (B) "Experience"

    (C) "Self-Reliance"

    (D) "The Divinity School Address"

    (E) "Man the Reformer"

21. William Carlos Williams was not only a poet, but also a(n)

    (A) insurance agent   (D) patent officer

    (B) lawyer   (E) physician

    (C) teacher

Questions 22–24

For wee must Consider that wee shall be as a **Citty upon a hill**. The eies of all people are upon Us, soe that if wee shall deale falsely with our god in this worke wee have undertaken, and soe cause him to with-drawe his present help from us, wee shall be made a story and a by-word through the world. We shall open the mouthes of enemies to speake evill of the ways of god, and all professours for God's sake.

22. The "wee" in line 1 refers to

    (A) preachers   (D) Quakers

    (B) New Englanders   (E) Puritans

    (C) Pilgrims

23. John Winthrop takes the "city upon a hill" image from Matthew 5:14. This literary device is often called a(n)

    (A) allusion   (D) metaphor

    (B) illusion   (E) simile

    (C) conceit

24. The title of this sermon given upon the ship *Arbella* in 1630 by John Winthrop is called

    (A) Magnalia Christi Americana

    (B) *"A Model of Christian Charity"*

    (C) *"Sinners in the Hands of an Angry God"*

    (D) *"The Wonders of the Invisible World"*

    (E) *"The Sovereignty and Goodness of God"*

25. Which author is NOT commonly considered a regional writer?

    (A) Mark Twain   (D) Stephen Crane

    (B) Willa Cather   (E) Kate Chopin

    (C) Jack London

Questions 26–27

    When I wrote the following pages, or rather the bulk of them, I lived alone, in the woods, a mile from any neighbor, in a house which I had built myself... in Concord, Massachusetts, and earned my living by the labor of my hands only. I lived there two years and two months. At present I am a sojourner in civilized life again.

26. The above excerpt was written by

    (A) Ralph Waldo Emerson

    (B) Allen Ginsberg

    (C) Edward Albee

    (D) Henry David Thoreau

    (E) Washington Irving

27. The excerpt is from which work of literature?

    (A) *On Golden Pond*   (D) *Concord Lake*

    (B) *Walden Pond*   (E) *Cape Cod*

    (C) *Lake Innisfree*

28. Interested in the mundane episodes of middle-class life, these types of novels tend to lean towards social reform. Writers took it upon themselves to critically comment on America's politics, economics, industry, social issues, as well as gender, class, and race issues. This type of novel is known as

    (A) realism

    (B) naturalism

    (C) sentimentalism

    (D) post-modernism

    (E) modernism

Questions 29–31

> The houses are haunted
> By white night-gowns.
> None are green,
> Or purple with green rings,
> Or green with yellow rings,
> Or yellow with blue rings.
> None of them are strange,
> With socks of lace
> And beaded ceintures.
> People are not going
> To dream of baboons and periwinkles.
> Only, here and there, an old sailor,
> Drunk and asleep in his boots,
> Catches tigers
> In red weather.

29. "The houses" that the speaker of the poem describes (and ridicules) are most likely located in

    (A) the country   (D) Europe

    (B) the city   (E) the future

    (C) the suburbs

30. According to the poem, which of the following probably does NOT dream?

    (A) A drunken sailor

    (B) Haunted houses

    (C) the speaker of the poem

    (D) the reader of the poem

    (E) poetry editors

31. The poem is called "Disillusionment of Ten O'Clock" and was written by

    (A) William Carlos Williams   (D) H.D.

    (B) Ezra Pound   (E) Wallace Stevens

    (C) Marianne Moore

32. Novels such as *The Portrait of a Lady* and *Daisy Miller* explore the adjustments Americans, especially women, face in European countries as they interact within different social structures and mores. These novels were written by

    (A) William Dean Howells   (D) Henry James

    (B) Theodore Dreiser   (E) William James

    (C) Frank Norris

Questions 33–34

   My view of Christianity is such, that I think no man can consistently profess it without giving the whole weight of his being against this monstrous system of injustice that lies at the foundation of all our society; and, if need be, sacrificing himself in the battle.

33. This passage comes from Harriet Beecher Stowe's *Uncle Tom's Cabin*. What does "this monstrous system" refer to?

    (A) Sexism   (D) The American government

    (B) Racism   (E) The church

    (C) Slavery

34. Who is the speaker of this quote?

    (A) Harriet Beecher Stowe   (D) Augustine St. Clare

    (B) Eva   (E) William Lloyd Garrison

    (C) Frederick Douglass

35. In Kate Chopin's "Story of an Hour," Mrs. Mallard dies of heart disease—"of joy that kills." This is an example of

    (A) allusion   (D) foreshadowing

    (B) verbal irony   (E) dramatic irony

    (C) cosmic irony

36. Sects of Christian reformers who struggled to "purify" the Church of England of any resemblance to Roman Catholicism and decided to immigrate to the new world in 1620 were known as

    (A) Pilgrims   (D) Puritans

    (B) Dissenters   (E) Quakers

    (C) Expatriates

37. Henry Wadsworth Longfellow's "The Song of Hiawatha" is an epic that romanticizes what group of people?

    (A) Colonial Americans   (D) Puritan settlers

    (B) European explorers   (E) French Jesuits

    (C) American Indians

Questions 38–39

> A Man said to the universe:
> "Sir, I exist!"
> "However," replied the universe,
> "The fact has not created in me
> A sense of obligation."

38. This Stephen Crane poem is a literary example of

    (A) naturalism   (D) allegory

    (B) realism   (E) modernism

    (C) satire

39. In order to give the universe a voice, this poem utilizes what literary device?

    (A) Onomatopoeia   (D) Allegory

    (B) Hyperbole   (E) Simile

    (C) Personification

40. Henry David Thoreau's essay, "Civil Disobedience," was written as the result of what crime for which Thoreau was forced to spend one night in jail?

    (A) Refusing to vote

    (B) Building a house on private property

    (C) Refusing to pay his poll tax

    (D) Refusing to enlist in the army

    (E) Writing slanderous satire

41. Ezra Pound's "A Station of the Metro" is an example of what poetic form that rejected long and elevated language in favor of crisp, clear language and precise images?

    (A) Objectivism   (D) Imagism

    (B) Surrealism   (E) Realism

    (C) Cubism

42. Which author is unique in his ability to tell stories of the Civil War because he actually served as a soldier in several of the war's most important and violent campaigns, including the Battle of Chickamauga and the Battle of Shiloh?

    (A) Stephen Ambrose   (D) Ambrose Bierce

    (B) Bret Harte   (E) Stephen Crane

    (C) Hart Crane

Questions 43–44

> I died for Beauty — but was scarce
> Adjusted in the Tomb
> When One who died for Truth, was lain
> In an adjoining room —
> He questioned softly "Why I failed"?
> "For Beauty", I replied —
> "And I — for Truth — Themself are One —
> We Brethren, are", He said —
> And so, as Kinsmen, met a Night —
> We talked between the Rooms —
> Until the Moss had reached our lips —
> And covered up — our names —

43. What implication does the poem NOT make about beauty and truth?

   (A) They are eternal.

   (B) They kill those who seek them.

   (C) They unify people.

   (D) They are as ephemeral as human life.

   (E) They are essentially the same thing.

44. What is the setting of this poem?

   (A) Heaven   (D) The imagination

   (B) Hell   (E) Purgatory

   (C) A cemetery

45. Instead of chapters, Mary Rowlandson's *A Narrative of the Captivity and Restoration of Mary Rowlandson* (also called *The Sovereignty and Goodness of God*) uses which of the following to distinguish movements and plot?

   (A) Sections   (D) People's names

   (B) Dates   (E) Places

   (C) Removes

46. In 1901, Booker T. Washington published his autobiography called

    (A) *The Souls of Black Folks*

    (B) *I Know Why the Caged Bird Sings*

    (C) *Autobiography of an Ex-Colored Man*

    (D) *Up from Slavery*

    (E) *Invisible Man*

47. Which of the following is the literary genre most noted as a pre-cursor for horror fiction?

    (A) Sentimental fiction   (D) Fantasy

    (B) Realist fiction   (E) Gothic fiction

    (C) Science fiction

48. From 1944–1946, three poetry collections, "*The Walls Do Not Fall*," "*Tribute to the Angels*," and "*The Flowering of the Road*" were written by H.D. These initials refer to

    (A) Henry David   (D) Hilda Dwight

    (B) Harriet Douglas   (E) Harriet Dwight

    (C) Hilda Doolittle

49. Willa Cather's novels and stories are predominantly set in what American state?

    (A) Kansas   (D) Arkansas

    (B) Oklahoma   (E) Nebraska

    (C) Missouri

50. "Call me Ishmael" is the opening line of what Herman Melville novel?

    (A) *Typee*   (D) *Moby-Dick*

    (B) *Omoo*   (E) *White-Jacket*

    (C) *Pierre*

51. Place each of the following authors beside the work of literature he/she is associated with.

     Sylvia Plath

     Zora Neale Hurston

     Toni Morrison

     _____ *The Bluest Eye*

     _____ *The Bell Jar*

     _____ *Their Eyes Were Watching God*

52. This genre is relatively formulaic: the author depicts his or her life as it progresses from a state of sin to a state of grace, detailing cycles of sin and repentance on the journey to salvation. The writer explores his or her relationship with God's natural world, the Bible, other believers and non-believers, and theological conflicts like "election" or "original sin." This genre is known as a(n)

     (A) sentimental novel   (D) jeremiad

     (B) realist fiction   (E) elegy

     (C) spiritual autobiography

53. The latter part of Edna St. Vincent Millay's life, like many of her contemporaries, turned political. She is most famous for participating in a protest against the execution of which two Italian anarchists?

     (A) Sacco and Vanzetti   (D) Medici and Bialetti

     (B) Sacco and Da Vinci   (E) Vanzetti and Bialetti

     (C) Capulet and Montague

Questions 54–55

        Safe upon the solid rock the ugly houses stand:
        Come and see my shining palace built upon the sand!

54. The allusive images of "rock" and "sand" in this poem were taken from what text?

     (A) The Koran   (D) The Odyssey

     (B) The Bible   (E) The Illiad

     (C) The Bhagavad Gita

55. In light of the allusion, the tone of this poem is

    (A) sarcastic   (D) nostalgic

    (B) mournful   (E) sardonic

    (C) tragic

56. In "Bartleby the Scrivener," a lawyer tells the story of one of his several scriveners, or copyists. Bartleby answers an ad for a job and is hired as a copyist in the lawyer's office. Conflict arises when the lawyer asks Bartleby to complete a simple task, and his response is merely

    (A) "As you wish."   (D) "No."

    (B) "I would prefer not to." (E) "In due time."

    (C) "Yes."

57. What modernist poet is most commonly known for breaking all of the following traditional poetic rules: capitalization, line spacing, spaces between words, and punctuation?

    (A) T.S. Eliot   (D) E.E. Cummings

    (B) Ezra Pound   (E) William Carlos Williams

    (C) H.D.

58. Writers like Gwendolyn Brooks, Amiri Baraka, and James Baldwin were the literary arm of the Black Power Movement that swept urban centers in the '60s and '70s and were part of the

    (A) Harlem Renaissance   (D) Black Arts Movement

    (B) Black Panthers   (E) Digital Underground

    (C) Chicago Renaissance

59. Not only does Charlotte Perkins Gilman's "The Yellow Wallpaper" verge on fantasy or horror, it is also a biting satire against nineteenth-century medical practice and

    (A) interior design   (D) urban fashion

    (B) New England hotels   (E) Christianity

    (C) marriage conventions

Questions 60–61

> If ever two or one, then surely we,
> If ever man were loved by wife, then thee;
> If ever wife was happy in a man,
> compare with me, ye women, if you can.

60. The previous stanza comes from the poem "To My Dear and Loving Husband" by

(A) Phillis Wheatley   (D) Edna St. Vincent Millay

(B) Mary Rowlandson   (E) Anne Bradstreet

(C) Christina Rossetti

61. The above stanza uses which type of meter?

(A) Iambic pentameter   (D) Trochaic tetrameter

(B) Iambic tetrameter   (E) Free verse

(C) Trochaic pentameter

62. Imagination over reason, fascination with the wild and uncivilized, and sensibility are all major tenets of

(A) the Age of Enlightenment

(B) Puritanism

(C) Realism

(D) Post-modernism

(E) Romanticism

63. Which of the following terms originally refers to art and sculpture that was bizarre, fantastic, abnormal, and symbolized the horror of being human in a very inhumane and distrustful world?

(A) Absurd   (D) Imagist

(B) Surreal   (E) Real

(C) Grotesque

64. Theodore Dreiser's *Sister Carrie*, like many of his novels, is set in what major American city?

    (A) New York   (D) Chicago

    (B) Los Angeles   (E) Cleveland

    (C) St. Louis

Questions 65–67

> I celebrate myself, and sing myself,
> And what I assume you shall assume,
> For every atom belonging to me as good belongs to you.

65. This opening stanza comes from what famous Walt Whitman poem?

    (A) Leaves of Grass

    (B) Song of Myself

    (C) I Heard a Learn'd Astronomer

    (D) Out of the Cradle Endlessly Rocking

    (E) O Captain! My Captain!

66. The preoccupation of the self (and seeking divinity within) is predominantly inspired by which American movement?

    (A) Transcendentalism   (D) Puritanism

    (B) Unitarianism   (E) Mormonism

    (C) Quakerism

67. This poem is also part of what larger collection?

    (A) Drum-Taps   (D) Calamus

    (B) Walden   (E) Children of Adam

    (C) Leaves of Grass

68. In F. Scott Fitzgerald's *The Great Gatsby*, what district of Long Island is most commonly associated with "new money"?

    (A) West Egg   (D) South Egg

    (B) East Egg   (E) The Valley of the Ashes

    (C) North Egg

Questions 69–70

> 'Twas mercy brought me from my Pagan land,
> Taught my benighted soul to understand
> That there's a God, that there's a Saviour too:
> Once I redemption neither sought nor knew.
>
> Some view our sable race with scornful eye,
> "Their colour is a diabolic die."
> Remember, Christians, Negros, black as Cain,
> May be refin'd, and join th' angelic train.

69.   What implication does this poem NOT make about Africans?

   (A)   Africans are not Christians.

   (B)   Africans are not enlightened.

   (C)   Africans have the opportunity to go to heaven.

   (D)   Africans are capable of creating great art.

   (E)   The target audience is white Christians.

70.   The poet Phillis Wheatley was

   (A)   an abolitionist

   (B)   a New England preacher's wife

   (C)   a young, slave girl

   (D)   illiterate

   (E)   Thomas Jefferson's mistress

71.   William Faulkner is famous for setting most of his fiction in what fictitious southern county?

   (A)   Ozaukee   (D)   Yoknapatawpha

   (B)   Tishomingo   (E)   Benton

   (C)   Licking

72. W.E.B. Du Bois, in his seminal book *The Souls of Black Folks,* coined an important term for race studies that refers to the act of only being aware of one's self through the eyes of others. The term is

    (A) double consciousness   (D) racism

    (B) double entendre   (E) cognizant trauma

    (C) mirrored consciousness

73. Ernest Hemingway penned all of the following novels EXCEPT

    (A) *All the King's Men*   (D) *The Sun Also Rises*

    (B) *A Farewell to Arms*   (E) *In Our Time*

    (C) *For Whom the Bell Tolls*

Questions 74–75

> I saw the best minds of my generation destroyed by
> madness, starving hysterical naked,
> dragging themselves through the negro streets at dawn
> looking for an angry fix,
> angelheaded hipsters burning for the ancient heavenly
> connection to the starry dynamo in the machinery of night,

74. The above passage utilizes what poetic form?

    (A) Imagism   (D) Open verse

    (B) Objectivism   (E) Clerihew

    (C) Sestina

75. The excerpt comes from what famous poem by Allen Ginsberg?

    (A) "A Supermarket in California"

    (B) "Sunflower Sutra"

    (C) "On the Road"

    (D) "Howl"

    (E) "Song of Myself"

76. In many of Nathaniel Hawthorne's prefaces to novels like *The Marble Faun* and *The House of the Seven Gables*, he explores the definition of what genre?

    (A)   Romance   (D)   Fantasy

    (B)   Gothic   (E)   Allegory

    (C)   Epic

77. *The Son of the Wolf, The Call of the Wild*, and *The Sea Wolf* were all written by

    (A)   Jack London   (D)   Louis L'Amour

    (B)   Robert Service   (E)   Zane Grey

    (C)   Stephen Crane

78. Which of the following authors does NOT explore issues revolving around the lives of American Indians?

    (A)   Sherman Alexie   (D)   Sandra Cisneros

    (B)   Louise Erdich   (E)   Leslie Marmon Silko

    (C)   N. Scott Momaday

79. John Smith was captured by Powhatan, chief of the Chesapeake Bay Indians, and then rescued by the chief's daughter, known as

    (A)   Sacajawea   (D)   Samson Occom

    (B)   Pocahontas   (E)   Mohegan

    (C)   Stands-with-Fists

80. Although some critics called it a pack of lies, John Steinbeck's novel *The Grapes of Wrath* was heralded for its realism and depiction of a very dark time in American history and is considered to be an American

    (A)   elegy   (D)   symbol

    (B)   epic   (E)   ode

    (C)   allegory

81. Walt Whitman is commonly referred to as the father of

    (A)   erotic poetry   (D)   free verse

    (B)   the catalog   (E)   confessional poetry

    (C)   America

82. Which of the following dramatists wrote the semi-autobiographical drama called *Long Day's Journey into the Night*, which was published posthumously due to its very personal content?

    (A) Tennessee Williams   (D) Tom Stoppard

    (B) Henry Miller   (E) Edgar Allan Poe

    (C) Eugene O'Neill

83. *The General History of Virginia, New England, and the Summer Isles* (1624) contains six books of collected and original writings by

    (A) William Bradford   (D) Edward Taylor

    (B) Miles Standish   (E) Christopher Columbus

    (C) John Smith

Questions 84–86

I am an invisible man. No, I am not a spook like those who haunted Edgar Allan Poe; nor am I one of your Hollywood-movie ectoplasms. I am a man of substance, of flesh and bone, fiber and liquids—and I might even be said to possess a mind. I am invisible, understand, simply because people refuse to see me.

84. The above passage is the beginning of *Invisible Man*. Why does the unnamed narrator state that people refuse to see him?

    (A) Because he is mentally disabled.

    (B) Because he is a member of an underground society.

    (C) Because he is poor.

    (D) Because he is literally invisible.

    (E) Because he is Black.

85. The phrase "and I might even be said to possess a mind" is a literary example of what device?

    (A) Sarcasm   (D) Allegory

    (B) Metaphor   (E) Symbol

    (C) Simile

86. What author penned *Invisible Man?*

    (A) James Baldwin   (D) Langston Hughes

    (B) H.G. Wells   (E) Ralph Ellison

    (C) Richard Wright

87. Hester Prynne, Arthur Dimmesdale, and Roger Chillingworth are all charac-
    ters in which Hawthorne novel?

    (A) *The Marble Faun*

    (B) *The Blithedale Romance*

    (C) *The House of the Seven Gables*

    (D) *The Scarlet Letter*

    (E) *Twice-Told Tales*

88. These works posit that humans are not that different from animals to the
    point that they merely respond to natural and environmental forces without
    fully understanding the forces or their reactions to them. Said to be a product
    of scientific determinism, these works are in the genre known as

    (A) Realism   (D) Post-modernism

    (B) Naturalism   (E) Modernism

    (C) Sentimentalism

89. What poetic device or convention is NOT commonly found in Emily Dick-
    inson's poetry?

    (A) Dashes

    (B) An abundance of capitalization

    (C) Metaphor

    (D) Hymn measure

    (E) Heroic couplet

90. This book tells the story of a young Massachusetts college student named Esther Greenwood who moves to New York to work as a magazine editor. She befriends and lives with many girls and finds herself torn between rebellion and conformity. The book is a semi-autobiographical novel written by Sylvia Plath and, because of its personal nature, was originally published under the pseudonym Victoria Lucas. The title of this book is

    (A) *Ariel*

    (B) *The Colossus*

    (C) *The Bell Jar*

    (D) *Dream Songs*

    (E) *Life Studies*

91. Place the following poets beside the title of their well-known poem.

    Carl Sandburg

    Robert Frost

    William Cullen Bryant

    _____ "Thanatopsis"

    _____ "The Fog"

    _____ "Fire and Ice"

92. In Tennessee Williams's *A Streetcar Named Desire*, who sexually assaults Blanche DuBois?

    (A) Stella's brother, Stanley

    (B) Stella's neighbor, Stanley

    (C) Stella's fiancée, Stanley

    (D) Stella's husband, Stanley

    (E) Stella's uncle, Stanley

93. In 1846, this author wrote "The Philosophy of Composition" for *Graham's Magazine*. One of the most enduring comments in that article was that "there is a distinct limit, as regards length, to all works of literary art—the limit of a single sitting." The author was

    (A) Walt Whitman

    (B) Margaret Fuller

    (C) Ralph Waldo Emerson

    (D) Nathaniel Hawthorne

    (E) Edgar Allan Poe

94. According to Richard Wright's *Native Son*, who is predominantly responsible for Bigger Thomas's violent acts?

   (A) Bigger's mother

   (B) The Chicago school system

   (C) Bigger

   (D) White, racist America

   (E) Bigger's employer

Questions 95–97

> The art of losing isn't hard to master;
> so many things seem filled with the intent
> to be lost that their loss is no disaster.
> Lose something every day. Accept the fluster
> of lost door keys, the hour badly spent.
>
> The art of losing isn't hard to master.
> Then practice losing farther, losing faster:
> places, and names, and where it was you meant
> to travel. None of these will bring disaster.
> I lost my mother's watch. And look! my last, or
> next-to-last, of three loved houses went.
>
> The art of losing isn't hard to master.
> I lost two cities, lovely ones. And, vaster,
> some realms I owned, two rivers, a continent.
> I miss them, but it wasn't a disaster.
> —Even losing you (the joking voice, a gesture
> I love) I shan't have lied. It's evident
> the art of losing's not too hard to master
> though it may look like (*Write* it!) like disaster.

95. Ultimately, according to the last two lines of the poem, the art of losing is

   (A) a disaster   (D) not hard to master

   (B) not a disaster   (E) lost

   (C) hard to master

96. The poem is an example of what traditional poetic form?

    (A) Sestina   (D) Rondelet

    (B) Villanelle   (E) Ballad

    (C) Sonnet

97. "One Art" was written by

    (A) Marianne Moore   (D) Elizabeth Bishop

    (B) H.D.   (E) Adrienne Rich

    (C) Sylvia Plath

98. What title is NOT an example of a slave narrative?

    (A) *The Narrative Life of Frederick Douglass*

    (B) *Solomon Northrup's Twelve Years a Slave*

    (C) *The Interesting Narrative of the Life of Olaudah Equiano*

    (D) *Incidents in the Life of a Slave Girl*

    (E) *The Autobiography of an Ex-Colored Man*

99. Which of the following poets is NOT considered a confessional poet?

    (A) Sylvia Plath   (D) Anne Sexton

    (B) Maxine Kumin   (E) John Berryman

    (C) Robert Lowell

100. The papers, now referred to as *The Federalist*, were penned by Alexander Hamilton, John Jay, and James Madison. At the time of publication, however, each essay was signed by

    (A) Noman   (D) Voltaire

    (B) Publius   (E) Nom de plume

    (C) Anonymous

Practice Test 1

CLEP American Literature

Answer Key

1. (C)	26. (D)	51. See below	76. (A)
2. (C)	27. (B)	52. (C)	77. (A)
3. (A)	28. (A)	53. (A)	78. (D)
4. (E)	29. (C)	54. (B)	79. (B)
5. (D)	30. (B)	55. (A)	80. (B)
6. (C)	31. (E)	56. (B)	81. (D)
7. See below	32. (D)	57. (D)	82. (C)
8. (C)	33. (C)	58. (D)	83. (C)
9. (B)	34. (D)	59. (C)	84. (E)
10. (E)	35. (E)	60. (E)	85. (A)
11. (C)	36. (A)	61. (A)	86. (E)
12. (D)	37. (C)	62. (E)	87. (D)
13. (B)	38. (A)	63. (C)	88. (B)
14. (C)	39. (C)	64. (D)	89. (E)
15. (B)	40. (C)	65. (B)	90. (C)
16. (E)	41. (D)	66. (A)	91. See below
17. (B)	42. (D)	67. (C)	92. (D)
18. (A)	43. (A)	68. (A)	93. (E)
19. (D)	44. (C)	69. (D)	94. (D)
20. (A)	45. (C)	70. (C)	95. (A)
21. (E)	46. (D)	71. (D)	96. (B)
22. (E)	47. (E)	72. (A)	97. (D)
23. (A)	48. (C)	73. (A)	98. (E)
24. (B)	49. (E)	74. (D)	99. (B)
25. (D)	50. (D)	75. (D)	100. (B)

7. The Romantic Period   1830–1870
    The Period of Realism and Naturalism   1870–1910
    The Modernist Period   1910–1945

51. Toni Morrison   *The Bluest Eye*
    Sylvia Plath   *The Bell Jar*
    Zora Neale Hurston   *Their Eyes Were Watching God*

91. William Cullen Bryant   "Thanatopsis"
    Carl Sandburg   "The Fog"
    Robert Frost   "Fire and Ice"

Detailed Explanations of Answers

Practice Test 1

1.   **(C)**   Hyperbole is the literary device that uses exaggeration. Similes (A) and metaphors (B) compare unlike items. A synecdoche usually refers to a word (a part) that is used to refer to a whole. Lastly, metonym refers to a term that is not referred to by its name, but by a term that is closely associated to that term (i.e., when we discuss the White House, we often mean the President).

2.   **(C)**   The passage is the first paragraph of Mark Twain's *Huckleberry Finn*, which is narrated by Huck Finn himself. Samuel Clemens (A) is the author of the novel, while Mark Twain (E) is his pseudonym. Jim (D) is the runaway slave that accompanies Huck on his adventure.

3.   **(A)**   Modernist poetry is established on the fact that poetry should exist without having to always mean something or to teach the reader anything. Therefore, MacLeish argued that a poem should just "be." This notion is a reaction to the nineteenth-century, which placed so much weight on the meaning and didactic nature of literature.

4.   **(E)**   Scholars tell us that the term "beat" was a shortened form of "beatnik," "beatified," and "beatific." Its roots are found in the world of jazz to refer to the down and out or the poor and exhausted. The Beats topics included drug experimentation, homosexuality and promiscuity, socialism and radical politics, and Eastern religions. The "hippies" (A) can claim to be descendents of the Beats.

5.   **(D)**   Unlike the other answers, Mather's *Magnalia Christi Americana* (usually translated as *The Ecclesiastical History of New England*) is a religious history. The key words in the question are "ecclesiastical" and "nostalgia." *Sinners in the Hands of an Angry God* (B) and *Personal Narrative* (E) were written by Jonathan Edwards; Mather's *The Wonders of the Invisible World* (C) explores, among other things, witchcraft and evil in America.

6.   **(C)**   It was very popular and even trendy for American authors in the twentieth century to move to Europe, usually London or Paris, to continue to write, research, and soak up the culture. Although "immigrants" (A) and "emigrants" (B) are the literal terms for someone who moves from one country to another, "expatriate" was the commonly used term to describe these writers. These writers chose to

move to Europe, and for the most part, did not obtain a different citizenship. They simply moved to Europe for an extended amount of time.

7.   The Romantic Period was from 1830 to 1870; the Period of Realism and Naturalism occurred between 1870 and 1910; and the Modernist Period lasted from 1910 to 1945.

8.   **(C)**   The spondee is the strongest poetic foot. It contains two stressed syllables that force the reader to emphasize that word over the others in the line. A trochee contains a stressed syllable followed by an unstressed syllable (A); an iamb contains an unstressed syllable followed by a stressed syllable (B); an anapest contains two unstressed syllables followed by a stressed syllable (D); and, a dactyl contains a stressed syllable followed by two unstressed syllables (E).

9.   **(B)**   If a phrase or passage is ambiguous, then it is capable of being understood or interpreted in multiple ways. These passages are intentionally vague or broad in order to allow readers to fill in the blank. If the phrase or passage is ambivalent (A), then that supposes that the author or writer could not (or would not) make up his or her mind.

10.   **(E)**   Robert Frost wrote many poems about nature and human relationships. He is most noted for his creative use of traditional forms, meter, and poetic structure. Robert Service (A) predominantly wrote ballads about the American west. T.S. Eliot (B) was a contemporary of Frost's, but he is better known for breaking traditional poetic conventions.

11.   **(C)**   Many scholars note that "Rip Van Winkle" is an allegorical tale about a man who goes to sleep while a British colonist in America and wakes up an American citizen. The story explores the tensions and difficulties of attaining and defining an American identity during the Revolutionary War. It is also noted that this tale was the first distinctly American story.

12.   **(D)**   You will come across the literary journal *Poetry: A Magazine of Verse* if you read any biography of a modern poet. This magazine (still in print today) fueled and encouraged many famous poetic careers. *The Atlantic Monthly* (A) and *Harper's* (B) were also famous during this time. However, these magazines predominantly published short stories and serialized novels. *The Dial* (E), on the other hand, was the strong arm of the Transcendental movement.

13.   **(B)**   The poetic voice is not necessarily that of the author but that of a "second self" that the poet uses to tell a particular story or to depict a particular event or person. Ventriloquism (A) is not a literary device. Narrative (E) is the story itself; the fiction equivalent of "persona" would be the narrator.

14. **(C)**   The key word in the question is "vernacular." Many regional and ethnic writers utilize dialects to paint a realistic picture of people, their culture, their place in time, and sometimes their education.

15. **(B)**   Dunbar was quite comfortable using dialect in his poetry to explore the lives of Blacks in America. So were Langston Hughes (A) and Gwendolyn Brooks (D). What is unique about Dunbar's use of dialect is that he forms some words that look very little like standard English, whereas, both Hughes's and Brooks's use of dialect was very easy for standard speakers to read. Both Countee Cullen (C) and Sterling Brown (E) wrote predominantly in traditional form and elevated poetic language.

16. **(E)**   The Age of Enlightenment is sometimes referred to as the Age of Reason. Although this movement began in Europe, its influence in America was profound. Some of our nation's greatest thinkers, including Jefferson, Franklin, and religious figure Jonathan Edwards, placed a heavy emphasis on the individual's right and necessity to reason. Romanticism (A) based much authority on the ability to feel and intuit, while Puritanism (D) based all authority on the soul and its relation to God.

17. **(B)**   In *"The Green Hills of Africa"* (1934), Hemingway wrote, "The good writers are Henry James, Stephen Crane, and Mark Twain. That's not the order they're good in. There is no order for good writers.... All modern American literature comes from one book by Mark Twain called *Huckleberry Finn*. If you read it you must stop where the Nigger Jim is stolen from the boys. That is the real end. The rest is just cheating. But it's the best book we've had. All American writing comes from that. There was nothing before. There has been nothing as good since." F. Scott Fitzgerald wrote *The Great Gatsby* (E).

18. **(A)**   There was actually a time in American history when families gathered around the fireplace and read poetry. These incredibly popular writers, The Fireside Poets, wrote poems that were appropriate for memorization and recitation. They were also called The Schoolroom Poets because of their popularity in schools as well as homes. Metaphysical poets (B) were 17th century British poets. Transcendentalists (E) and Romantics (C) were terms used during this same time, but the key term is "famous." These writers were heralded by their readers and critics.

19. **(D)**   Although there are volumes and volumes written about Lincoln's presidency, poet Carl Sandburg's works about Lincoln are still the most read and best-selling. The key word in the question is "Chicago." Sandburg spent his career writing about Illinois—the good, the bad, and the ugly.

20. **(A)**   Margaret Fuller was also a transcendentalist. She is most noted for editing the transcendental journal called *The Dial*. What makes her unique in the movement was her ability to write about transcendental ideas from a feminist angle. "The Great Lawsuit" was later expanded into her book called *Woman in the Nineteenth Century*.

21. **(E)**   There is a legend that states that Williams wrote his famous poem "The Red Wheelbarrow" while tending to a sick patient in an old farm house. Wallace Stevens worked as an insurance agent (A), and as a lawyer (B) for most of his literary career.

22. **(E)**   This is a tricky, but important question. Remember that the term "pilgrims" was given to the group of puritans who immigrated to America in 1620. Those immigrants were dissenters of the Church of England. Scholars note that the puritans, who immigrated in 1630, were traveling for capital and religious reasons. This sermon by John Winthrop was given in 1630 aboard the *Arbella*.

23. **(A)**   A work that references another work (usually classic or biblical) is called an allusion. Don't confuse that word with illusion (B), which is merely a false appearance.

24. **(B)**   "A Model of Christian Charity" is the only work listed written by John Winthrop. The other works were written by Cotton Mather (A) and (D), Jonathan Edwards (C), and Mary Rowlandson (E).

25. **(D)**   Crane is better known for writing realism and naturalism than he is for writing about a particular region. The majority of Twain's work (A) explores the Midwest and Willa Cather (B) is known for her fiction set in Nebraska and the American Southwest. Jack London (C) set most of his fiction in the American Northwest, Alaska, and Canada. Kate Chopin (E) used Louisiana for much of her fiction.

26. **(D)**   The key phrase in this passage is "I lived alone, in the woods." Emerson (A) lived in Concord at the same time, but not alone, in the woods.

27. **(B)**   Thoreau titled his seminal work on the simple life, *Walden*, after the pond where he lived for two years. Students must remember that this sojourn was an experiment. As the passage states, Thoreau returned to civilized life.

28. **(A)**   Realism was a reaction to the ideals of Romanticism. Realism merely explored the realities of human existence. These works are more objective than sentimental novels (C), yet they do maintain a centralized notion of truth, unlike modernism (E) and post-modernism (D). Naturalism (B) is an extension and con-

temporary of realism. Although very similar, those works were inspired by Darwinian thought, and the supposition that humans are controlled by their environment.

29. **(C)**   This poem was written during a time that held traditional, suburban American ideals with much skepticism. According to the poem, dreams and imagination cannot exist in the tranquilized and domestic spaces of the suburbs. Students should note the affluence of the details in the poem like "socks of lace/ And beaded ceintures."

30. **(B)**   This question forces the student to read the poem literally. The question asks students to interpret these "white night-gowns," and asks the reader to follow the "plot" of the poem. Although the poem may implicate the reader (D), the speaker (C), and even poetry editors (E), the poem speaks of people actually living in the houses.

31. **(E)**   Like many modernist poets, Stevens was known for his gentle critiques of modern American life. The more traditional line structures and linear plot movement should cancel Williams (A), Ezra Pound (B), and even H.D. (D).

32. **(D)**   The key phrase in the question is "face in European countries." Exploring differences between American and European cultures is unique to Henry James among the others listed. Howells (A) and Dreiser (B) explored tensions between classes and genders in America. William James (E) was a famous psychologist and Henry's brother.

33. **(C)**   The author and title of the novel should give away this answer. Although the novel implicitly addresses issues concerning sexism (A), racism (B), the American government (D), and even the church (E), the explicit purpose of the novel was to eradicate slavery from America.

34. **(D)**   Augustine St. Clare is the antagonistic, agnostic slave owner who questions the institution of slavery throughout the novel. His young daughter, Eva (B), an innocent abolitionist in her own right, has just died. Her influence on his life is profoundly evident in this passage. Stowe (A), Douglass (C), and Garrison (E) were all ardent abolitionists during this time.

35. **(E)**   Dramatic irony occurs when the readers know more than the characters. We tend to laugh (or at least grin) at this passage because we know Mrs. Mallard is not happy to see her husband again. She was up in her room romanticizing a life without him. Verbal irony (B) occurs when someone says one thing, but means something quite the opposite. This is not the case in this scene. Cosmic irony (C) occurs when the gods or fate have a hand in the outcome of the story.

36. **(A)**   Dissenters, known as Pilgrims, decided to immigrate to the New World in 1620. Other Puritan groups (D) left in 1630. Quakers were also extant in the seventeenth century, as well as separate from Roman Catholicism. They did not, however, immigrate to the New World at this time in history.

37. **(C)**   The prophet Hiawatha is sent by the Mohican master of life, Gitche Manito, to bring peace to the warring Indian nations. Set among the tribes near Lake Superior, Hiawatha and his bride Minnehaha serve the good of humanity and bring a golden age to the natives—that is until the Europeans arrive and send Hiawatha to other adventures. Although the other answers are implicated in American Indian life during colonization, the epic predominantly explores the lives of these Indian tribes.

38. **(A)**   The key theme of this poem is that the natural world shows no compassion, care, or concern for human beings. This is a key concept in naturalism: humans are controlled by an impersonal, uncaring universe. Realism (B) is closely related to naturalism, but it does not maintain philosophical/scientific underpinnings like naturalism. Modernism (E) might even question the veracity of a phrase like "Sir, I exist."

39. **(C)**   Personification is used to give life and human characteristics to inanimate objects. Allowing the universe to respond in human language is an example of personification. Onomatopoeia (A) refers to sound words like "buzz" or "pop." Hyperbole (B) refers to poetic exaggeration.

40. **(C)**   Thoreau did not pay the poll tax because these funds were used to support the institution of slavery and bankroll the war against Mexico. In his mind, this individual act against the government was monumentally just and civil.

41. **(D)**   Mentioning Ezra Pound should give away the answer to this question. Imagism was a part of modernist poetry, but seems to have had a short and brief history. Objectivism (A) was a term used by William Carlos Williams, who also used imagism in his poetry. Visual artists and painters such as Salvador Dali and Pablo Picasso used Cubism (C) and surrealism (B) predominantly.

42. **(D)**   Ambrose Bierce is the only listed author that served in the war and wrote about it. His tales "Chickamauga" and "The Occurrence at Owl Creek Bridge," were influenced by his time as a soldier and are still widely read and anthologized. Stephen Crane (E) was born after the war ended. Bret Harte (B) lived during the Civil War, but his fiction explores the American West, especially California. Hart Crane (C) wrote poetry at the turn of the century.

43. **(A)**   This famous Emily Dickinson poem is a response (and reaction) to John Keats's "Ode on a Grecian Urn" where he argues in the last two lines that "Beauty is truth, truth beauty,—that is all / Ye know on earth, and all ye need to know." This poem supposes that beauty and truth are eternal, identical, and life giving. Dickinson, however, makes the point that beauty and truth kill those who seek them (B), unify seekers in death (C), and are ephemeral (D). What the poem does not argue is that these entities are eternal: "Until the Moss had reached our lips—/ And covered up—our names."

44. **(C)**   Very literally, this poem is set in a tomb and explores the conversation between two dead people.

45. **(C)**   In 1676, several Indian tribes attacked Lancaster, Massachusetts, killing and capturing colonists at will. Mary Rowlandson and some of her children survived the attack only to be "removed" from one location to the next until she was finally ransomed and returned to her home and family. Her narrative is made up of twenty removes. This way of separating sections of the narrative is very unique to Rowlandson's narrative.

46. **(D)**   Booker T. Washington's autobiography *Up from Slavery* is arguably the seminal work on the Black experience at the turn of the century. The title not only refers to Washington's progress from a son of a slave to a college president and internationally known writer and orator, but it also refers to his ideals for all former slaves and their descendents. His book can be read as an argument for how free Blacks should interact with white-dominated America. W.E.B. Du Bois wrote *The Souls of Black Folks* (A). Maya Angelou wrote *I Know Why the Caged Bird Sings* (B). James Weldon Johnson wrote *Autobiography of an Ex-Colored Man* (C), and, Ralph Ellison wrote *Invisible Man* (E).

47. **(E)**   Stories of the gothic fiction genre are mysterious, suspenseful, and terrifying. Its many conventions include dark castles or homes, storms, supernatural appearances, psychological issues, victimized women, and lots of screaming. This genre was made famous in eighteenth-century Britain (especially Mary Shelley's *Frankenstein*). However, this genre also has an important American presence, especially in southern literature. Charles Brockden Brown, Edgar Allan Poe, Henry James, William Faulkner, and even Harriet Beecher Stowe used the genre to create suspenseful and frightening scenes. Sentimental (A) and realist (B) fiction were not always scary in the same way. Moreover, fantasy (D) and science fiction (C) are also considered products of gothic fiction.

48. **(C)**   Historians tells us that Ezra Pound sent Doolittle's poems to Harriet Monroe, publisher of *Poetry*, using the simple moniker H.D. These three collections, together, became known as *Trilogy*.

49. **(E)** Willa Cather is predominantly known as a Midwestern writer. Her books, *O! Pioneers* and *My Antonia,* were set in Nebraska. Although Cather was born in Virginia, as a young girl, she moved with her family to Nebraska. Red Cloud, Nebraska, still makes the claim of being Cather's hometown.

50. **(D)** Although *Typee* (A), *Omoo* (B), and *White-Jacket* (E) are all considered sea narratives, *Moby-Dick* is regarded as one of the greatest American novels. The narrator, Ishmael, takes the reader along a journey with Captain Ahab to kill the elusive white whale.

51. Toni Morrison wrote *The Bluest Eye*; Sylvia Plath authored *The Bell Jar*; and Zora Neale Hurston penned *Their Eyes Were Watching God.*

52. **(C)** The spiritual autobiography was made popular in the seventeenth century with texts like Jonathan Edwards' *Personal Narrative* and Anne Bradstreet's "To My Dear Children." Puritanism influenced these texts greatly. The genre continued to grow and evolve as the country (and its religious atmosphere) grew and evolved. Scholars argue that *The Autobiography of Benjamin Franklin* is the deistic/enlightenment's version of the spiritual autobiography. The jeremiad (D), which was also popular during the seventeenth century, is a lament that combines religious obedience with civic responsibility.

53. **(A)** Sacco and Vanzetti were Italian immigrants who were convicted and executed for murder in Massachusetts. Their political leanings became as controversial as their crime. Millay organized a group of writers to protest the executions. She tried to persuade the governor of Massachusetts to pardon the men.

54. **(B)** The parable now called "The Wise and Foolish Builders" can be found in the Bible. The gospels according to Matthew and Luke each tell the story of a man who foolishly builds his house on sand (only to watch a storm destroy it) and the man who wisely builds his house upon a rock. The parable explores what foundations upon which humans build their lives.

55. **(A)** Millay writes several poems where she plays lightly with biblical truths and other societal morals. In this poem, she seems to argue that although building a house on the rock would be more practical and responsible, the house built on the sand will be much more beautiful and artistic.

56. **(B)** Bartleby is a complicated figure for most scholars. He politely, yet assertively, replies, "I would prefer not to" to any request the Lawyer makes. The key to answering this question correctly is knowing that, although Bartleby refused to do anything for the Lawyer, he kept his job until almost the end of the story. "As

you wish" (A) was the common response given by Wesley in the popular movie *The Princess Bride*.

57. **(D)** Each poet on the list is considered a modernist poet and each poet did play with traditional poetic conventions. However, Cummings is most noted for his ability to combine words and ignore rules regarding capitalization and line spacing. A few of his famous poems were "In just-," "Buffalo Bill's," and "i thank You God for most this amazing."

58. **(D)** The key phrase in this question is "literary arm of the Black Power Movement." This movement was highly politically and sometimes militantly charged. The Harlem Renaissance (A) is known more for its exploration of Black life in America, while the Black Arts Movement (D) was known more for its political engagement. The Black Panthers (B) were a militant group in the 1960s that promoted political and social agitation for Black rights.

59. **(C)** Although the story takes place in a New England hotel (B), and the title of the story deals with interior design (A), one of the major sub-plots of the story explores how the husband patronizes and belittles his wife in the name of "helping" her. One can argue that the woman's lack of agency and power in her own marriage drives her to insanity.

60. **(E)** Of the listed writers, Bradstreet, a Puritan wife and mother, is the only one to be known for her positive marital poetry. Millay (D) certainly talked about romantic relationships, but she never mentions husbands. Rowlandson (B) did not write poetry. And, Phillis Wheatley's (A) most famous poetry was written and published before she married.

61. **(A)** Iambic pentameter is the most common meter in traditional poetry. Each line contains five feet, and each foot contains an unstressed syllable followed by a stressed syllable (i.e., buh-bump, buh-bump, etc.). Remember, a trochee (C) and (D) is a foot that contains a stressed syllable followed by an unstressed syllable.

62. **(E)** Romanticism was a direct reaction to the Age of Enlightenment (A), and the Age of Enlightenment, with its focus on reason, was a reaction to the Puritans' (B) focus on the soul and its relation to God. Students should note that realism (C) reacted to romantic idealism with a healthy dose of realism.

63. **(C)** The grotesque is a common trope in modern American literature. Southern writers like Faulkner, Welty, and O'Connor, all used the grotesque to characterize and comment on southern culture. The absurd (A) is a term usually applied to drama, and surreal (B) is a term usually applied to the visual arts.

64. **(D)** This is an important question because Dreiser is commonly associated with a group of writers who, at the beginning of the twentieth century, put Chicago on the literary map. Writers who wrote during the Chicago Renaissance include Edgar Lee Masters, Sherwood Anderson, Theodore Dreiser, Upton Sinclair, and Carl Sandburg.

65. **(B)** This poem was untitled in the first edition of *Leaves of Grass* (A). However, in subsequent editions, Whitman titled it "Song of Myself." These lines reflect Whitman's wish to "absorb the nation and also be absorbed by it." The other poems listed can be found in *Leaves of Grass*.

66. **(A)** Emersonian transcendentalism focuses on the divinity of the individual. This idea eventually caused Emerson to denounce the divinity of Christ, which at the time (1830s) was still a part of Unitarian (B) theology. Both the Puritans (D) and the Quakers (C) believed that humans were not divine.

67. **(C)** Whitman's *Leaves of Grass* went under a number of revisions before his death in 1892. At his death, *Leaves of Grass* contained sub-sections: "Drum-Taps" (A), "Calamus" (D), and "Children of Adam" (E).

68. **(A)** Gatsby and the narrator, Nick, lived in West Egg (A), which was commonly associated with "new money." East Egg (B) symbolized the traditional aristocracy of New York or "old money." The Valley of the Ashes (E) was the industrial and impoverished strip between West Egg and East Egg and came to symbolize the moral degradation of America.

69. **(D)** Wheatley's poem about slavery and being brought to America is quite poignant and assertive for its time. The poem does imply that Africans cannot be Christians (A) and that Africans are not enlightened (B). Targeting white audiences (E), the poem also implies that Africans can (and will) go to heaven (C). Lastly, scholars argue whether the poem's implications were Wheatley's intention. Although this poem is a great example of African art, the poem does not imply this truth.

70. **(C)** Wheatley wrote all of her poems while a slave in the home of an upper-class Boston family. She famously defended the authenticity of her work to a group of New England dignitaries before she was allowed to publish her work.

71. **(D)** Yoknapatawpha is the fictional setting of most of Faulkner's fiction. Most scholars agree that this county and its seat, Jefferson, are loosely based on Faulkner's home county in Mississippi, Lafayette, and the county seat, Oxford.

72. **(A)**   There is nothing sexual (B) about Du Bois's vision of racism (D). Nor does the term have to do with mental illness (E). His words are best to define double consciousness: "The history of the American Negro is the history of this strife,—this longing to attain self-conscious manhood, to merge his double self into a better and truer self."

73. **(A)**   Robert Penn Warren wrote *All the King's Men.*

74. **(D)**   Allen Ginsberg, like his spiritual/poetic mentor Walt Whitman, was known for breaking traditional poetic forms. His use of open (or free) verse allowed him to play with the length of poetic lines to mimic human breath and speech patterns. Imagism (A) and objectivism (B) were poetic forms applied by modernist poets like Pound and Williams, respectively. Sestinas (C) and clerihews (E) are two other types of poetic forms.

75. **(D)**   The excerpt is the opening stanza of "Howl"—the poem that made Ginsberg famous and infamous at the same time. Jack Kerouac wrote *On the Road* (C), and Walt Whitman wrote "Song of Myself" (E).

76. **(A)**   Although much of Hawthorne's work is symbolic or allegoric (E), he is most noted for his work in Romance. In the preface to *The House of the Seven Gables*, he writes, "The point of view in which this tale comes under the Romantic definition lies in the attempt to connect a bygone time with the very present that is flitting away from us . . . the book . . . having a great deal more to do with the clouds overhead than with any portion of the actual soil of the County of Essex."

77. **(A)**   All of the writers listed, except for Stephen Crane, were known for writing tales of the west and uncharted territories. However, London's *The Call of the Wild* is still widely read and appreciated.

78. **(D)**   Cisneros is most widely known for her collection of vignettes titled *The House on Mango Street*. This work explores the lives of a Mexican-American family moving around the neighborhoods of Chicago. The other writers on the list predominantly write about the lives of twentieth-century American Indians.

79. **(B)**   Much of this history is cloaked in myth and legend. Scholars, however, are certain that the woman's name was Pocahontas. Sacajawea (A) joined the Lewis and Clark expeditions between 1804-1806.

80. **(B)**   Although there are strict conventions that help define the classic epic, modern novels like *The Grapes of Wrath* have been labeled epics because of their "largeness." In essence, the novel encapsulates the epic spirit by exploring the identity of a nation during a trying time, and especially the identity of a central

figure as he struggles to find his place within that particular cultural moment. The novel does mourn death (A), contains many symbols (D), and can be read as an allegory of American ideals (C). Scholars are clear, however, that Steinbeck's epic best depicts America during the Great Depression.

81. **(D)** Whitman rejected traditional poetic forms. It was labeled "free verse" by many writers because this type of poetry seemed to free the poet from the confines of traditional poetic forms. Whitman did explore eros (A) in his poetry. Additionally, he utilized the catalog (B), confession (E), and the American identity (C), but his use of free (or open) form changed American poetry forever.

82. **(C)** Eugene O'Neill grew up in a troubled, complex family and many of his dramas are about the modern American family.

83. **(C)** The date 1624 is the key to answering this question correctly. Christopher Columbus (E) was dead. Edward Taylor (D) wasn't born yet. Miles Standish (B) and William Bradford (A) were Puritans who immigrated to America in 1620. John Smith, historians note, helped colonize Virginia as early as 1607.

84. **(E)** Ralph Ellison's *Invisible Man* is a scathing exploration of what it means to be a Black man in mid-twentieth-century America. The unnamed narrator does become a member of an underground society (B), but this membership is not what makes him invisible. In actuality, he creates quite a public persona while associated with that group. Students should not confuse this novel with H.G Wells's *The Invisible Man*, which tells the story of a man who actually becomes invisible (D).

85. **(A)** The key phrase in this question is "literary example." Sarcasm is not necessarily only a literary device, so the narrator uses sarcasm to prove a point that although invisible (Black), he still possesses intellect. The other answers are actual literary devices.

86. **(E)** *Invisible Man* was Ralph Ellison's only published novel while he lived. James Baldwin (A) is known for books like *Going to Meet the Man*. Richard Wright (C) wrote *Black Boy* and *Native Son*. H.G. Wells (B) wrote *The Invisible Man*. Langston Hughes (D) was a poet during the Harlem Renaissance.

87. **(D)** The characters are found in *The Scarlet Letter* and not in any of the other Hawthorne texts listed.

88. **(B)** Literary naturalism was heavily influenced by the increasing importance of scientific discovery in the twentieth century, especially the work of Charles Darwin. Realism (A) is closely related to naturalism, yet it does not have scientific determinism attached to it.

89. **(E)**   Like Whitman, Dickinson's poetry changed the way Americans wrote and understood poetry. Although she commonly used traditional poetic conventions like rhyme and meter, she is most famous for her abundant use of the dash (A), capitalization (B), metaphor (C), and hymn measure (D).

90. **(C)**   Although the other works on the list are products of the confessional era of literature, *The Bell Jar* is the only novel. Robert Lowell's *Life Studies* (E) does, however, contain small pieces of prose. The other three works are all poetry collections: John Berryman's *Dream Songs* (D) and Plath's *The Colossus* (B) and *Ariel* (A).

91.   William Cullen Bryant wrote "Thanatopsis"; Carl Sandburg penned "The Fog"; and Robert Frost wrote "Fire and Ice."

92. **(D)**   Blanche lives with her sister Stella and Stella's husband Stanley.

93. **(E)**   Poe wrote much more than scary short stories. He was known as a dramatist, a fine essayist, and a literary critic. The other authors on the list did write essays, but Poe is the only one known for his work on literary criticism.

94. **(D)**   The novel is quite clear that although Bigger did commit the crimes (C), his mother was not an exemplary parental figure (A), and his employer (E) was a hypocritical philanthropist who gave money to Black organizations, but made sure that those people never left the "projects." The real evil of the novel belongs to the racist American institutions already set in place before Bigger's birth.

95. **(A)**   The key phrase in this poem is the parenthetical, italicized, and emphatically punctuated plea "Write it!" This should give the reader plenty of clues that writing that last word would be incredibly difficult. Although the speaker tries to play off losing as not a disaster (B), it is the placement of the phrase and its use of punctuation and italics that encourages readers to question everything the speaker has argued thus far.

96. **(B)**   Traditionally, the villanelle contains 19 lines with a strict repetitive pattern. The villanelle repeats the first and third lines throughout the poem. The sestina (A) is a 39-line poem that uses the same six words to end the lines of each sestet. The sonnet (C) only contains fourteen lines, and no repetition is used.

97. **(D)**   The key to answering this question is knowing that Bishop did, more so than the others listed, play with traditional poetic forms throughout her career. Rich (E) gave up formal poetry for free verse early in her career.

98. **(E)** James Weldon Johnson wrote *The Autobiography of an Ex-Colored Man* anonymously in 1912, and then published it under his name in 1927. Scholars note that this text bridged the gap between slave narratives of the previous century and the modern Black novel of the latter twentieth century. Harriet Jacobs wrote *Incidents in the Life of a Slave Girl* (D).

99. **(B)** Although Maxine Kumin was a good friend to Anne Sexton until Sexton's death, Kumin's poetry was never labeled strictly confessional. She did write about personal experiences, but her poems always contained a universal flavor.

100. **(B)** When originally published, the essays were signed "Publius." Noman (A) was the name Odysseus gave the Cyclops. Nom de plume (E) is another term used for pseudonym, and Voltaire (D) was an eighteenth-century, European satirist.

PRACTICE TEST 2

CLEP American Literature

Also available at the REA Study Center (*www.rea.com/studycenter*)

This practice test is also offered online at the REA Study Center. Since all CLEP exams are administered on computer, we recommend that you take the online version of the test to receive these added benefits:

- **Timed testing conditions** – Gauge how much time you can spend on each question.
- **Automatic scoring** – Find out how you did on the test, instantly.
- **On-screen detailed explanations of answers** – Learn not just the correct answers, but why the other answer choices are incorrect.
- **Diagnostic score reports** – Pinpoint where you're strongest and where you need to focus your study.

Practice Test 2

CLEP American Literature

Answer Sheet

1. Ⓐ Ⓑ Ⓒ Ⓓ Ⓔ	35. Ⓐ Ⓑ Ⓒ Ⓓ Ⓔ	69. Ⓐ Ⓑ Ⓒ Ⓓ Ⓔ
2. Ⓐ Ⓑ Ⓒ Ⓓ Ⓔ	36. Ⓐ Ⓑ Ⓒ Ⓓ Ⓔ	70. Ⓐ Ⓑ Ⓒ Ⓓ Ⓔ
3. Ⓐ Ⓑ Ⓒ Ⓓ Ⓔ	37. Ⓐ Ⓑ Ⓒ Ⓓ Ⓔ	71. Ⓐ Ⓑ Ⓒ Ⓓ Ⓔ
4. Ⓐ Ⓑ Ⓒ Ⓓ Ⓔ	38. Ⓐ Ⓑ Ⓒ Ⓓ Ⓔ	72. Ⓐ Ⓑ Ⓒ Ⓓ Ⓔ
5. Ⓐ Ⓑ Ⓒ Ⓓ Ⓔ	39. Ⓐ Ⓑ Ⓒ Ⓓ Ⓔ	73. Ⓐ Ⓑ Ⓒ Ⓓ Ⓔ
6. Ⓐ Ⓑ Ⓒ Ⓓ Ⓔ	40. Ⓐ Ⓑ Ⓒ Ⓓ Ⓔ	74. Ⓐ Ⓑ Ⓒ Ⓓ Ⓔ
7. Ⓐ Ⓑ Ⓒ Ⓓ Ⓔ	41. Ⓐ Ⓑ Ⓒ Ⓓ Ⓔ	75. Ⓐ Ⓑ Ⓒ Ⓓ Ⓔ
8. Ⓐ Ⓑ Ⓒ Ⓓ Ⓔ	42. Ⓐ Ⓑ Ⓒ Ⓓ Ⓔ	76. Ⓐ Ⓑ Ⓒ Ⓓ Ⓔ
9. Ⓐ Ⓑ Ⓒ Ⓓ Ⓔ	43. Ⓐ Ⓑ Ⓒ Ⓓ Ⓔ	77. Ⓐ Ⓑ Ⓒ Ⓓ Ⓔ
10. Ⓐ Ⓑ Ⓒ Ⓓ Ⓔ	44. Ⓐ Ⓑ Ⓒ Ⓓ Ⓔ	78. Ⓐ Ⓑ Ⓒ Ⓓ Ⓔ
11. Ⓐ Ⓑ Ⓒ Ⓓ Ⓔ	45. Ⓐ Ⓑ Ⓒ Ⓓ Ⓔ	79. Ⓐ Ⓑ Ⓒ Ⓓ Ⓔ
12. Ⓐ Ⓑ Ⓒ Ⓓ Ⓔ	46. Ⓐ Ⓑ Ⓒ Ⓓ Ⓔ	80. Ⓐ Ⓑ Ⓒ Ⓓ Ⓔ
13. Ⓐ Ⓑ Ⓒ Ⓓ Ⓔ	47. Ⓐ Ⓑ Ⓒ Ⓓ Ⓔ	81. Ⓐ Ⓑ Ⓒ Ⓓ Ⓔ
14. Ⓐ Ⓑ Ⓒ Ⓓ Ⓔ	48. Ⓐ Ⓑ Ⓒ Ⓓ Ⓔ	82. Ⓐ Ⓑ Ⓒ Ⓓ Ⓔ
15. Ⓐ Ⓑ Ⓒ Ⓓ Ⓔ	49. Ⓐ Ⓑ Ⓒ Ⓓ Ⓔ	83. Ⓐ Ⓑ Ⓒ Ⓓ Ⓔ
16. Ⓐ Ⓑ Ⓒ Ⓓ Ⓔ	50. Ⓐ Ⓑ Ⓒ Ⓓ Ⓔ	84. Ⓐ Ⓑ Ⓒ Ⓓ Ⓔ
17. Ⓐ Ⓑ Ⓒ Ⓓ Ⓔ	51. Ⓐ Ⓑ Ⓒ Ⓓ Ⓔ	85. Ⓐ Ⓑ Ⓒ Ⓓ Ⓔ
18. Ⓐ Ⓑ Ⓒ Ⓓ Ⓔ	52. Ⓐ Ⓑ Ⓒ Ⓓ Ⓔ	86. Ⓐ Ⓑ Ⓒ Ⓓ Ⓔ
19. Ⓐ Ⓑ Ⓒ Ⓓ Ⓔ	53. Ⓐ Ⓑ Ⓒ Ⓓ Ⓔ	87. Ⓐ Ⓑ Ⓒ Ⓓ Ⓔ
20. Ⓐ Ⓑ Ⓒ Ⓓ Ⓔ	54. Ⓐ Ⓑ Ⓒ Ⓓ Ⓔ	88. Ⓐ Ⓑ Ⓒ Ⓓ Ⓔ
21. Ⓐ Ⓑ Ⓒ Ⓓ Ⓔ	55. Ⓐ Ⓑ Ⓒ Ⓓ Ⓔ	89. Ⓐ Ⓑ Ⓒ Ⓓ Ⓔ
22. Ⓐ Ⓑ Ⓒ Ⓓ Ⓔ	56. Ⓐ Ⓑ Ⓒ Ⓓ Ⓔ	90. Ⓐ Ⓑ Ⓒ Ⓓ Ⓔ
23. Ⓐ Ⓑ Ⓒ Ⓓ Ⓔ	57. Ⓐ Ⓑ Ⓒ Ⓓ Ⓔ	91. Ⓐ Ⓑ Ⓒ Ⓓ Ⓔ
24. Ⓐ Ⓑ Ⓒ Ⓓ Ⓔ	58. Ⓐ Ⓑ Ⓒ Ⓓ Ⓔ	92. Ⓐ Ⓑ Ⓒ Ⓓ Ⓔ
25. Ⓐ Ⓑ Ⓒ Ⓓ Ⓔ	59. Ⓐ Ⓑ Ⓒ Ⓓ Ⓔ	93. Ⓐ Ⓑ Ⓒ Ⓓ Ⓔ
26. Ⓐ Ⓑ Ⓒ Ⓓ Ⓔ	60. Ⓐ Ⓑ Ⓒ Ⓓ Ⓔ	94. Ⓐ Ⓑ Ⓒ Ⓓ Ⓔ
27. Ⓐ Ⓑ Ⓒ Ⓓ Ⓔ	61. Ⓐ Ⓑ Ⓒ Ⓓ Ⓔ	95. Ⓐ Ⓑ Ⓒ Ⓓ Ⓔ
28. Ⓐ Ⓑ Ⓒ Ⓓ Ⓔ	62. Ⓐ Ⓑ Ⓒ Ⓓ Ⓔ	96. Ⓐ Ⓑ Ⓒ Ⓓ Ⓔ
29. Ⓐ Ⓑ Ⓒ Ⓓ Ⓔ	63. Ⓐ Ⓑ Ⓒ Ⓓ Ⓔ	97. Ⓐ Ⓑ Ⓒ Ⓓ Ⓔ
30. Ⓐ Ⓑ Ⓒ Ⓓ Ⓔ	64. Ⓐ Ⓑ Ⓒ Ⓓ Ⓔ	98. Ⓐ Ⓑ Ⓒ Ⓓ Ⓔ
31. Ⓐ Ⓑ Ⓒ Ⓓ Ⓔ	65. Ⓐ Ⓑ Ⓒ Ⓓ Ⓔ	99. Ⓐ Ⓑ Ⓒ Ⓓ Ⓔ
32. Ⓐ Ⓑ Ⓒ Ⓓ Ⓔ	66. Ⓐ Ⓑ Ⓒ Ⓓ Ⓔ	100. Ⓐ Ⓑ Ⓒ Ⓓ Ⓔ
33. Ⓐ Ⓑ Ⓒ Ⓓ Ⓔ	67. Ⓐ Ⓑ Ⓒ Ⓓ Ⓔ	
34. Ⓐ Ⓑ Ⓒ Ⓓ Ⓔ	68. Ⓐ Ⓑ Ⓒ Ⓓ Ⓔ	

Practice Test 2

CLEP American Literature

(Answer sheet on facing page.)

TIME: 90 Minutes
100 Questions

DIRECTIONS: Each of the questions or incomplete statements below is followed by five possible answers or completions. Select the best choice in each case and fill in the corresponding oval on the answer sheet. Some questions will ask you to match terms with one another or to put a list in chronological order.

---

1. Willa Cather's novels, especially *O! Pioneers*, is a good example of

    (A) naturalism   (D) allegory

    (B) satire   (E) propaganda

    (C) regionalism

Questions 2–4

   "Leave my loneliness unbroken—quit the bust above my door!
   Take thy beak from out my heart, and take thy form from off my door!"
   Quoth the raven, "Nevermore"

2. Who is the author of the excerpt?

    (A) Edgar Allan Poe   (D) Sylvia Plath

    (B) Zora Neale Hurston   (E) James Fenimore Cooper

    (C) Ralph Ellison

3. For whom does the speaker of this poem mourn?

    (A) Faith   (D) Lenore

    (B) Annabel Lee   (E) The raven

    (C) Evangeline

4. The raven is sitting on top of the bust of what Greek god?

    (A) Zeus   (D) Venus

    (B) Athena   (E) Hermes

    (C) Vulcan

5. Which of the following authors is NOT considered a southern writer?

    (A) Flannery O'Connor   (D) Toni Morrison

    (B) Eudora Welty   (E) Carson McCullers

    (C) William Faulkner

Questions 6–7

> 'Twas mercy brought me from my Pagan land,
> Taught my benighted soul to understand
> That there's a God, that there's a Saviour too:
> Once I redemption neither sought nor knew.
>
> Some view our sable race with scornful eye,
> "Their colour is a diabolic die."
> Remember, Christians, Negros, black as Cain,
> May be refin'd, and join th' angelic train.

6. Phillis Wheatley's "On Being Brought from Africa to America" utilizes which metrical device?

    (A) Hymnal measure   (D) Caesura

    (B) Trochaic substitution   (E) Endstop

    (C) Heroic couplets

7. "Cain" is an allusion to what ancient text?

    (A) *Gilgamesh*   (D) *The Bible*

    (B) A Jean Toomer novel   (E) *The Odyssey*

    (C) *The Bhagavad Gita*

8.   Which of the following authors is NOT considered part of the Beat Genera-
     tion?

     (A)   Allen Ginsberg   (D)   Lawrence Ferlinghetti

     (B)   William S. Burroughs   (E)   Andy Warhol

     (C)   Jack Kerouac

Questions 9–11

   "When Caroline Meeber boarded the afternoon train for Chicago,
her total outfit consisted of a small trunk, a cheap imitation alligator-
skin satchel, a small lunch in a paper box, and a yellow leather snap
purse, containing her ticket, a scrap of paper with her sister's address
in Van Buren Street, and four dollars in money. It was August, 1889.
She was eighteen years of age, bright, timid, and full of the illusions of
ignorance and youth."

9.   The title of this Theodore Dreiser novel is taken from Caroline's nickname,
     Sister

     (A)   Christian   (D)   Meebs

     (B)   Carrie   (E)   Carol

     (C)   Liney

10. What American literary movement would the year 1889 be part of?

     (A)   Romanticism

     (B)   The Age of Enlightenment

     (C)   Modernism

     (D)   Realism

     (E)   Surrealism

11. What lucrative career did Caroline embark upon, after many failed attempts
     with common laborer jobs, in New York City?

     (A)   Actor   (D)   Dancer

     (B)   Painter   (E)   Mayor

     (C)   Prostitute

12. In the second part of *The Autobiography of Benjamin Franklin*, he desires to embrace each of the following virtues: Temperance, Silence, Order, Resolution, Frugality, Industry, Sincerity, Justice, Moderation, Cleanliness, Tranquility, Chastity, and Humility. During the Age of Enlightenment, the individual who perfected these virtues would reach

    (A)   nirvana   (D)   moral perfection

    (B)   a transcendent state   (E)   the inner light

    (C)   salvation

13. Allen Ginsberg's poem "A Supermarket in California" references what famous American poet in the following line: "I saw you, _____, childless, lonely old grubber, poking among the meats in the refrigerator and eyeing the grocery boys"?

    (A)   Ralph Waldo Emerson   (D)   T.S. Eliot

    (B)   Walt Whitman   (E)   Emily Dickinson

    (C)   Robert Frost

Questions 14–15

> Often I think of the beautiful town
> That is seated by the sea;
> Often in thought go up and down
> The pleasant streets of that dear old town,
> And my youth comes back to me.   5
> And a verse of a Lapland song
> Is haunting my memory still:
> 'A boy's will is the wind's will,
> And the thoughts of youth are long, long thoughts.'

14. Which of the following does NOT describe the possible themes of Henry Wadsworth Longfellow's "My Lost Youth"?

    (A)   The connection between the past and the present

    (B)   The fleeting childhood

    (C)   Mourning and death

    (D)   Differences between boys and girls

    (E)   Romantic immortality of youth

15. What famous twentieth-century poet titled his first poetry collection, *A Boy's Will*, after this Longfellow poem?

    (A) T.S. Eliot   (D) Robert Frost

    (B) Langston Hughes   (E) Shel Silverstein

    (C) Carl Sandburg

16. Place the name of each of the following African American authors beside the title of the book he/she authored.

    Phillis Wheatley

    W.E.B. DuBois

    Ralph Ellison

    _____ *Invisible Man*

    _____ *The Souls of Black Folks*

    _____ *Poems on Various Subjects, Religious and Moral*

17. In John Winthrop's "A Model of Christian Charity," he urges his Puritan listeners to become

    (A) the salt of the earth

    (B) a city on a hill

    (C) a light to the world

    (D) a voice on the mountaintop

    (E) purified

18. Many scholars refer to Augie in Saul Bellow's *The Adventures of Augie March* as the *everyman*—he experiences poverty, wealth, love, loss, education, and ignorance. It is the quintessential story of man versus society. This novel is a genre of fiction that uses elements of satire and realism to explore the adventures of a lower class citizen in a corrupt or jaded society and is often referred to as a(n)

    (A) jeremiad   (D) fabliaux

    (B) allegory   (E) epiphany

    (C) picaresque

Questions 19–21

"The God that holds you over the pit of hell, much as one holds a spider, or some loathsome insect, over the fire, abhors you, and is dreadfully provoked; his wrath towards you burns like fire; he looks upon you as worthy of nothing else, but to be cast into the fire; he is of purer eyes than to bear to have you in his sight; you are ten thousand times so abominable in his eyes as the most hateful venomous serpent is in ours."

19. The passage above is notable chiefly for its use (sometimes referred to as a conceit) of

   (A) extended metaphor   (D) hyperbole

   (B) alliteration   (E) onomatopoeia

   (C) allusion

20. The "you" in this excerpt most probably refers to

   (A) the Queen of England

   (B) Quakers

   (C) Shakers

   (D) sinners in a local Puritan church

   (E) the Plymouth Bay colony

21. Some historians/scholars note that Jonathan Edwards' sermons contained healthy mixtures of what two eras?

   (A) Enlightenment and Realism

   (B) Enlightenment and Romanticism

   (C) Enlightenment and Puritanism

   (D) Enlightenment and Sentimentality

   (E) Enlightenment and Transcendentalism

22. Toni Morrison's first novel, *The Bluest Eye*, tells the story of little Pecola Breedlove, who wants nothing more than to

   (A) be loved   (D) have blonde hair

   (B) have a boyfriend   (E) have blue eyes

   (C) get along with her parents

23. Mary Rowlandson's *A Narrative of the Captivity and Restoration of Mary Rowlandson* (also called *The Sovereignty and Goodness of God*) is best referred to as a(n)

    (A) spiritual autobiography   (D) captivity narrative

    (B) jeremiad   (E) epistolary novel

    (C) diary

24. Arthur Miller's play *The Crucible* tells the story of what historical event?

    (A) The trial of Nat Turner

    (B) The Scopes Trial

    (C) The Salem Witch Trials

    (D) The Trials of Sacco and Vanzetti

    (E) John Brown's trial

25. In 1630, John Winthrop delivered his sermon "A Model of Christian Charity" on which ship that was anchored in the Massachusetts Bay?

    (A) *Arbella*   (D) *San Dominick*

    (B) *Mayflower*   (E) *Nina*

    (C) *Pinta*

26. William Cullen Bryant's famous poem "Thanatopsis" concerns itself with

    (A) the walking dead

    (B) life after death

    (C) contemplation of death

    (D) a death dream

    (E) one's last words before death

Questions 27–30

Whenever Richard Cory went down town,
We people on the pavement looked at him:
He was a gentleman from sole to crown,
Clean favored, and imperially slim.

And he was always quietly arrayed,
And he was always human when he talked;
But still he fluttered pulses when he said,
"Good-morning," and he glittered when he walked.

And he was rich, richer than a king—
And admirably schooled in every grace:
In fine, we thought that he was everything
To make us wish that we were in his place.

So on we worked, and waited for the light,
And went without the meat, and cursed the bread;
And Richard Cory, one calm summer night,
Went home and put a bullet through his head.

27.   The last two lines create a powerful end by using what literary device?

   (A)   Verbal irony   (D)   Situational irony

   (B)   Dramatic irony   (E)   Hyperbole

   (C)   Cosmic irony

28.   This poem is an example of a(n)

   (A)   lyric   (D)   ode

   (B)   elegy   (E)   ballad

   (C)   narrative

29.   "Richard Cory" was written by

   (A)   T.S. Eliot   (D)   Edgar Lee Masters

   (B)   Shel Silverstein   (E)   Carl Sandburg

   (C)   Edwin Arlington Robinson

30.   Which poem was NOT written by Edwin Arlington Robinson?

   (A)   "Miniver Cheevy"   (D)   "Mr. Flood's Party"

   (B)   "Luke Havergal"   (E)   "Eros Turannos"

   (C)   "Ezra Bartlett"

31. Elizabeth Bishop had a longstanding poetic/professional relationship with a Confessional poet that produced many wonderful poems that could be read as a conversation between the two. Two poems that explore that relationship are "The Armadillo" and "Skunk Hour." Bishop composed "The Armadillo." Who wrote "Skunk Hour"?

   (A) John Berryman   (D) Anne Sexton

   (B) Sylvia Plath   (E) Allen Ginsberg

   (C) Robert Lowell

Questions 32–34

> Do not weep, maiden, for war is kind.
> Because your lover threw wild hands toward the sky
> And the affrighted steed ran on alone,
> Do not weep.
> War is kind.
>
> Hoarse, booming drums of the regiment,
> Little souls who thirst for fight,
> These men were born to drill and die.
> The unexplained glory flies above them,
> Great is the battle-god, great, and his kingdom —
> A field where a thousand corpses lie.
>
> Do not weep, babe, for war is kind.
> Because your father tumbled in the yellow trenches,
> Raged at his breast, gulped and died,
> Do not weep.
> War is kind.
>
> Swift blazing flag of the regiment,
> Eagle with crest of red and gold,
> These men were born to drill and die.
> Point for them the virtue of slaughter,
> Make plain to them the excellence of killing
> And a field where a thousand corpses lie.
>
> Mother whose heart hung humble as a button
> On the bright splendid shroud of your son,
> Do not weep.
> War is kind.

32. Which of the following statements are TRUE?

    (A) This poem is ironic.

    (B) This poem is not ironic.

    (C) This poem was written by a war nurse.

    (D) This poem was written by a war general.

    (E) This poem was written by a European.

33. "These men were born to drill and die" is an excellent example of what literary movement?

    (A) Realism   (D) Modernism

    (B) Naturalism   (E) Romanticism

    (C) Regionalism

34. This poem was inspired by what American war?

    (A) The Spanish-American War (D) The Revolutionary War

    (B) The War of 1812   (E) World War I

    (C) The French-Indian War

35. *Of Plimoth Plantation*, written over a period of 20 years, recalls the history of the Plymouth colony. *Of Plimoth Plantation* was written by

    (A) John Smith   (D) Miles Standish

    (B) Edward Taylor   (E) John Winthrop

    (C) William Bradford

Questions 36–37

> "First having read the book of myths,
> and loaded the camera,
> and checked the edge of the knife-blade,
> I put on/the body-armor of black rubber
> the absurd flippers
> the grave and awkward mask."

36. Using the images and word choices of the poem, how would you describe the speaker's relationship with diving?

    (A) Novice

    (D) Loving

    (B) Expert

    (E) Apprehensive

    (C) Intermediate

37. Adrienne Rich's poem "Diving into the Wreck" uses scuba diving as an extended metaphor for

    (A) American publishing

    (D) romantic relationships

    (B) American Christianity

    (E) homosexuality

    (C) parenthood

38. William Bradford was the leader of these seventeenth-century separatists who immigrated to the New World in 1620. They were known as

    (A) dissenters

    (D) colonists

    (B) Pilgrims

    (E) New Englanders

    (C) Puritans

39. Ralph Waldo Emerson, Margaret Fuller, and, to some extent, Henry David Thoreau, were all a part of what literary/philosophical movement?

    (A) Realism

    (B) The Age of Enlightenment

    (C) Romanticism

    (D) Transcendentalism

    (E) Modernism

40. This Kate Chopin novel (or novella) follows Edna Pontellier as she navigates the social conventions of her day, which centered on repressed emotional and sexual desires. The name of this novel is

    (A) *Age of Innocence*

    (D) "The Yellow Wallpaper"

    (B) *Ethan Frome*

    (E) "A White Heron"

    (C) *The Awakening*

Questions 41–42

"Young Goodman Brown came forth at sunset into the street at Salem village; but put his head back, after crossing the threshold, to exchange a parting kiss with his young wife. And Faith, as the wife was aptly named, thrust her own pretty head into the street, letting the wind play with the pink ribbons of her cap while she called to Goodman Brown."

41.   This Hawthorne story is commonly referred to as a(n)

    (A)   symbol   (D)   lyric

    (B)   allegory   (E)   gothic

    (C)   allusion

42.   What is Young Goodman Brown's wife's name?

    (A)   Grace   (D)   Faith

    (B)   Joy   (E)   Mrs. Brown

    (C)   Love

Questions 43–45

        The fog comes
        on little cat feet.

        It sits looking
        over harbor and city
        on silent haunches
        and then moves on.

43.   The above poem utilizes what literary device?

    (A)   Simile   (D)   Extended simile

    (B)   Onomatopoeia   (E)   Symbol

    (C)   Extended metaphor

44.   What early twentieth-century poet wrote "The Fog"?

    (A)   Robert Frost   (D)   T.S. Eliot

    (B)   Carl Sandburg   (E)   William Carlos Williams

    (C)   E.E. Cummings

45. By reading the poem and knowing the poet, the words "harbor and city" most probably refer to

(A) New York
(D) Chicago

(B) Boston
(E) St. Louis

(C) San Francisco

46. Hawthorne's short stories "The Maypole at Merrymount" and "Young Goodman Brown" chiefly explore and describe experiences with which type of people?

(A) Mormons
(D) Revolutionaries

(B) Pilgrims
(E) American Indians

(C) Puritans

47. Place each of the following authors beside the geographical area he/she is most associated with.

Mark Twain

Willa Cather

Kate Chopin

_____ Louisiana

_____ Nebraska

_____ The Midwest

48. Which anti-slavery writer was actually a former slave?

(A) John Greenleaf Whittier
(D) Ralph Waldo Emerson

(B) Frances Harper
(E) Harriet Beecher Stowe

(C) Harriet Jacobs

49. Mark Twain is the pseudonym of

(A) Huck Finn
(D) Roger Clemens

(B) William Dean Howells
(E) Samuel Clemens

(C) Sam Perkins

50. Wallace Stevens was not just a poet. After working as a lawyer for many years, he worked for which company for the remainder of his career?

   (A) New York Life

   (B) Mutual Insurance

   (C) Hartford Accident and Indemnity

   (D) GEICO Insurance

   (E) State Farm Insurance

51. William Carlos Williams rejected imagism as a mode of writing poetry. Which of the following terms means the poet views the poem as an object, and that object allows the poet to see the world more critically, analytically, and clearly?

   (A) Objectivism   (D) Realism

   (B) Surrealism   (E) Post-modernism

   (C) Cubism

52. *The Scarlet Letter* begins with an introduction by an anonymous narrator who happened upon a bundled manuscript while working in a

   (A) government post office

   (B) Massachusetts Custom House

   (C) Puritan preacher's manse

   (D) Protestant church basement

   (E) Virginia Custom House

53. Although these poets used very different poetic forms, techniques, and subject matter, which one of them is NOT considered a modernist?

   (A) Amy Lowell   (D) Edna St. Vincent Millay

   (B) H.D.   (E) Julia Ward Howe

   (C) Marianne Moore

54. Which Herman Melville novel was published posthumously?

   (A) *Twice-Told Tales*   (D) *Billy Budd*

   (B) *The Blithedale Romance*   (E) *Pierre*

   (C) *The Piazza Tales*

Questions 55–57

> I think I should have loved you presently,
> And given in earnest words I flung in jest;
> And lifted honest eyes for you to see,
> And caught your hand against my cheek and breast;
> And all my pretty follies flung aside
> That won you to me, and beneath your gaze,
> Naked of reticence and shorn of pride,
> Spread like a chart my little wicked ways.
>
> I, that had been to you, had you remained,
> But one more waking from a recurrent dream,
> Cherish no less the certain stakes I gained,
> And walk your memory's halls, austere, supreme,
> A ghost in marble of a girl you knew
> Who would have loved you in a day or two.

55.   The above is an example of which poetic form?

   (A)   Petrarchan Sonnet   (D)   Shakespearean Sonnet

   (B)   Villanelle   (E)   Ballade

   (C)   Sestina

56.   The predominant tone of this poem is

   (A)   anger   (D)   love

   (B)   shame   (E)   lust

   (C)   regret

57.   What modernist commonly used traditional forms to explore contemporary issues such as love and relationships?

   (A)   Marianne Moore   (D)   Phillis Wheatley

   (B)   Elizabeth Bishop   (E)   Edna St. Vincent Millay

   (C)   Anne Bradstreet

58. William Faulkner used this literary device (made famous by James Joyce's *Ulysses*), which focused on the mental-emotional life of the characters instead of the external. This device is called

   (A) extended metaphors

   (B) stream of consciousness

   (C) double consciousness

   (D) the subconscious narrator

   (E) extended similes

59. Which section is NOT included in Walt Whitman's *Leaves of Grass*?

   (A) "Nature"

   (B) "Drum-Taps"

   (C) "Calamus"

   (D) "Children of Adam"

   (E) "Sea-Drift"

Question 60

> Did God mould up this Bread in Heaven, and bake,
> Which from his Table came, and to thine goeth?
> Doth he bespeak thee thus, This Soule Break take.
>
> Come Eate thy fill of this thy Gods White Loafe?
> Its Food too fine for Angells, yet come, take
> And Eate thy fill. Its Heavens Sugar Cake.

60. Edward Taylor's "Meditation 8" refers to which holy sacrament?

   (A) Marriage

   (B) Baptism

   (C) Confession

   (D) Communion/Eucharist

   (E) Lent

61. "The Legend of Sleepy Hollow" and "Rip Van Winkle" are early Romantic short stories written by

(A) Washington Irving

(B) Diedrich Knickerbocker

(C) James Fenimore Cooper

(D) Henry Wadsworth Longfellow

(E) Rip Van Winkle

62. Which Harlem Renaissance poet wrote the poem "I, Too, Sing America" that responded to Walt Whitman's poem "I Hear America Singing"?

(A) Countee Cullen   (D) Jean Toomer

(B) Sterling Brown   (E) Langston Hughes

(C) Paul Laurence Dunbar

Questions 63–65

I heard a Fly buzz—when I died-
The Stillness in the Room
Was like the Stillness in the Air-
Between the Heaves of Storm-

63. The stanza above uses what metrical structure?

(A) Short hymn measure

(B) Long hymn measure

(C) Hymn measure/common measure

(D) Heroic couplets

(E) Ballade

64. The abundant use of dashes and capitalization are typical conventions of whose poetry?

(A) Walt Whitman   (D) Emily Dickinson

(B) Sylvia Plath   (E) Adrienne Rich

(C) Anne Bradstreet

65. The following words are all synonyms of "heave." Which synonym best applies to the context of this poem?

    (A) To hoist

    (B) To rise and fall

    (C) To throw

    (D) To vomit

    (E) To breathe

66. All of the following writers are considered part of the Harlem Renaissance EXCEPT

    (A) Langston Hughes

    (B) Zora Neale Hurston

    (C) Sterling Brown

    (D) Countee Cullen

    (E) James Baldwin

67. Henry James's *Daisy Miller: A Study* is commonly referred to as a

    (A) novel

    (B) novella

    (C) short story

    (D) prose poem

    (E) vignette

68. This work, by Jean Toomer, was published in 1923 and, as an example of high modernism, is often cited as one of the most influential works for other, younger writers in the Harlem Renaissance. The series of poems and short stories is called

    (A) *Cane*

    (B) *The Autobiography of an Ex-Colored Man*

    (C) *Black Boy*

    (D) *Up from Slavery*

    (E) "Sweat"

69. Insert each of the terms below to the best definition.

    Hyperbole

    Personification

    Onomatopoeia

    _____ Poetic exaggeration

    _____ Words that imitate the sounds associated with the objects or actions to which they refer

    _____ Giving human characterizations to inanimate objects

70. The Age of Enlightenment heavily influenced the minds of American revolutionaries, including Benjamin Franklin, Thomas Paine, Thomas Jefferson,
James Madison, and Alexander Hamilton, among others. As Puritanism, and
the authority of the Bible and the Church, began to lose hold on the colonies,
many popular thinkers considered themselves to be

   (A) dissenters   (D) atheists

   (B) deists   (E) pagans

   (C) agnostics

71. American Transcendentalism is argued to stem from what American
religion?

   (A) The Society of Friends   (D) Unitarianism

   (B) Mormonism   (E) Christian Science

   (C) Shakers

Questions 72–74

> "If we must die, let it not be like hogs
> Hunted and penned in an inglorious spot,
> While round us bark the mad and hungry dogs,
> Making their mock at our accurse lot.
>
> If we must die, O let us nobly die . . .
> So that our precious blood may not be shed
> In vain; then even the monsters we defy
> Shall be constrained to honor us though dead!
>
> O kinsmen we must meet the common foe!
> Though far outnumbered let us show us brave,
> And for their thousand blows deal one deathblow!
> What though before us lies the open grave?
>
> Like men we'll face the murderous, cowardly pack,
> Pressed to the wall, dying, but fighting back!"

72. The "we" in the first line of the poem most likely refers to whom?

   (A) Slaves   (D) Latinos

   (B) Foreigners   (E) African Americans

   (C) Immigrants

73. The above poem is an example of what poetic form?

    (A) Elizabethan Sonnet   (D) Sestina

    (B) Italian Sonnet   (E) Ballade

    (C) Villanelle

74. Although born in Jamaica, the poetry of "If We Must Die," Claude McKay, is commonly associated with which literary movement?

    (A) Romanticism

    (B) Realism

    (C) The Harlem Renaissance

    (D) Surrealism

    (E) The Chicago Renaissance

75. Scholars often cite this person as Booker T. Washington's antithesis because he was born in Massachusetts to free parents and found his calling in the intellectual and educational world instead of the vocational world. The name of this man is

    (A) Charles W. Chesnutt   (D) W.E.B. Du Bois

    (B) Martin Luther King Jr.   (E) Frederick Douglass

    (C) Malcolm X

76. A famous review of Nathaniel Hawthorne's *Mosses from an Old Manse* was called "Hawthorne and his Mosses" and was written by

    (A) Margaret Fuller   (D) Herman Melville

    (B) Ralph Waldo Emerson   (E) Edgar Allan Poe

    (C) Robert Lowell

77. "A Jury of Her Peers" is the short story adaption of what famous Susan Glaspell play?

    (A) *12 Angry Men*

    (B) *The Glass Menagerie*

    (C) *Trifles*

    (D) *A Streetcar Named Desire*

    (E) *Cat on a Hot Tin Roof*

Questions 78–79

Heaven is "a place where the wicked cease from troubling you with talk of their personal affairs, and the good listen with attention while you expound on your own."

78. This definition of "heaven" is an example of what literary device?

   (A) Denotation   (D) Synecdoche

   (B) Connotation   (E) Metonym

   (C) Satire

79. The above passage is quoted from

   (A) *The Devil's Dictionary*

   (B) *The Art of Fiction*

   (C) *Peculiar Treasures: A Biblical Who's Who*

   (D) *The Oxford English Dictionary*

   (E) *Wikipedia*

80. What is the name of the impotent, yet very masculine, wine-loving narrator of Hemingway's *The Sun Also Rises,* who introduces readers to the raucous and vibrant lives of expatriates living in Europe?

   (A) Nick Carraway   (D) Israel Potter

   (B) Jay Gatsby   (E) Henry Flemming

   (C) Jake Barnes

81. The slave Olaudah Equiano was renamed Gustavus Vassa after

   (A) a British slave trader   (D) a Norwegian prince

   (B) a Swedish king   (E) his slave master

   (C) an American Diplomat

Questions 82–84

> "I shall grow old . . . I shall grow old . . . / I shall wear the bottoms of my trousers rolled."

82. This T.S. Eliot excerpt comes from what famous poem?

   (A) *The Waste Land*

   (B) "The Love Song of J. Alfred Prufrock"

   (C) *The Four Quartets*

   (D) "The Journey of the Magi"

   (E) *Ariel*

83. What is the ending to the following lines from the poem quoted above?

> "In the room the women come and go
> Talking of _____."

   (A) Vertigo   (D) Da Vinci

   (B) Politics   (E) The Alamo

   (C) Michelangelo

84. What is implied in much modernist writing is the youthful energy of change and rebellion. The protagonist of this poem commonly represents the nightmare of modernism, which is

   (A) the law   (D) settling down

   (B) getting married   (E) getting a job

   (C) getting old

85. The whiteness of the white whale in Herman Melville's *Moby-Dick* is commonly seen as a symbol of

   (A) neutrality   (D) emptiness

   (B) purity   (E) the sea

   (C) evil

Question 86

> "I, too dislike it.
> Reading it, however, with a perfect contempt for it, one discovers in
> it, after all, a place for the genuine."

86. What does the "it" represent in this Marianne Moore poem?

   (A) The Bible   (D) Novels

   (B) Newspapers   (E) Proverbs

   (C) Poetry

87. In which Stephen Crane novel does Henry Fleming, a young Union soldier, desire the glory that battle provides, but runs during his second battle?

   (A) *An Episode of War*

   (B) *The Little Regiment*

   (C) *The Red Badge of Courage*

   (D) *The Veteran*

   (E) *A Mystery of Heroism*

88. During this literary era, good literature remained slightly beyond the grasp of general readers and became complex and abstract systems of art that pre-occupied itself with its own meaning. Which literary era is referred to?

   (A) Realists   (D) Post-modernists

   (B) Romantics   (E) Surrealist

   (C) Modernists

89. Which of the following, founded by Ralph Waldo Emerson and later edited by Margaret Fuller, was the flagship newspaper of the Transcendentalists?

   (A) *The Liberator*

   (B) *The Dial*

   (C) *The North Star*

   (D) *The Atlantic Monthly*

   (E) *Harper's Magazine*

90. Which of the following writers does NOT explore Jewish-American issues in his fiction?

    (A)   John Updike   (D)   Bernard Malamud

    (B)   Saul Bellow   (E)   Isaak Singer

    (C)   Philip Roth

91. "So you're the little woman who wrote the book that started this great war."

    Legend has it that these words were spoken to Harriet Beecher Stowe, author of *Uncle Tom's Cabin,* when first met by

    (A)   Ulysses S. Grant   (D)   Abraham Lincoln

    (B)   Jefferson Davis   (E)   Frederick Douglass

    (C)   Robert E. Lee

92. Willy Loman, his wife Linda, and their sons Biff and Happy, are all characters in Arthur Miller's famous play

    (A)   *The Crucible*   (D)   *Death of a Salesman*

    (B)   *Cat on a Hot Tin Roof* (E)   *A Streetcar Named Desire*

    (C)   *Raisin in the Sun*

93. As a Christian convert, this Mohegan Indian, ministered to several New England Indian tribes, including the Montauks of Long Island. He was known as

    (A)   Pocahontas   (D)   Jim Thorpe

    (B)   Sacajawea   (E)   Samson Occom

    (C)   Powhatan

Questions 94–96

> The whiskey on your breath
> Could make a small boy dizzy;
> But I hung on like death:
> Such waltzing was not easy.
>
> We romped until the pans
> Slid from the kitchen shelf;
> My mother's countenance
> Could not unfrown itself.
>
> The hand that held my wrist
> Was battered on one knuckle;
> At every step you missed
> My right ear scraped a buckle.
>
> You beat time on my head
> With a palm caked hard by dirt
> Then waltzed me off to bed
> Still clinging to your shirt.

94. The meter of this poem matches what popular ballroom dance?

   (A) Foxtrot   (D) Waltz

   (B) Swing   (E) Salsa

   (C) Two-step

95. Readers argue whether this poem explores child abuse, or if the poem is the description of an innocuous, although rambunctious, dance between a father and a child. This tension in a poem is usually called

   (A) ambiguity   (D) a conceit

   (B) ambivalence   (E) a symbol

   (C) satire

96. What is the title of the poem and who is its author?

   (A) "The Dance" by William Carlos Williams

   (B) "Elegy for Jane" by Theodore Roethke

   (C) "My Papa's Waltz" by Theodore Roethke

   (D) "The Disillusionment of Ten O'Clock" by Wallace Stevens

   (E) "Fire and Ice" by Robert Frost

97. Sparked by the French Revolution in 1789 and also influenced by the Industrial Revolution, this movement rejected scientific reasoning as the only way to understand the universe or human nature and claimed the idyllic life of the rural areas of America instead of the growing urban section. The movement was

    (A) Realism

    (B) The Age of Enlightenment

    (C) Romanticism

    (D) Transcendentalism

    (E) Modernism

98. In Rebecca Harding Davis's "Life in the Iron Mills," Hugh Wolfe is a common laborer who hides what particular artistic talent?

    (A) Painting   (D) Writing

    (B) Sculpting   (E) Photography

    (C) Drawing

99. In which Flannery O'Connor story does Manly Pointer convince Joy Hopewell (who calls herself Hulga) to remove her prosthetic leg and then runs off with it, leaving her alone in the attic of a barn?

    (A) "Revelation"

    (B) "A Good Man is Hard to Find"

    (C) "Everything that Rises Must Converge"

    (D) "A Well-Lighted Place"

    (E) "Good Country People"

100. In the Leatherstocking series, James Fenimore Cooper reveals the underbelly of American nationalism, especially as it conflicted with the American Indians. Which novel is NOT part of James Fenimore Cooper's popular Leatherstocking series?

    (A) *The Last of the Mohicans*

    (B) *The Song of Hiawatha*

    (C) *The Prairies*

    (D) *The Pioneers*

    (E) *The Deerslayer*

Practice Test 2

CLEP American Literature

Answer Key

1. (C)	26. (C)	51. (A)	76. (D)
2. (A)	27. (D)	52. (B)	77. (C)
3. (D)	28. (C)	53. (E)	78. (C)
4. (B)	29. (C)	54. (D)	79. (A)
5. (D)	30. (C)	55. (D)	80. (C)
6. (C)	31. (C)	56. (C)	81. (B)
7. (D)	32. (A)	57. (E)	82. (B)
8. (E)	33. (B)	58. (B)	83. (C)
9. (B)	34. (A)	59. (A)	84. (C)
10. (D)	35. (C)	60. (D)	85. (C)
11. (D)	36. (A)	61. (A)	86. (C)
12. (D)	37. (D)	62. (E)	87. (C)
13. (B)	38. (B)	63. (C)	88. (C)
14. (D)	39. (D)	64. (D)	89. (B)
15. (D)	40. (C)	65. (B)	90. (A)
16. See below	41. (B)	66. (E)	91. (D)
17. (B)	42. (D)	67. (B)	92. (D)
18. (C)	43. (C)	68. (A)	93. (E)
19. (A)	44. (B)	69. See below	94. (D)
20. (D)	45. (D)	70. (B)	95. (B)
21. (C)	46. (C)	71. (D)	96. (C)
22. (E)	47. See below	72. (E)	97. (C)
23. (D)	48. (C)	73. (A)	98. (B)
24. (C)	49. (E)	74. (C)	99. (E)
25. (A)	50. (C)	75. (D)	100. (B)

16. Ralph Ellison   *Invisible Man*
     W.E.B. DuBois   *The Souls of Black Folks*
     Phillis Wheatley   *Poems on Various Subjects, Religious and Moral*

47. Kate Chopin   Louisiana
     Willa Cather   Nebraska
     Mark Twain   The Midwest

69. Hyperbole   Poetic exaggeration
     Onomatopoeia   Words that imitate the sounds associated with the objects or actions to which they refer
     Personification   Giving human characterizations to inanimate objects

Detailed Explanations of Answers

Practice Test 2

1.   **(C)**   Like most of Cather's work, *O! Pioneers* is the story of European immigrants trying to create a life for themselves in the barren farmlands of southern Nebraska. The region is as much a part of the novel as are the characters. Although the novel may poke fun at certain institutions and beliefs, it is not known as a satire (B). The novel contains strong symbols, but it is not an allegory (D).

2.   **(A)**   Edgar Allan Poe is the author of this narrative poem, "The Raven." First published in 1845, it is often noted for its musicality, stylized language, and supernatural atmosphere.

3.   **(D)**   The key to answering this question is knowing that Poe maintained a strict rhyming pattern in the poem. Also, remember that the speaker's mourning is induced by the loss of his love, Lenore. Annabel Lee (B) is the title of another Poe poem.

4.   **(B)**   Athena was the goddess of wisdom. By placing the raven on the bust of this god, Poe could be using the raven (a symbol of death or demise) to squash all hopes of wisdom. It is fitting that the speaker would have the goddess of wisdom above the door of his study. Zeus (A) is considered the father of the gods. Vulcan (C) was known to forge Zeus's lightning bolts. Venus (D) was the goddess of beauty and Hermes (E) was the messenger god.

5.   **(D)**   To answer this question correctly, you must know that Morrison was born in, and sets some of her fiction in, northern Ohio. She is placed in company with writers like Faulkner (C) and O'Connor (A) because of her use of the grotesque. However, Morrison does not hold one of the key elements of being a southern writer—she's not from the south.

6.   **(C)**   The heroic couplet contains two rhyming lines that both use iambic pentameter. It is called "heroic" because it was commonly used in classic epic poems that followed the journeys of a national hero. Scholars love to point out the irony of a young slave girl who used the heroic couplet to explore the life of a slave. Hymnal measure (A) uses alternate rhyming and an alternation between three and four foot lines. The caesura (D) is a poetic pause in a line. The trochaic substitution

(B) uses a trochee (a stressed syllable followed by an unstressed syllable) in a line that is predominantly iambic.

7.   **(D)**   In the Book of Genesis, Cain kills his brother Abel in a jealous rage. God condemns Cain to a life of wandering but does promise to protect him by marking him in an unspecified way. Unfortunately, many readers during Wheatley's lifetime used this story to fuel their prejudice toward Africans. They claimed that Cain was the ancestor of the Black race, and was therefore banished from God's favor. That's just bad theology. Do not confuse the spelling with Jean Toomer's novel, *Cane* (B). Even though *The Odyssey* (E) is an epic poem, and Wheatley does use heroic couplets, the allusion does not come from Homer.

8.   **(E)**   Although Andy Warhol was an avant-garde artist and champion of pop art, his popularity did not peak until the 1960s. In some way, Warhol was influenced by the underground and subversive works of writers like Ginsberg (A) and Kerouac (C).

9.   **(B)**   *Sister Carrie* is sometimes referred to as the flagship of American realism and naturalism. Dreiser paints a very realistic picture of industrial Chicago and the trials of those trying to make a living and climb the social ladder. Although each of the characters dreams big dreams, they are ultimately controlled by their social status, gender, or personality. Sister Christian (A) was a hit record by the '80s band Night Ranger.

10.   **(D)**   Dreiser's masterpiece, *Sister Carrie*, had a hard time getting published and it did not sell well during its first printing. The plot and characters were just too real. Dreiser critiques the American dream by exploring a rags-to-riches story that ends in tragedy. It is the tale of real people with real jobs trying to make it in a really tough Chicago and New York atmosphere. There is nothing romantic (A) or surreal (E) about this novel.

11.   **(D)**   Although Hurstwood and Drouet took care of Carrie financially, and it is implied that she had romantic relations with these men, it would not be fair to call her a prostitute (C). Her career as a dancer took off when she moved (was kidnapped by Hurstwood) to New York City. There she became famous, but she lost her ability to be intimate with other people, which was her tragedy.

12.   **(D)**   One of the major tenets of the Age of Enlightenment was the belief that the individual, through work and progress, could attain moral perfection. This entire section of Franklin's autobiography explores his desire to perfect the listed virtues. Also, note that the autobiography is considered a great example of Enlightenment thinking. Salvation (C) would be aligned with orthodox Christianity;

nirvana (A) with Buddhism; a transcendent state (B) with transcendentalism, and the inner light (E) with Quakerism.

13.   **(B)**   Students should be very cognizant of the fact that many modern and contemporary poets, especially the Beat poets, were fascinated with Walt Whitman. The passage alludes to Whitman's bachelorhood and his questionable homosexuality, which connected the great poet to Ginsberg. Emerson (A), Frost (C), and Eliot (D) were all married.

14.   **(D)**   The speaker reflects on his childhood in a harbor town. Each stanza ends with these two phrases: "A boy's will is the wind's will, / And the thoughts of youth are long, long thoughts." The poem explores the connection between the past and the present (A), the speaker's fleeting childhood (B), those who have passed on (C), and according to the repeating stanza, the romance of being young and thinking your thoughts will last forever (E). "My Lost Youth" does not address gender issues.

15.   **(D)**   Like Longfellow, there is something very regional and domestic about Frost.

16.   Phillis Wheatley is the author of *Poems on Various Subjects, Religious and Moral*; W.E.B. DuBois wrote *The Souls of Black Folks*; and *Invisible Man* was written by Ralph Ellison.

17.   **(B)**   Students should remember this all-important metaphor used by the Puritans to distinguish them in the new world. It was common to think that the whole world would be watching this rag-tag group of Puritans and their experiment in America. The metaphor is used in the Book of Matthew (5:14): "You are the light of the world. A city on a hill cannot be hidden." This metaphor had civic and religious importance to the Puritans.

18.   **(C)**   The picaresque genre was popular in Spain and Italy during the Renaissance, but many modern novels use the picaresque to explore the maturation of a young protagonist. The fabliaux (D) is a comic, bawdy tale usually filled with dramatic irony, double-crossing, and sex. Chaucer applied the form to his *Canterbury Tales*.

19.   **(A)**   Students should remember that the CLEP test often uses the term "conceit" to refer to an extended metaphor that helps better explain and explore the poem.

20.   **(D)**   Although the Puritan sermons (sometimes called jeremiads) combined religious obedience and civic responsibility, it is also important to remember that

these preachers were concerned first with their congregation and community. This excerpt from a Jonathan Edwards sermon is not a political attack (A), nor was it given to Shakers (C) or Quakers (B).

21. **(C)**   It is often argued among scholars that Edwards was born after the end of Puritan domination in colonial America. That is true. However, Edwards was a type of nostalgic preacher that used much of Puritan history and Calvinist theology to craft his sermons. Edwards lived during the Age of Enlightenment, so reason played an important role in his theology.

22. **(E)**   Although blue eyes certainly symbolize love (A) and acceptance (B) and (C), the novel explores Pecola's life as she searches and dreams for blue eyes like Shirley Temple's. In the last scene of the novel, readers must decide whether Pecola actually receives her wish, or whether she is mentally unstable.

23. **(D)**   The captivity narrative genre explores the captivity, temptation, and spiritual redemption of a colonial woman by American Indians. Although captivity narratives are a type of spiritual autobiography (A), and they can include diary entries (C), letters (E), and even sermonic tendencies (B), Rowlandson focuses her narrative on the Indians and their treatment of her and her family.

24. **(C)**   The key word in the question is "crucible." According to dictionary definitions, the crucible was a pot used to melt metals. Culturally, we get melting pot from this definition. The meaning is two-fold. Literally, the "witches" were burned, which makes the crucible an appropriate title. However, the play also explores the community's (Puritan) unwillingness to allow people of differing opinions and lifestyles to live among them. It was not a melting pot.

25. **(A)**   Historians argue whether Winthrop gave this famous sermon aboard the *Arbella* or on the pier before departure. Regardless, the sermon was not delivered upon the *Pinta* (C) or the *Nina* (E), which are ships most commonly associated with Christopher Columbus. Nor was Winthrop aboard the *Mayflower* (B) that left England in 1620.

26. **(C)**   A little knowledge of Greek roots helps here. "Thanato" is Greek for death. The context of the poem is a contemplation or exposition of death and human communities.

27. **(D)**   Situational irony occurs when an incident occurs that opposes what we expected to happen. Initially, readers are blindsided by the fact that a well-respected, well-to-do man of society would take his own life. Verbal irony (A) occurs when someone says one thing but means the opposite. Dramatic irony (B) occurs when the audience knows more than the characters.

28. **(C)** The poem simply tells the story of Richard Cory. An elegy (B) is a funeral poem of sorts. Although this poem discusses death, the key convention of the elegy is that its tone is full of lament. "Richard Cory's" irony leaves little room for genuine lament. An ode (D) usually contains ten lines.

29. **(C)** Edward Arlington Robinson's narratives are recognizable because they are usually short, traditionally-structured poems that contain much irony. Silverstein (B) wrote fun, playful poems for children. Masters (D) wrote poems that did contain irony, but Masters was not known for using traditional rhyme schemes and meter.

30. **(C)** "Ezra Bartlett" is one of Edgar Lee Masters' poems from *Spoon River Anthology*. In this collection, each poem is told from the perspective of a deceased member of the community. The cemetery is named Spoon River.

31. **(C)** Although all of the poets listed are considered confessional poets (or at least use various conventions of confessional poetry), Bishop had a longstanding poetic/professional relationship with Robert Lowell, author of "Skunk Hour." The poets' relationship as well as the relationship between "Skunk Hour" and "The Armadillo" should be discussed in American Literature classes.

32. **(A)** This is one of Stephen Crane's most famous war poems. Crane saw the front lines as a war correspondent, not as a nurse (C) or officer (D). He grew strongly skeptical of war, and especially of the politics that surrounded war. Note that the repetition of "Do not weep/War is kind" is always preceded by images of extreme violence. This technique sets up the irony.

33. **(B)** Not only was Crane born after the American Romantic movement (E), but "War Is Kind" actually was among Crane's works signalling the beginning of modern American Naturalism. Naturalism promoted a deterministic outlook on life, as seen in the second stanza: "These men were born to drill and die." American Realism (A) and Modernism (D) are predominantly twentieth-century movements.

34. **(A)** Students should be able to connect authors with historical moments. Crane, who had been a war correspondent on the front lines of both the Greco-Turkish War (1897) and the Spanish-American War (1898), was deeply disturbed at how war is entered into and conducted.

35. **(C)** William Bradford coined the term "puritan." His history of Plymouth colony was lost for many years before a copy of it was rediscovered in the mid-nineteenth century. Edward Taylor (B) and John Winthrop (E) were Puritan preach-

ers who mainly wrote sermons. John Smith (A) traveled to the New World well before the Puritans and is better known for writing histories of the settlement of Virginia.

36. **(A)** Although the details of the scuba gear may lead readers to think that the diver is an intermediate diver (C) or even an expert diver (B), pay close attention to the modifiers that the speaker uses. Words like "absurd," "grave," "awkward," and even the phrase "First having read the book" exemplify that the diver is not that familiar or intimate with the act of diving.

37. **(D)** This is one of Rich's most famous and highly anthologized poems. At first, the reader is convinced that the poem is about diving, but as the poem continues, the comparisons the speaker makes to the act of diving and exploring a wreck to romantic relationships become stronger and stronger.

38. **(B)** It is important to know the differences among these terms. "Dissenters" (A) simply refers to the people who explicitly act against a particular authority. Puritans (C) also wanted to purify Christianity from Roman Catholic influences in England. However, the biggest difference between the Puritans and the Pilgrims is that the Puritans did not desire to separate from the church. They merely wanted to change the church from within.

39. **(D)** The term "transcendentalism" refers to the ability to transcend, or to rise above. The implication is that individuals have the ability to rise above the doctrines, dogmas, and teachings of the present to reach a more ideal spiritual state—one found within themselves. The individual mind can obtain spiritual truths without help from the senses or guidance from past institutions or religious dogmas. Autonomy and individuality are the center of this ideology. Transcendentalism surfaced during the Romantic movement (C). However, remember that Transcendentalism was a reaction to the Age of Enlightenment (B), and that Transcendentalism came before Realism (A) and Modernism (E).

40. **(C)** All of the titles listed were written by nineteenth-century women. Edith Wharton wrote *Age of Innocence* (A) and *Ethan Frome* (B). Charlotte Perkins Gilman wrote the short story "The Yellow Wallpaper" (D). Sarah Orne Jewett wrote "A White Heron" (E).

41. **(B)** The key to answering this question is understanding the difference between allegory and symbol. A symbol is a literal object that represents an abstract idea. For example, to many Americans, the bald eagle represents freedom. An allegory is a piece of literature that is entirely symbolic: every character, scene, event, and conflict represents something beyond itself. Notice the names in the excerpt: Young *Goodman* Brown and *Faith*.

42. **(D)** Believe it or not, the CLEP test will give you some questions that are just this easy. Be sure to read the excerpts slowly and carefully. The answer to this question is explicitly mentioned in the passage.

43. **(C)** The fog is compared to a cat in the entire poem without using the words "like" or "as." Therefore, it is a metaphor that is extended throughout the whole poem.

44. **(B)** Carl Sandburg was famous for composing urban poems. He wrote many poems about Chicago and the city. Robert Frost (A) wrote many poems about rural settings in New England.

45. **(D)** It is important to connect authors with regions of the country. Not all nineteenth- and twentieth-century writers were regional writers, but much of Sandburg's poetry referred to Chicago.

46. **(C)** Hawthorne was fascinated by the settling of America and the Calvinist theology that influenced many Puritans. He often used satire, allegory, allusion, and symbol to make remarks about Puritan ideologies and their influences on nineteenth-century America. Most often these remarks were disparaging.

47. Geographically-speaking, Mark Twain is associated with the Midwest, Willa Cather is known for writing about Nebraska, and Kate Chopin was a regional writer from Louisiana.

48. **(C)** Abolitionists were a minority group predominantly living in New England, and most of them were white and upper class. Whittier (A), Emerson (D), and Stowe (E) were ardently opposed to slavery. However, they also wrote about other things, including New England life. Frances Harper (B) was Black but she was born to free parents and never served as a slave.

49. **(E)** Samuel Clemens chose the penname "Mark Twain," which is a steamboat term that means "safe water." The name referred to his years as a steamboat pilot on the Mississippi River and to his years as a journalist and political humorist when pseudonyms were popular and necessary.

50. **(C)** This seemingly tricky question is made much easier when students realize that Stevens lived most of his life in Connecticut. The businesses listed are major American insurance agencies; however, only one was founded in Connecticut and named after its capital.

51. **(A)** Sometimes objectivism and imagism are used to describe the same movement. However, note that imagism reached its height of popularity during

World War I, while Williams and Pound began working in objectivism in the early 1930s. Surrealism (B) and cubism (C) were movements predominantly associated with painting and the visual arts.

52. **(B)**   After the 1846 publication of *Mosses from an Old Manse*, the Hawthornes fell on hard financial times, so a friend secured a position for Nathaniel at the Salem Custom House. It was there that he wrote his introduction "The Custom House" for *The Scarlet Letter*.

53. **(E)**   Howe is most famous for writing the "Battle Hymn of the Republic" during the Civil War. She was born in 1819 and died in 1910. Lowell (A), H.D. (B), Moore (C), and Millay (D) did use a variety of traditional forms and conventions, but are most noted for their resistance to traditional forms and poetic topics.

54. **(D)**   Melville died in 1891, leaving an unfinished sea narrative, *Billy Budd*. The novel was not finished and published until 1924. Upon publication, the novel increased interest in Melville's previous works and literary career. *Twice-Told Tales* (A) and *The Piazza Tales* (C) are both short story collections. *The Blithedale Romance* and *Pierre* were published in 1852.

55. **(D)**   The key to answering this question correctly is first noticing that a fourteen-line poem with a traditional rhyme scheme is almost always a sonnet. Secondly, the Shakespearean/Elizabethan sonnet always ends with a rhyming couplet. The villanelle (B) contains 19 lines and the sestina (C) contains 36 lines.

56. **(C)**   The speaker discusses all the ways she should have acted toward her lover. The line "And walk your memory's halls" implies that she regrets her actions and spends much time reminiscing about those days.

57. **(E)**   The key word in the question is "modernist." While most modern poets resisted, and even rejected, traditional poetic forms, Millay used the sonnet to explore issues of love, loss, and desire from a woman's point of view. Both Bradstreet (C) and Wheatley (D) did use traditional forms. However, Bradstreet wrote in the seventeenth century and Wheatley wrote in the eighteenth century.

58. **(B)**   In stream-of-consciousness writing, the narrative mimics what a character thinks and not just what he says. This type of writing is highly recognizable because of its resistance to standard spelling, punctuation, dialogue tags, and sentence structure. "Double consciousness" (C) is a term coined by W.E.B. DuBois in *Souls of Black Folks* and refers to a split identity.

59. **(A)**   "Nature" was an essay written by Ralph Waldo Emerson that attempted to define and explain the major tenets of transcendentalism. "Drum-Taps" (B)

includes Whitman's Civil War poems. "Calamus" (C) and "Children of Adam" (D) are most famous for poems that explore homosexual themes. "Sea-Drift" (E) is a shorter section that includes several poems of nature and life near the sea.

60. **(D)** The image of bread is most commonly associated with the Lord's Supper, also known as communion and the Eucharist. In the New Testament, Jesus broke bread and poured wine to give to His disciples as a symbol of his broken body and spilled blood for their (and the world's) sins. In the Protestant tradition, only baptism (B) and communion are holy sacraments. Roman Catholicism also includes marriage (A) and confession (C).

61. **(A)** Washington Irving became the first American international literary superstar. His famous works include a satirical magazine called *Salmagundi* that he wrote in 1807 with his brother; *A History of New-York from the Beginning of the World to the End of the Dutch Dynasty by Diedrich Knickerbocker (1809)*, a parody and political satire; and his most famous work, *The Sketch Book of Geoffrey Crayon*, which was written during a seventeen-year stay in Europe and published in a two-volume set in 1820. This work houses Irving's most enduring and mythologized stories, "The Legend of Sleepy Hollow" and "Rip Van Winkle."

62. **(E)** Langston Hughes's poem is a response to Whitman's seemingly egalitarian "I Hear America Singing" which lists the many occupations and personalities that constitute America. Hughes simply reminds readers that African-Americans are Americans, too.

63. **(C)** This type of measure was often called "common measure" because of its popular use. (I tell my students to hum the tune of "Amazing Grace" when they read a Dickinson poem. It works most of the time.) Using iambs, lines 1 and 3 contain four feet, and lines 2 and 4 contain three feet. Short hymn measure (A) contains only one four-foot line, while long hymn measure (B) utilizes four feet in each line.

64. **(D)** Students should quickly recognize an Emily Dickinson poem because of these distinctions. Whitman (A) predominantly used long, bumbling lines with relatively little rhyme.

65. **(B)** "Heave" in this poem refers to the time between great tumult. This metaphor implies that there is a sense of rising and falling during the time just before death.

66. **(E)** Although James Baldwin was born and raised in Harlem, he did not begin his writing career until 1953 with his autobiographical novel, *Go Tell It On*

the Mountain. Most scholars note that the Harlem Renaissance reached its peak in the 1920s and early 1930s.

67. **(B)** Conveniently, the novella is usually defined as a work of fiction that is longer than a short story, but shorter than a novel. Most novellas contain about one hundred pages.

68. **(A)** The book *Cane* became central to African-American literature. Fearing being pigeonholed as a "Black" writer, Toomer refused to include his writings in Black anthologies and spent his literary energies on spirituality and philosophy. James Weldon Johnson wrote *The Autobiography of an Ex-Colored Man* (B); Richard Wright wrote *Black Boy* (C); Booker T. Washington wrote *Up From Slavery* (D); and Zora Neale Hurston wrote the short story "Sweat."

69. Hyperbole is defined as poetic exaggeration; personification is defined as giving human characteristics to inanimate objects; and onomatopoeia is the use of words that imitate the sounds associated with the objects or actions they refer to.

70. **(B)** Unlike many atheists (D) and even agnostics (C), deists believed in a God. The famous analogy that followed deistic thought was that God was much like a clockmaker: He created the earth and then set it in motion to work on its own.

71. **(D)** Literary historians argue that every major transcendental thinker started as a Unitarian. Unitarians believe in the single nature of God and that Jesus was an exemplar, not divine. This idea translated well into transcendentalism as many thinkers, especially Emerson, preached about the divinity of the individual soul.

72. **(E)** The key to knowing the answer to this question is recognizing its author and place in American history. Claude McKay was a Jamaican-born poet who wrote during the Harlem Renaissance in the 1920s. Thus, the answer cannot be slaves (A), and, since we know that the subject of the poem is African Americans, foreigners (B), immigrants (C), and Latinos (D) cannot be correct.

73. **(A)** Shakespearean and Elizabethan sonnets are synonymous terms and both refer to a 14-line, iambic poem with an ending rhyming couplet, much like Italian and Petrarchan sonnets.

74. **(C)** Claude McKay began his education at Booker T. Washington's Tuskegee Institute in Alabama, but transferred to Kansas State College. He eventually dropped out of school to further his literary career in the Harlem district of New York City. McKay's first collection of poetry, *Harlem Shadows* (1922), is considered the collection that began the Harlem Renaissance.

75. **(D)** W.E.B. Du Bois earned undergraduate degrees from Fisk University and Harvard. He was the first African-American to receive a doctorate from Harvard. His seminal work is titled *The Souls of Black Folks*. One of the key differences between Booker T. Washington and W.E.B. Du Bois was that Washington encouraged a vocational education while Du Bois encouraged an intellectual education.

76. **(D)** Melville's essay is almost as famous as Hawthorne's. Melville and Hawthorne began their relationship when the Melvilles purchased a home in Pittsfield, Massachusetts, in 1850. Although their correspondence and friendship only lasted a couple of years, it is obvious that Hawthorne's work had a strong influence on Melville.

77. **(C)** The short story's title is more transparent than the play's title, *Trifles*. The plot revolves around Minnie Wright who has been arrested for the murder of her distant and abusive husband. The audience, however, never meets Minnie. The play takes place in the Wright's kitchen. The men are investigating the crime scene while their wives discuss the horrible act and Minnie's depressive life with the deceased man.

78. **(C)** The tone of the definition is one of scorn and ridicule, which are common to satire. The satirist uses humor (sometimes light and other times sardonic) to make fun of particular institutions and ideologies in the hopes that it will change.

79. **(A)** In 1911, Ambrose Bierce published *The Devil's Dictionary*, which is still very popular and widely quoted. In it, he offers alterative definitions for common words, ultimately ridiculing human assumptions, the government, society in general, and common prejudices. The original title of the work was supposedly the *Cynic's Dictionary*, but Bierce preferred the more irreverent association with the Devil than a cynic. Henry James wrote the *The Art of Fiction* (B) and Frederick Buechner wrote the very religious (and not at all satiric) *Peculiar Treasures* (C).

80. **(C)** Jake Barnes is the narrator of *The Sun Also Rises*. Hemingway's burgeoning passion and admiration for bullfighting was revealed in this novel. He noted once "bullfighting is the only art in which the artist is in danger of death and in which the degree of brilliance in the performance is left to the fighter's honor." Nick Carraway (A) and Jay Gatsby (B) are characters in F. Scott Fitzgerald's *The Great Gatsby*; Israel Potter (D) is the protagonist in Melville's eponymous novel; and Henry Flemming (E) is the protagonist in Stephen Crane's *The Red Badge of Courage*.

81. **(B)** Equiano's history beginning in America and England is fully confirmed by historical evidence. Although it was very common for slaves to inherit their

master's name (E), Equiano's master, Michael Henry Pascal, renamed him Gustavus Vassa—the first Swedish King who led his people in rebellion against Danish rule. Equiano was educated in London, served in the Navy, and sold back into slavery. His next master was a Quaker named Robert King who allowed Equiano to purchase his freedom for forty pounds in 1766. In 1789, he wrote and published *The Interesting Narrative of the Life of Olaudah Equiano, or Gustavus Vassa the African,* a strongly abolitionist autobiography.

82. **(B)** The poem is a loose narrative about Prufrock's love for a woman. It is an internal monologue about the state of love, his doubts and moments of inferiority, and ultimately, his isolation as an individual from society. In a popular passage, Prufrock intimates on the dismal punishment of old age as he states, "I shall grow old . . . I shall grow old . . . / I shall wear the bottoms of my trousers rolled." The other famous poem on the list is *The Waste Land* (A). It draws on many different religions and ancient cultures in an attempt to comment on the current state of the world. It is highly allusive, multi-lingual, and incredibly fragmented; it is a modern text. Some argue, much like "Prufrock," *The Waste Land* is a treatise against modernity and a tale of detachment, isolation, and fragmentation that only leads to demise. *Ariel* (E) was written by Sylvia Plath.

83. **(C)** Although the long poem does not utilize many traditional poetic conventions, Eliot does use rhyme in this famous repetitious couplet to explore the illusive and culturally-astute women of the poem.

84. **(C)** Although it was clear that modernists resisted most of what represented a bourgeoisie existence, such as getting married (B), settling down (D), or even maintaining a steady job (E), the poem explores the great fear of getting old and losing the vitality and youthfulness that art, culture, and sex offer.

85. **(C)** Whiteness is a peculiar metaphor in *Moby-Dick*. It is the color of evil, as it represents absence or unnaturalness. This resists common associations of white: purity (B), neutrality (A), or emptiness (D).

86. **(C)** This particular poem went through many revisions and editions, but the theme stays the same—what should a poem look like? Although the speaker ridicules much about poetry, it is clear that the poem, according to the speaker and to Moore, should explore imagination and reality. Famously, the speaker argues that poetry should contain "imaginary gardens with real toads in them."

87. **(C)** Crane is most recognizable for his famous novel of the Civil War, *The Red Badge of Courage,* even though Crane was born several years after the War concluded. His Civil War novel was first serialized in many newspapers across the country before it was published in book form in 1895. *The Red Badge of Courage*

is one of the first depictions of battles and soldiers from a realist perspective. The other titles on the list are Crane's short stories about the Civil War.

88. **(C)** Modernists attack much of nineteenth-century literary for its accessibility and trite conventions. Modernists were not interested in didactic literature that proposed to promulgate a particular meaning. According to Archibald MacLeish, in summary, "a poem should not mean, but be." Both realists (A) and romantics (B) were very interested in the human condition and in encouraging readers to feel for humanity.

89. **(B)** Henry David Thoreau, Margaret Fuller, and Ralph Waldo Emerson published their transcendental ideas in *The Dial*, a journal that ran from 1840-1844. *The Liberator* (A), published by William Lloyd Garrison, and *The North Star* (C), published by Frederick Douglass, were both considered abolitionist newspapers. *The Atlantic Monthly* (D) and *Harper's Magazine* (E) were and still are popular lifestyle and literary magazines.

90. **(A)** Updike grew up in Pennsylvania and later moved to New York where he wrote for *The New Yorker* for many years. Many of his novels and stories explore Protestant Christians or their theology as it interacts with gender, class, and institutions of marriage and parenthood. The other authors on the list are known predominantly for exploring Jewish-American issues during the twentieth century.

91. **(D)** After its publication in 1852, *Uncle Tom's Cabin* produced many vehement responses from its readers. It was lauded as the perfect description of slave life and northern apathy. However, it was also ridiculed as one-sided and inaccurate. Regardless, the novel sold over 500,000 copies within five years and held the attention of many famous Americans . . . even Lincoln.

92. **(D)** The play *Death of a Salesman* begins with Willy returning from a failed business trip. At home, Willy journeys through several flashbacks and daydreams that introduce the viewers to the past, when life was manageable and the boys were young, energetic, and optimistic. These daydreams and flashbacks become central to the plot. It becomes clear to the viewer that the realities of the present and of the past are beginning to mix with fictional daydreams in Willy's mind. Ultimately, Willy's daydreaming, fake optimism, and disillusionment drive him away from his family and eventually to his own death. The play is a wonderful comment on the stresses of American capitalism, but it is also the story of a struggling family in a time when every family desires (yet also questions) the American Dream. Arthur Miller also wrote *The Crucible* (A); Tennessee Williams wrote *Cat on a Hot Tin Roof* (B) and *A Streetcar Named Desire* (E); and Lorraine Hansberry wrote *A Raisin in the Sun* (C).

93. **(E)** Occom's autobiography, *A Short Narrative of My Life* (1768), was originally written as a ten-page manuscript and details his life as an Indian minister. It was found in the Dartmouth College archives. The other famous American Indians on the list were never ordained ministers.

94. **(D)** The key to answering this question is knowing that the waltz is a three-step dance and that each line in the poem contains three metrical feet.

95. **(B)** Students should remember that ambiguity connotes the writer's intention to leave interpretation open to multiple conclusions. Ambivalence (B) usually implies that the writer just doesn't know what to think. This poem shows a writer intentionally creating tension between dance and abuse.

96. **(C)** This is one of the most famous and highly anthologized poems of the twentieth century. In "My Papa's Waltz," the speaker depicts a child dancing with his drunken father. The structure of the lines and rhyme of the poem signifies the waltz and the dark word choices force the reader to take pause and closely analyze the scene. Many student readers debate whether it is a poem about a dance or about abuse. Written in iambic trimeter (3 beats), the poem takes on the physical nature of a waltz, but words like "death" and "whiskey" create wonderful ambiguity and tension.

97. **(C)** The *individual* is at the heart of any definition of romanticism. And, although this idea is similar to the Enlightenment, the Romantics reacted against a life of reason for a life of sentiment and feeling. For the Romantics, individuals are the very center of the literary act; therefore, expressing feeling, emotion, and attitude are the key components of the literary act. Both Realism (A) and Modernism (E) were reactions to Romanticism and Transcendentalism (D) was an offspring of romantic ideals.

98. **(B)** The story follows a Welsh immigrant iron worker by the name of Hugh Wolfe. He spends what free time he has at the mill sculpting figures out of scrap iron called korl. One evening, a group of businessmen walks through the factory and notice a beautiful sculpture of a korl woman. Hugh asks the men to help him financially with his sculpting and his artistic dreams. Deborah, Hugh's cousin, overhears the men reject Hugh's requests. In a desperate effort to help Hugh and herself, she takes one of the men's wallets and offers it to Hugh as a way out of poverty. Eventually, they both land in jail where they are forgotten.

99. **(E)** "Good" is the key, and ironic, word in the title and in the description. Manly is a traveling Bible salesman who uses his "good southern boy" charm to manipulate and deceive his customers. Each of the stories listed were also written by O'Connor.

100. **(B)**   *The Song of Hiawatha* is an epic poem, written by Longfellow, about the Ojibway Indians of the American North and is not a part of Cooper's Leather-stocking series. *The Song of Hiawatha* follows an Indian youth named Hiawatha and his love Minnehana. Scholars assert that Longfellow used the style of Finnish folk-epics to create his "American" epic, namely the Kalevala. Scholars also note that Longfellow used another source for the content of his poem: the journalistic work by Henry Schoolcraft, the superintendent for Indian Affairs in Michigan from 1836 to 1841. Undoubtedly, the poem is also about the Indians' assimilation into white, colonized America. Hiawatha leaves his people in a mythical departure, but leaves them with the charge to take off the war paint and light the peace pipe in honor of the strangers from abroad.

Glossary

Allegory A story in which characters and events are used as symbols for ideas about life.

American Renaissance A literary movement that began in the 1830s and spanned to the Civil War. It has been described as focusing more on humanism and imagination, as it moved away from Calvinism and Puritanism. It also included, and is closely associated with, the tenets of Transcendentalism.

American Romanticism A literary movement in America that stemmed from opposition to the Age of Reason and placed the individual at the center of the literary act, which the movement maintained should be full of feeling, emotion, and attitude. It emphasized freedom of expression.

"Beat" A term often associated with Jack Kerouac and the Beat Movement, it was a shortened form of the term "dead-beats," "beatified," or "beaten down."

Black Arts Movement The Black power movement that swept urban centers in the 1960s and 1970s.

Bradford, William Landed in 1620 in Plymouth, Massachusetts, with the Pilgrims on the *Mayflower*; in 1621, he became the Pilgrims' leader and was named the first governor of the Plymouth colony.

Bread and Cheese Club A literary club of New York that James Fenimore Cooper helped found. It housed the Romantic painters of the Hudson River School, including William Cullen Bryant.

Brent, Linda The pseudonym Harriet Jacobs used to protect her children.

Bronson Alcott's Temple School Prestigious school in Boston, Massachusetts, where Margaret Fuller taught with Elizabeth Peabody. The school was founded by Bronson Alcott in 1834 and taught students using a teaching style based on conversation. Corporal punishment as a method of discipline was forbidden in the school.

Brook Farm A utopian community dedicated to social reform and Transcendentalist teaching. Nathaniel Hawthorne lived there for a year and used his experiences at Brook Farm as a basis for his novel *The Blithedale Romance*, which satirized utopian communities and Transcendentalism.

Captain Ahab The protagonist in Herman Melville's novel *Moby-Dick*. He was in search of the great white whale called Moby Dick, which ultimately kills him.

Captivity narrative A narrative that was written while the author is in captivity. **Mary Rowlandson's** narrative is the first identified as such. The genre is associated with the sixteenth to nineteenth century and is organized into removes or episodes. The narrative can be identified by the author's reliance on God's power for deliverance and the use of the Indians and their lifestyles as metaphors for evil, sin, and godlessness.

Catskill Mountains A mountainous region in southeastern New York where Rip Van Winkle lived among the descendants of Dutch immigrants.

Chillingsworth, Roge The husband of **Hester Prynne** in Nathaniel Hawthorne's novel *The Scarlet Letter*. He seeks revenge upon **Arthur Dimmesdale**.

"City upon a hill" This phrase comes from Jesus' parable of Salt and Light in the Sermon on the Mount (Matthew 5:14). It was also **John Winthrop's** vision for the Massachusetts Bay Colony.

Coleridge, Samuel Taylor A famous English Romantic writer who influenced the American Romantic movement. He is known for "Kubla Khan" and "The Rime of the Ancient Mariner."

Conceit (also known as **extended metaphor**) When an author carries an analogy throughout a text using multiple images or vehicles.

Confessional poetry (also known as **post-confessional poetry**) Poetry that is dedicated to, and preoccupied with, the "self." It is intensely personal and attempts to connect the "self" with the larger world. Adrienne Rich and Sylvia Plath were confessional poets.

Declaration of Independence The document drafted by Thomas Jefferson in 1776 which states that the thirteen colonies considered themselves separate from the British Empire.

Deists These thinkers believed in a Supreme Being, but they believed that the Supreme Being did not interfere in the actions of humans. Numbers of these thinkers increased as Puritanism decreased in the colonies.

Dimmesdale, Arthur The local minister in Nathaniel Hawthorne's novel *The Scarlet Letter*. He has relations with **Hester Prynne** and is the father of Pearl.

Double-consciousness This term was invented by W.E.B. Du Bois and refers to the act of being aware of one's self through the eyes of others. Du Bois believed that African Americans' identity was defined by how white people saw them.

Edwards, Jonathan One of the most anthologized preachers of colonial America, he was part of the second generation of Puritans influenced by the **Enlightenment** and tied to the **Great Awakening**. He is most known for his 1741 sermon titled "Sinners in the Hands of an Angry God."

Enlightenment A cultural movement of the late seventeenth and early eighteenth centuries that used reason to challenge tradition and faith. It played a large role in the American Revolution and had an influence on Benjamin Franklin and Thomas Jefferson. Its influence can be seen in some of the early government documents, such as the Declaration of Independence and the U.S. Bill of Rights.

"Errata" A term used by Benjamin Franklin to describe his youthful errors.

Extended metaphor (also known as **conceit**) When an author carries an analogy throughout a text using multiple images or vehicles.

Fireside (Schoolroom) Poets A label given to a group of poets whose poetry was easy to memorize and recite. The following poets were among this group: John Greenleaf Whittier, Oliver Wendell Holmes Sr., James Russell Lowell, and Henry Wadsworth Longfellow.

Formalists (also known as **New Critics**) Literary theorists who used close reading and explication to find meaning in a text. New Criticism dominated the middle to late decades of the twentieth century.

Gothic novel A literary term used to describe fiction that preceded horror fiction. These stories are usually suspenseful, mysterious, and terrifying; the stories also often include dark castles or houses, storms, and the supernatural. Edgar Allan Poe's work is an example.

Grotesques A term used by Sherwood Anderson to describe his characters, who were usually sad, tragic, comic, and endearing. The term was originally used to describe art that was bizarre, fantastic, abnormal, and horrific. It symbolized the horror of being human in an inhumane world. Flannery O'Connor and William Faulkner also had grotesque characters.

Great Awakening A spiritual revival of increased religious zeal that made its way through the colonies in the mid-1730s and 1740s.

Great Migration A term used to describe the Puritans' migration to America. After many years of dissent, conflict, and unrest in attempting to purify the Church of England, a group of Puritans (led by **John Winthrop**) left England aboard a fleet of ships in 1630 and landed in Massachusetts Bay.

Hamilton, Alexander He is most known for the 85 essays he wrote with **James Madison** and John Jay from 1787 to 1788 in New York newspapers that advocated support for strong federal government. He signed his essays "Publius."

Harlem Renaissance A period during which a boom of art, social commentary, and politics was produced in Harlem, New York, by African-American artists—stretching to other urban areas with the purpose of upholding Black dignity, history, and experiences.

Imagism A term used to describe a type of poetry embraced by modernist poets, such as Pound and Doolittle. This form of poetry rejected long and elevated language and used crisp, clear, and precise images.

Ishmael The narrator of Herman Melville's novel *Moby-Dick*.

Jamestown A new colony of Virginia established by the Virginia Company and governed by John Smith; the first permanent settlement in the Americas. It was situated in the native homeland of the Powhatan Indians, also called Tsenacommacah.

Jazz Age A term used by F. Scott Fitzgerald in his short story collection *Tales of the Jazz Age* (1922) to describe and define the years between World War I and the Great Depression.

Jeremiad A term invented and made popular by scholars Perry Miller and Sacvan Bercovitch. It is a loud lament against all that is morally wrong with society.

Kant, Immanuel The central figure of German philosophy; published his major work, *The Critique of Pure Reason,* in 1781. Kant believed that the human mind shapes and structures experience, and thus humans create categories and concepts that structure their view of the world and its laws. His work had a large influence on **Ralph Waldo Emerson** and **Transcendentalism**.

King Philip's War An attack (1675) in New England led by **Metacomet** (also known as King Philip by the colonists) in which colonists were killed and their houses were burned. Many colonist women and children were captured.

Knickerbocker, Diedrich A persona created by Washington Irving for satirical purposes. The character appears in "Rip Van Winkle" and *A History of New-York*.

Leatherstocking series A series of five novels written by James Fenimore Cooper that reveals the underbelly of

American nationalism, especially as it conflicted with the American Indians.

Locke, John Considered one of the first British empiricists. His influence can be found in the Declaration of Independence. He was a physician, and was known as the first philosopher to define "self" through a continuity of consciousness.

Lyric poem A literary term used to describe a poem that is song-like in quality and often expressive of emotions. It may vary in meter and rhyme schemes.

Madison, James Most known for the 85 essays (known as the Federalist Papers) he wrote with **Alexander Hamilton** and John Jay from 1787 to 1788 in New York newspapers that advocated support for a strong federal government. He signed his essays "Publius."

Massachusetts Bay Company A joint stock trading company that was chartered by the English Crown in 1629 to colonize a large area of land in New England. **John Winthrop** quickly became the leader of the company and was joined by other Puritans who wished to create a religious order in the New World.

Massasoit The leader of the **Wampanoag Indians,** the tribe the Puritans encountered in the New World. Massasoit helped the Puritans get through their first harsh winter.

Mather, Cotton Most known for his 1702 publication of the history of Christianity in New England, *Magnolia Christi Americana*. He is also known for his involvement in the **Salem Witch Trials**.

Mather, Increase The father of Cotton Mather; a prominent figure in the Massachusetts colonies. Like Cotton, he is known for his involvement in the **Salem Witch Trials**.

Metacomet The son of the chief of the **Wampanoag Indians**; also called King Philip by the colonists. He led the attacks against the colonists in 1675 in what was known as **King Philip's War**.

Middle Passage The in-between stage of the triangular slave trade in which Africans were shipped across the Atlantic to the New World from Africa.

Modernity A term used to describe an era that resists its past in a variety of ways. This happens when the era's writers, thinkers, artists, architects, musicians, and others do not view the present as relatively aligned with its past.

Monticello The primary plantation of Thomas Jefferson. He built it just outside of Charlottesville, Virginia, on the summit of an 850-foot mountain peak.

Moral Perfection The section of Benjamin Franklin's autobiography where he commits to perfecting temperance, silence, order, resolution, frugality, industry, sincerity, justice, moderation, cleanliness, tranquility, chastity, and humility.

Myths Stories used by the ancient Greeks, Native Americans, and other cultures to explain cultural, historical, religious, and scientific happenings.

Narrative poem A literary term used to describe poetry that tells a story. It does not always include rhyming.

New Critics (as called **Formalists**) Literary theorists who used close reading and explication to find meaning in a text. New Criticism dominated the middle to late decades of the twentieth century.

New England Unitarianism A theology begun in the 1780s by James Freeman; grew to be more popular than Calvinist theology. It rejected the Trinity and did not believe in the divinity of Jesus. Although Ralph Waldo Emerson was a member of the church, he eventually broke away from it.

Objectivism A term used by William Carlos Williams to describe his form of poetry which used the poem as an object through which to see the world more clearly, critically, and analytically.

Open verse A literary term used to describe poetry that does not use a consistent rhyme or meter.

Pequod The whaling ship in Herman Melville's novel *Moby-Dick*.

Picaresque A genre of fiction that uses elements of satire and realism to explore the adventures of a lower-class citizen in a corrupt or jaded society.

Pilgrims The name that William Bradford gave to the settlers who landed near Plymouth, Massachusetts, and disembarked from the *Mayflower* in late 1620. The Pilgrims founded the first permanent European settlement. They also formed independent churches, which King James considered treasonous.

Plymouth, Massachusetts The name that John Smith gave to the area where the *Mayflower* landed in 1620.

Poetic persona The literary term for the poetic voice of a poem that the author uses as another voice to tell the narrative or depict an event, experience, or person in a poem.

Pontellier, Edna The protagonist in *The Awakening* by Kate Chopin.

Post-confessional poetry (also known as **confessional poetry**) Poetry that is dedicated to, and preoccupied with, the "self." It is intensely personal and attempts to connect the "self" with the larger world. Adrienne Rich and Sylvia Plath were confessional poets.

Powhatan The chief of the Chesapeake Bay Indians. He is known for a popular narrative that describes John Smith being captured by him and rescued by his daughter, Pocahontas. Scholars are not in agreement on the veracity of the narrative.

Provincetown Players A theater group founded by Susan Glaspell in New York that included Eugene O'Neill and Edna St. Vincent Millay. The group produced socially conscious, feminist, and satirical pieces.

Prynne, Hester The protagonist in Nathaniel Hawthorne's novel *The Scarlet Letter.* As retribution for her adultery, the Puritan community forces her to wear the letter *A* on her chest.

Puritans Those belonging to the puritanism reform movement of the sixteenth and seventeenth centuries were known as Puritans. Influenced by Calvinists, they sought to purify the Church of England (especially Roman Catholicism) and to use their efforts to also bring reform throughout the entire nation.

Queequeg The Polynesian harpooner in Herman Melville's novel *Moby-Dick*.

Removes These were used to organize the Captivity narratives; also called episodes.

Romantic Painters of the Hudson River School These mid-nineteenth-century painters embraced the literary tenets of Romanticism, as their pastoral paintings of the Hudson River Valley often reflected themes of discovery, exploration, and settlement where humans and nature coexisted in peace and harmony. Thomas Cole is often acknowledged as the founder.

Rowlandson, Mary The first identified author of the genre known as the **captivity narrative**. She was captured by the **Wampanoag Indians** during **King Philip's War**.

Salem Witch Trials A series of trials and hearings in which people were accused, tried, and condemned of witchcraft in colonial Massachusetts in 1692.

San Francisco Circle A small group of writers in California who met to discuss their writing. Among the group members were Ambrose Bierce, Mark Twain, and Bret Harte.

Sketch The product of literary experimentation that developed in the period between the two world wars. It is preoccupied with a single scene, moment, character, or image and grounded in precise imagery and sensory detail. Stein is known for using sketches, often called "still-life studies."

Slave narrative A type of story that was written between 1830 and 1865 by slaves with the hope of exposing the horrors of slavery to a white audience. Slave narratives contain religious themes and biblical allusions—often with the purpose of showing religious hypocrisy and violence.

Spiritual autobiography A formulaic genre in which the author details his or her life as it moves from a state of sin to one of grace, detailing cycles of sin and repentance on the journey to salvation. St. Augustine's *Confessions* is a classic example.

Spondee The literary term for a poetic foot with two stressed syllables; it is used to emphasize a word.

Squanto A Patuxet Indian who spoke English and was instrumental, as interpreter and guide, in helping the Puritans through their first harsh winter in the New World.

Stream of consciousness A literary technique used by William Faulkner and made famous in James Joyce's *Ulysses*. In this technique, the narrative flows as though the character is thinking and allows readers to identify the mental or emotional life of the character. It lacks standard spelling, grammar, and punctuation.

Swedenborg, Emanuel A Swedish scientist and inventor who had spiritual revelations and visions and was inspired to write a series of religious books. His most famous publication was *Heaven and Hell* (1758). His writings influenced the Transcendentalist writers.

Symbol A literary device in which an object is used to represent something else, such as an idea, belief, image, or action.

Taylor, Edward A Puritan who immigrated to America in 1668 from England because of his refusal to sign an oath of loyalty to the Church of England; he is most famous for his religious poems, *Preparatory Meditations*.

Transcendental Club A group of New England intellectuals who met for informal meetings to discuss and exchange Transcendentalist ideas.

Underground Railroad A network of people and safe houses that helped slaves escape to the North and Canada.

Villanelle A poetic form that includes 19 lines, which are broken into five triplets and a quatrain. The first line is repeated in the sixth, twelfth, and eighteenth lines, while the third line is repeated in the ninth, fifteenth, and nineteenth lines.

Virginia Company Two stock companies that were chartered by James I in 1606. The two companies were founded to settle establishments on the coasts of North America. John Smith joined the company in 1607 when he landed in Virginia.

Vorticism A term invented by Ezra Pound to describe a particular type of avant-garde art that was heavily influenced by cubism and futurism; this type of art was usually abstract with harsh lines and angles and focused on urban areas and industry.

Wampanoag Indians Native American tribe encountered by the Pilgrims upon landing in Plymouth, Massachusetts. The tribe embraced about 3,000 Algonquian-speaking Indians who inhabited southeastern Massachusetts and subsisted on corn, beans, and squash. The leader of the tribe was **Massasoit.** This tribe helped the Pilgrims through their first harsh winter in the New World.

War of 1812 A 32-month conflict between the United States of America and Great Britain that resulted from British attempts to restrict U.S. trade.

Winthrop, John Leader of the group of Puritans who chose to migrate to America in 1630 and landed in the Massachusetts Bay.

Wolfgang von Goethe, Johann A German politician, natural scientist, and author of many different types of literary works. Most know him for his drama *Faust* (1808), which was not published until after his death. He had a large influence on Margaret Fuller.

Yoknapatawpha The fictional Mississippi county invented by William Faulkner.

Index

Notes

Notes

Notes

Notes

Notes

Notes

Notes

Notes